Changing Job Structures

Books by the same author:
New Firm Formation and Regional Development
US Corporate Personnel Reduction Policies
Managing Workforce Reduction: An International Survey
Towards the Flexible Craftsman

Changing Job Structures

Techniques for the design of new jobs and organizations

Michael Cross
*Senior Visiting Fellow in Manufacturing Practice
Manchester Business School*

Heinemann Newnes

Heinemann Newnes
An imprint of Heinemann Professional Publishing Ltd
Halley Court, Jordan Hill, Oxford OX2 8EJ

OXFORD LONDON MELBOURNE AUCKLAND SINGAPORE
IBADAN NAIROBI GABORONE KINGSTON

First published 1990

© Michael Cross 1990

British Library Cataloguing in Publication Data
Cross, Michael
  Changing job structures.
  1. Companies. Organization structure
  I. Title
  658.1

ISBN 0 434 90284 5

Typeset by Hope Services (Abingdon) Ltd.
and printed and bound by Billing & Sons Ltd, Worcester

Contents

Preface	x
Acknowledgements	xi
1 WHY CHANGE JOB AND ORGANIZATION STRUCTURES?	1
Introduction	1
Technological change	1
Resources	2
External conditions	3
Structure of the book	4
Summary	5
2 WHAT DO EXISTING APPROACHES OFFER?	7
Introduction	7
Change management and the process of change	8
Existing approaches to job analysis and organization design	15
Criteria for a method to design and develop job content and organization structures	24
Summary	28
3 THE STRUCTURE OF THE APPROACH	29
Introduction	29
The overall structure of the approach	32
Summary	35
4 ESTABLISHING A START POINT	36
Introduction	36
Detailed preparation for the initial launch of a change initiative	36
Developing the terms of reference and rules for the proposed change	73
Definition and scoping of the problems and issues to be tackled	88
Selection of an appropriate method	106
Summary	108
5 DATA AND INFORMATION COLLECTION	111
Introduction	111
Measurement of work	112
The task statement	115

Task attributes	123
Development of the task listing	134
Development of task-related data	149
Summary	153

6 DATA ANALYSIS

	154
Introduction	154
Step 1. Task data cleaning and validation	154
Step 2. Task data validation	156
Step 3. Task data – first plots	157
Step 4. Task data reduction	158
Step 5. Task data – second plots	158
Step 6. Design principles and evaluation criteria	159
Step 7. Task data – rules for analysis	166
Step 8. Task data – third plots	171
Step 9. Possible new combinations/configurations of roles and structure of the organization	171
Step 10. Task data reduction	185
Step 11. Task data – fourth plots	186
Summary: Designing an efficient and effective organization	186

7 SELECTING THE 'BEST OPTION'

	194
Introduction	194
Step 1. Developing evaluation criteria	194
Step 2. Sorting and weighting of the evaluation criteria	201
Step 3. Applying the evaluation criteria	204
Step 4. Esimating the benefits	215
Step 5. Estimating the costs	229
Step 6. The balance sheet	241
Summary	249

8 IMPLEMENTATION

	251
Introduction	251
Implementation of the method (Stages 1 to 7)	251
Training	299
Pay and rewards	303
Monitoring and evaluating the changes	309
Summary	318

9 COMMUNICATIONS

	320
Introduction	320
Key questions about communications	320
Questions about change raised by those affected	322

Lessons learnt about communications from companies 338
  introducing new jobs and organization structures
Summary 339

10 WHERE NEXT? 340

Bibliography 343
Index 346

Preface

The need to change job and organizational structures has been at the top of most companies' agendas over the last decade. Factors such as increased competition on cost, quality and service and technical change have forced companies to seek out new ways of doing old tasks. Until recently many companies had fallen for the 'productivity paradox' whereby they had reduced costs 'in order to raise efficiency'. Costs were reduced, but gains in medium to short term efficiency were not achieved. The requirement for raised levels of performance called for new ways of working, often radically different from current practices.

In seeking to develop and introduce new ways of working, companies have too often relied upon adversarial routes: directly forcing changes through, threatening job security during negotiations etc. While such approaches have resulted in introducing changes in job and organization structures, it was not an easy nor a low risk strategy.

One learning point to emerge from these exercises in the 'management of change' is that there must be a better way. This book is born out of this belief. It is the product of ten years of change in working practices in manufacturing and the service sectors, and it seeks to offer a practical and commonsense method for participative development of future ways of working.

The methods and examples in this book are of particular relevance to people or organizations engaged in any of the following initiatives, or just interested in the ideas behind them: business unit development, core and non-core work, contractor base workload, flexible working practices, flexibility, focused factories, group working, industry worker concept, job and organization design and development, manufacturing centre formation, multi-skilling, polyvalency, primary and secondary skilling, team working, and total productive maintenance.

By far the greater part of the book has grown out of the joint work of management and unions, operators and craftsmen, supervisors and managers, lab. technicians and filing clerks, cleaners and scientists, and personnel managers and word processing operators. In all it draws on the experience of over 10,000 job holders and over 250 different jobs.

It is a book rich in empirical evidence and is based on material used in the actual achievement of changes in job and organization structures.

Ealing
May 1990

Michael Cross

Acknowledgements

In the writing of this book, and in particular in the compiling of the material since October 1981, I would like to acknowledge the help and assistance of the following people:

Terry Ponting, Mike Hornby, Vic Raby, Terry Palmer, Keith Ruffle, Chris Storrar, the late David Webb, Ken Butt, Jim Cross, Mike Day, Bruce Norman, Steve Lee, Mike Holt, Alan Winn, Sue Bleasdale, Jacqui Daly, Harry Frackelton, Bill Grogan, Carmel Higgins, Alan Hough, Margaret Jones, Janet Marsden, John Molyneux, Kevin Smith, Kingsley Chesworth, Jim Browne, Tom Lindsay, Keith Patterson, Mike Raywood, Jim Soulsby, Mike Griffin, Jeremy Kent, Reg Collingwood, Robin Stewart, Terry Dickens, Ian Foden, Richard Bliss, Bob Meston, Julian Amey, John Hoggett, Chris Corder, David Russell, Viv Cotton, Don Carnall, Jim Beckford, John Flynn, Dave McKee, Dave Holden, Dick Kemp, John Barnes, the late Dennis Toon, Bert Hirst, Jim Flemming, Chris Gillies, Howie Jones, Barry Kimber, Terry Morgan, Phil Worsley, Paul Mitchell, Keith May, Paul Litchfield, Keith Lindsay, Mike Bucknell, George Guy, Bryan Amesbury, Alan Owen, Mike Webber, Sarah Holmes and Sir Bruce Williams.

They have all done something to improve the work that forms the basis of this book: to them all, many thanks and the usual absolution from responsibility.

I hope that the contents and spirit of the book go some way to repaying the kindness and generosity of those named above and of the many others who have helped me.

I would also like to record my thanks to the following companies that have materially affected the contents of this book:

Albright and Wilson, Whitehaven
Alcan Plate, Birmingham
Applefords, Wrexham
BP Chemicals, Grangemouth
Barclays Bank, London
Batchelors Foods, Ashford
British Nuclear Fuels, Capenhurst and Sellafield
British Pipeline Agency, Hemel Hempstead
British Tissues, Oughtibridge

Cadbury, Somerdale
Ciba-Geigy, Paisley
Coca-Cola Schweppes Beverages, Uxbridge
Courages, Reading
Crosfield Chemicals, Warrington
Cryoplants, Edmonton
Cummins Engines, Darlington
Cussons, Nottingham
Dornay Foods, Kings Lynn
Elida Gibbs, Leeds
Esso Petroleum, Fawley
Exxon Chemicals, Fawley and Mossmoran
Fibreglass, St Helens
Glaxo Operations, Barnard Castle, Speke and Ware
Heinz, Harlesden and Kitt Green
ICI Pharmaceuticals, Macclesfield
Kellogg, Manchester
Kimberley-Clark, Prudhoe
Kodak, Harrow and Kirkby
Komatsu, Birtley
Lever Brothers, Port Sunlight and Warrington
Lyons Tetley, Greenford
3M, Gorseinon
Mars Confectionery, Slough
Michelin, Stoke
Metal Box, Neath
Mobil Oil, Coryton
Pedigree Petfoods, Melton Mowbray
Pilkington Flat Glass, Cowley Hill and Greengate
PLM Redfern, Barnsley
Reed Corrugated Cases, Edinburgh, Hartlepool, Cambridge, Thatcham and Aylesford.
Roche Products, Dalry
Ross Foods, Grimsby
Rothmans International, Darlington and Spennymoor
Rowntree, York
Scottish and Newcastle Beer Production, Edinburgh, Manchester and Newcastle
Shell Chemicals, Carrington
Shell Lubricants, Stanlow
Shell UK, Stanlow
Trebor, Maidstone
United Biscuits, Harlesden
Van den Berghs and Jurgens, Bromborough and Purfleet

Again, to each of these companies sincere thanks – and also a 'thank you' to those not named.

M.C.

1
Why change job and organization structures?

Introduction

Walk into almost any workplace and ask people to describe the strengths and weaknesses of their factory, office or warehouse. You will quickly be told about the pay and other conditions of work, but also that 'people are not listened to'. They will point out improvements that need to be made, but 'there is no way of making any of them happen'. Yet if you were to go to one of the plants of Digital Equipment, Mars, General Foods, Volvo etc. you would be told a different story. Leaving one of these companies' plants, the overriding memory is of a workplace whose success depends on the development of their people. How have these organizations achieved the appropriate culture and organization structure? How have they designed their jobs and organization?

This book explains one practical method that allows high-performance jobs and organizations to be designed and developed. Companies no longer have the choice as to whether or not to try to develop a high-performance organization. All organizations are facing challenges from changes in their 'task environment', particularly in the areas of technology, availability and use of resources, and the industrial and economic climate external to the company.

Technological change

1 New technology is becoming increasingly important in the provision of products and services, and their use, and hence affects most organizations in some way.
2 The rapid and successful uptake of product and process technologies is a key requirement for any successful company.
3 It is not the acquisition of a technology alone that is important; it is its subsequent use and enhancement which makes the difference between an average and a successful company.

4 The integration of separate stages of the production process into a single machine or processing unit, which itself combines different technologies, has led to increased complexity in the operation and maintenance of machines.
5 Failure to adopt and use successfully the appropriate technology in the provision of a product or service is having increasing direct impact on the viability of the whole organization.
6 Social, technical, political and economic factors combine to indicate strongly the benefits of designing work systems, organization and technology in a balanced way that respects and acknowledges the unique contribution of people.
7 With the shift to a greater degree of mechanization and automation, more and more organizations are becoming dependent upon the operation of a series of technologies. In the event of failure of these technologies, the organization cannot supply its customers with products and services.
8 The move to 'informate' (a term coined by Zuboff, 1989) manufacturing processes has had a major impact upon the jobs of key process and other workers. In the cases of paper and steel manufacturing, many of the tacit skills have been in large part incorporated into the production technology. In the car manufacturing industry, routine assembly workers have been upgraded to what Renault call 'rainbow-collar workers'. Such changes in technology need to be positively planned to ensure that new skill mixes do not result in low-grade work.

These eight factors are operating to a greater or lesser extent on all organizations. One of the main keys to the successful management of a technology for the benefit of the organization and its members is the ability to assess and balance external demands with internal resources in the form of robust and competent job-holders and an appropriate organization structure.

Resources

1 Changes in the supply of new entrants to the labour market, reductions in the availability of labour (due to shorter working week, working year and working life), and lack of a readily available pool of labour with up-to-date skills are all leading to an increased reliance on the existing staff of organizations. These factors are now affecting most of the major Western economies.
2 The introduction of 'Total Quality Management' (TQM) and 'Just-in-Time' (JIT) methods is raising awareness of the waste of all types of

resources. To reduce waste and use resources productively, 'Employee Involvement' (EI) and 'Total Productive Maintenance' (TPM) initiatives are needed. Both of these support initiatives rely on tapping existing labour resources and channelling the job-holders into new ways of working together.

Both reduced resource availability and the effective management of resources are of increasing importance to all organizations. Yet, at a time of rapid technological change and diffusion, existing resource mixes need to be modified to serve new demands. Managing the transition from the existing resource mix to the new one is crucial to the successful development of an organization.

External conditions

1. The widely publicized examples of radical change introduced on existing and on new sites have highlighted the significant improvements that can be achieved. Examples of the former include Shell Chemicals, Norsk Hydro and Monsanto: of the latter, Nissan, News International, Pirelli, Exxon Chemicals, General Foods and Digital Equipment. Such companies provide working and successful examples of 'ideal organizations'.
2. *In Search of Excellence* (Peters and Waterman, 1983) has raised awareness in many people that there are alternative ways of designing, developing and running an organization. For some this approach to methodology has encouraged efforts to improve; for others (such as Kodak) it has provided the way to a blueprint against which to audit the existing organization.
3. Both the value and benefits of investment in training have come to be widely accepted in most Western economies. There are signs even in lagging economies of awareness that action must be taken to increase the level of investment in training.
4. In the economies of Western Europe, the USA, Australia and elsewhere there are initiatives at national, local and industrial levels to develop high-quality vocational education and training systems. In the UK, for example, a national framework has been established by the National Council for Vocational Qualifications which is supported by the setting of national and industry standards (e.g. City & Guilds qualifications) and by local 'delivery bodies' (e.g. Training and Enterprise Councils). This approach is similar to that established in West Germany.
5. Even though on a number of sites significant progress has been made in establishing the most progressive forms of working and organization, the majority have tended to adopt a minor modification of traditional

structures and practices. This is in large part due to the lack of an integrated approach to the design and project management of the new sites. The building of a new site is now increasingly recognized to be one of the 'best' times to introduce changes in job and organization structures.
6 In the recession of the late 1970s and early 1980s many organizations reduced their staffing levels. With the recovery of most economies since 1983–84, more and more organizations have sought to establish a balance between a full-time workforce and some form of subcontracting and temporary labour.

Together these factors suggest *what* should be the characteristics of the new jobs and organizations, in general terms. The missing part of the process is the *how*: what is the process by which the new jobs and organizations will be designed and developed?

In order for companies to respond successfully to the changes in their task environment, they need clear goals and an appropriate strategy. Once a strategy has been agreed, there are available within the organization various tactical means to carry it out and influence its success. These can be broadly grouped (Aguilar, 1988: 49–50) as:

Organization structure.
Planning and allocation of resources systems.
Information and control systems.
Reward systems.
Staffing and people development.
Leadership.

The effectiveness of each of these instruments for change is dependent on the content and structure of the jobs and organization being designed and developed to support the goals and strategy of the company. Companies thus need to design their organization around their 'core purpose' and to ensure that all jobs and roles support and move toward that core purpose and its achievement.

This book describes one tried and tested method for achieving just this – an organization designed with its core purpose as the prime design criterion.

Structure of the book

In Chapter 2 the content and structure of the method are developed through a consideration of existing methods and general approaches to the design of jobs and organizations. A series of design criteria is also developed by combining the process (how to start, who to involve, when to communicate etc.), the method (what approach to adopt, what data to collect, how to analyse and interpret that data etc.), and the objective (what is to be achieved). By bringing these two complementary approaches together the basis of the method is developed.

Building directly upon the design criteria for a successful method, Chapter 3 provides a description of the eight-stage method. The next five chapters chart specific parts of the eight-stage method. Chapter 4 deals with establishing a start point covering the development of a 'sound basis for change', which includes: the detailed preparation required for the initial launch of a change initiative/project; the development of the terms of reference; the definition (scoping) of the issues under study; and the selection of an appropriate method. Chapter 5 examines and describes what information is required and how it can be collected. It also illustrates how much detail is required, depending on the focus of the study. This is followed in Chapter 6 with the detailed steps to be taken in analysing the data, and how a range of options can be generated. How to select the most appropriate or 'best' option is the focus of Chapter 7, while Chapter 8 considers the possible routes and strategies by which the selected option can be implemented.

The remaining two chapters consider two important topics: communications (Chapter 9) and 'Where next?' (Chapter 10). Throughout each of the eight stages of the method, communication is a key concern. How do you involve and raise understanding, interest and commitment to support and implement a particular change? Chapter 9 brings together the various elements of communication noted in the preceding chapters, and highlights the vital importance of effective communications in achieving change. In the final chapter, job and organization design and development are considered as a continuous process, and one which must be a key objective from the outset of any job and organization change initiative.

Summary

While some individuals in some companies convince themselves that change of almost any kind is impossible, there is ample evidence that radical and continuous improvement is possible: Companies such as Digital Equipment, Mars and General Foods all serve to illustrate that there is a better way: there is an alternative. However, in seeking to adapt an existing organization to become a 'high-performance work system' it is necessary to deal with the wide range of interrelated factors which shape and influence the work an organization performs. In order to deal with the complexity of the situations emerging in many organizations there is a need for a structured approach that can deal with a wide range of inputs in a simple, straightforward way.

This book offers one such method in a series of easy-to-follow steps which have been mainly developed in twenty British, North American, Japanese and European multinational companies drawn from manufacturing (chemicals, food, pharmaceuticals, engineering, paper and oil), banking and transportation since October 1981. The method has now reached a free-standing form which can be applied without any 'expert' assistance. This book represents the first version of the method to be published for more widespread application and to allow its further refinement and development.

2

What do existing approaches offer?

Introduction

From the discussion in Chapter 1, one clear need emerges: the need for a method that can deal with the myriad factors, internal and external to a company, which will result in some form of change in the work performed by the members of that organization. The purpose of this chapter is to describe how the method that is detailed in the rest of this book was developed. From the outset the search has been for a method which, when applied, will result in developing jobs and an organization which are superior to those that exist. It is also an objective from the outset to combine a technique of job and organization design with a process that aids the introduction of the jobs and organization, once designed.

The approach adopted to resolve this problem is made up of two distinct elements: first, a search of the literature on 'change' – what is change? How can it be achieved? Are some strategies more successful than others? Is there a practical model of change based on empirical evidence rather than organization development theory? Here a number of contributions proved to be useful: that of John Hunt of the London Business School; Jim Macrae's and ICI's Lostock model; the 7-C model of Peter Savage (then of Exxon Chemicals, now of Harrison and Crosfield's Chemicals Division); the teaching material of John Schermerhorn; finally, the work of Jay Galbraith. Taken together, these five practitioners of 'change management' helped to form the process requirement of any job and organization method.

Second, a review was made of the available job and organizational design methods using a categorization method described by Pearn and Kandola (1988) in their book, *Job Analysis*. In all 26 methods are reviewed and their specific and general strengths and weaknesses are summarized in tabular form.

By combining the output of these two exercises it is possible to generate design criteria upon which the method will be based. These are used in Chapter 3, where the whole study method is outlined stage by stage.

In the present chapter each of three main parts deals with one aspect of how the method was developed. The first takes the process of change and derives a list of key elements of any method that seeks to bring about change in job content and organization structure. The second part builds upon Chapter 1 in terms of the complexity of the issues involved and the questions raised above. Is the approach or technique under review, by means of its methodology and/or the mechanics of its application, able to satisfy the list of process criteria? This serves to eliminate a large number of methods in terms of their stand-alone application, i.e. their application in isolation from, and with no reference to, any other method. It can also indicate other methods which, if combined with other techniques, or developed in themselves, would prove useful. Overall, a general approach emerges from this part of the chapter together with a number of useful techniques. The third and final part of the chapter combines the 'process' and 'method/technique' criteria lists in order to derive an overall list of criteria for method design. The validity and importance of the criteria are illustrated with reference to the real situations in which the method has been developed.

Change management and the process of change

'Change' is mainly concerned with positioning, mobilizing, moving through a series of temporary stages, and consolidating. Many models of the change process and the categorization of change by type or position within an organization structure are not content-specific. They offer a series of very broad generalizations, and contain within themselves a series of key markers with regard to how to implement change. On the printed page the various categorizations of change (see, for instance, Table 2.1 and Figure 2.1) appear rational and mechanistic. It is important to realize that they are only broadly illustrative of the key aspects of change, leaving a lot unsaid.

Very briefly, in the material drawn upon here change is classified in two ways: the Hunt and Lostock categorizations help to describe change in terms not only of its magnitude but also of its level within an organization. Hunt (1986) distinguishes four orders of change:

Routine.
To meet crises.
Innovative.
To transform the organization into a different social system.

The Lostock model (named after an ICI chemical works in Cheshire, UK) builds up an organization layer by layer (Figure 2.2), each layer having a

What do existing approaches offer?

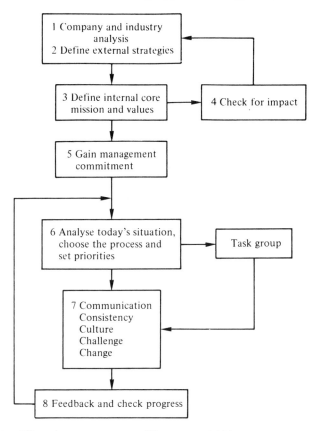

Figure 2.1 *The change process (Savage, 1987)*

different balance in terms of internal/external focus and its role in relation to improvement. The longer-term, large-scale, more complex and strategic changes are handled at the top of the organization (the 'raising capability' and 'business linking' levels), while the day-to-day operations and their improvement are handled by the bottom three levels (from the bottom upward, 'maintenance', 'improving' and 'adapting').

It is the maintenance level that is concerned with the day-to-day operation and control of a particular work process within a series of given parameters, i.e. rules, programmes and procedures – the 'known tasks'. The immediately upper two levels are concerned with the shorter ('improving' level) and longer term ('adapting' level) improvement of the existing process. Both of these levels are directly linked to the day-to-day structure as they both learn from it, and apply that learning to improving the process. The key linking layer between the day-to-day operation and its longer-term development is 'improving', which seeks to manage and improve the day-to-day operation by means of small modifications and

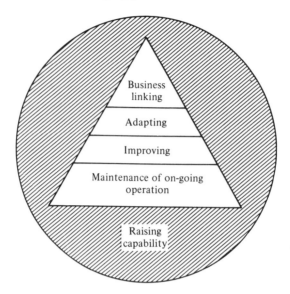

Figure 2.2 *Macrae/Lostock model of the key processes operating within an organization*

adjustments which are not sufficient to require large-scale resources or expertise, and do not deflect the bottom levels from their prime task of producing an output.

The Lostock model shows each of the five functions occurring within an organization in a hierarchical form, but it is better to regard them as overlapping, or as the five sides of a pentagon – i.e. they are in partnership with one another. The key issue for any company is to ensure that all of the five levels of function exist and are in balance with each other, and that the other elements of the organization – its skills, shared values, style, structure, staff and systems (six of the McKinsey 7 S's (Waterman *et al.*, 1980) – are acting in a supportive fashion.

Within the framework offered by the Lostock model, which also reflects Galbraith's ideas on the design of organizations based on their ability to process information, it is possible to place Hunt's four orders of change. His routine and innovative changes would correspond with the improving and adapting levels in the Lostock model; the 'to meet crises' and 'to transform the organization into a very different social system' are very much part of the 'raising capability' level of the Lostock model.

We now have a composite framework which combines the types of change described in Figures 2.1 and 2.2 with responsibility for change in terms of organization (non-hierarchical) levels. It is within this framework that the process of change can be placed, remembering that the process to achieve change might well be the same at all five levels – all that is different being the magnitude of the change being handled.

The two models of the process of change offered in Figure 2.1 and Table 2.1 are typical of the many described in the growing literature on the 'management of change'. The three change strategies with their associated managerial behaviours/styles and predicted outcomes detailed in Table 2.1 provide a very broad summary of the change options available to a company. At one extreme is the force–coercion strategy which literally is the imposition of change almost irrespective of the consequences. It is underpinned by a series of beliefs that people are selfish, not trustworthy, are always seeking benefits for themselves, are generally lethargic and will not listen to reasoned argument. There remains doubt about how long imposed changes will stay in place: their benefits might be quickly realized, but be shortlived or difficult to maintain over time.

Table 2.1 *Change strategies, management behaviour and predicted change outcomes (based on Schermerhorn (1985: 637); see also Schermerhorn (1986: 517–519)*

Change strategy	Managerial behaviour	Predicted outcomes
1 Force–coercion	Unilateral action Command	Temporary compliance
2 Empirical–rational	Rational persuasion Expert testimony Demonstration projects	Longer-term internalization
3 Normative–re-educative	Shared power Participative decisions Group process	Longer-term internalization

The middle-ground change strategy is the 'empirical–rational' option. Here the basic approach is to provide information, expert testimony, experimental and demonstration projects in order to raise awareness, improve understanding etc. of individuals within an organization. This strategy relies upon the premise that information, however presented, is open to only one interpretation, and that the 'reasonable person', if given that information, will come to the same conclusion as the presenters of the information. Such an educational approach to change has its merits, and can be effective if used at an appropriate moment.

Of the three change strategies the third is the only one that seeks to challenge, develop and build upon the values, beliefs and assumptions that underlie individual and group behaviour. It seeks to establish on an open and joint basis a 'set of rules' (at the crudest level) and a 'vision and value statement' (at the most refined level) by which the organization will seek to change itself. The basis of this model lies in applied research which indicates that the only way to change behaviour significantly in the long term is to consider in detail the influences upon an individual's behaviour. A wide range of factors shape the behaviour of an individual, many of which are under the direct control of an organization, e.g. management style, pay and rewards system, conditions of work, quality of communications, training and development opportunities, career progression possibilities etc. Each of these factors form part of an organization's management strategy to control, develop and direct the applied behaviour, i.e. the work, of individuals, teams and the organization as a whole.

The third change strategy recognizes both the need to examine the beliefs and values that underlie behaviour and the complex mix of factors deployed within an organization to shape and direct behaviour. This strategy therefore seeks to bring about changes in job content and organization structure not by imposition or education, but by changing the behaviour of individuals who will themselves bring about the appropriate changes. It is a strategy which is also based on a series of assumptions about people and their needs. For example, the following list was generated by one group of senior production, engineering and personnel managers drawn from a large multi-national manufacturing company in order to make explicit their assumptions about people, as a step in developing their vision for the future.

Most people want to learn and develop.
Most people like to take a pride in what they do.
Most people want to help others.
Most people like to work in effective and successful teams.
Most people want their own contribution to be recognized by others.
Most people want to achieve realistic targets/goals.
Most people want to be well informed.
Most people will contribute to worthwhile tasks/goals.
Most people want to help in the improvement of their company.
Most people want responsibility, not accountability.
Most people have ideas of value to contribute.
All people like to be rewarded commensurate with their contribution.
Most people like stability/certainty but will adapt to purposeful change.
Most people can be led, some need to be pushed.
Most people need a challenge/stimulation.
Most people want to influence/have direct control of their work.

Most people need to work to and for a purpose.
Most people need some direction but understand the purpose of their activities.
All people like job security.
Most people want to compete and win.
Most people want to respect and trust good leaders/managers.
Most people are loyal.

Apart from these assumptions about people, it is also implicit in the third change strategy that the most effective and, in fact, probably the only way to change an individual's behaviour is to create a situation in which they can change their own behaviour. Because of this, almost invariably the normative change strategy takes longer to show a significant return on the input but in the long term can yield huge benefits.

In describing these three very broad change strategies it is too easy to give the impression that they are mutually exclusive. This is not the case. Over the period of a few years it is quite possible for a company to shift its general approach towards introducing change from, say 'force–coercion' to 'empirical–rational'. Such a shift in approach occurs not because the management of a company have radically changed their beliefs about people (though this is not unknown), but because the trading position of the company has changed. In fact, too many companies switch between two basic approaches to change, depending on their trading position. First, many company managements consider that during a recession the only way to survive is to impose a series of changes, e.g. to reduce the numbers employed, introduce temporary employment contracts etc. The urgency does not allow any alternative, it is believed. (It is noteworthy, however, that a number of companies which imposed cost-cutting changes in the early 1980s and which have been continuously trying to raise productivity have been forced to realize the need to change the very basis of their methods of operation and their organizations: they are now trying to change attitudes and behaviour.) Second, during periods of more buoyant trading these companies adopt a different change strategy by means of either the 'rational' or the 'normative' route. This shift again reflects a management view that 'we can afford to take longer and, anyway, we wouldn't get away with imposing any changes'. Unfortunately this switching between two or more change strategies reflects the misunderstanding by many managers of the very nature of successful long-term change.

The final contribution to this discussion of the process of change is a model developed by Peter Savage when he was Manufacturing Director and Site Manager of the Exxon Chemicals facility at Fawley, near Southampton. In 1979 he adopted the last of the three change strategies described above and proceeded to devise an eight-element model of the change process (Figure 2.2). In all, eight key ingredients made up the successful change strategy at Fawley. For example, it was vital to build, upon a sound business plan for the site, a core mission and value statement. There then follow six key concepts embodied in Steps 5 and 7: commitment, communication, consistency, culture, challenge and change. Note that the main emphasis of the process is on the creation of the conditions for, and the facilitation of, change. The simple idea is that the bulk of the effort in any change process should be devoted to moving the mass, not the tip, of the iceberg. This, once achieved, makes the implementation of 'change' a relatively simple matter.

From this brief discussion of 'change' in terms of process and organization structure, what can be learnt to help formulate a method whose purpose is to design and change job contents and organization structures? The following are the main learning points that can influence the development and design of the method. A method is required that can:

1 Handle a wide range of changes in terms of source, volume and complexity.
2 Involve everyone potentially affected by the outcome of the change process, as everyone has a role in the implementation of change and most people want to participate.
3 Handle both the current, familiar situation and 'the unknown', in terms of market uncertainties, work volume fluctuations etc.
4 Both handle complex situations and also facilitate the initiation of a series of parallel and related change initiatives.
5 Build upon the organization structure and result in a robust model which is explicable to those affected by the resulting changes.
6 Be used in a way that recognizes that change is of necessity a long-term process.
7 Show that it can build upon and/or develop a stated mission and value statement, and also show how the resulting job and organization structures relate to that mission and value statement.
8 Cope with an ill-defined problem in such a way that it sifts both internal and external factors in the process of focusing a study.
9 Adapt to different local circumstances and conditions: that is, the method should be rigorous but not over-mechanistic nor dependent upon only a single means of moving forward.
10 Include, in the initial focusing of the study and subsequent stages, both the 'physical attributes' of the organization and the attitudes of its members.
11 Build upon and channel the ease and readiness with which weaknesses in the current organization can be identified and general willingness to find ways to overcome them.

12 Cope with a continuous process of communication with those who may be affected by the changes following the method's application (it also follows that the method must be able to produce 'communicable' material, e.g. its output should be presentable in diagrammatic form).
13 Act, if necessary, as part of a positioning and change-presentation process thereby preparing people for the output of the method's application.

These thirteen requirements help to direct the consideration of the available methods and also assist the overall development of the study method.

Existing approaches to job analysis and organization design

Before using the factors identified above as being important in the design and operation of a method that seeks to structure the design of jobs and organizations, it is necessary to consider briefly what methods already exist. The following review of existing methods is only illustrative: it does not claim to be comprehensive. We then move forward by taking the list of thirteen points developed above and begin to focus on a number of existing methods which meet most of the 'change process' design criteria.

Table 2.2 lists job analysis and related methods and techniques with brief evaluations across eight broad categories. This presentation is based on that used in the Institute of Personnel Management's *Job Analysis: A Practical Guide for Managers* (Pearn & Kandola, 1988). It is useful to expand slightly on these categories:

Orientation
    Task   Focuses on the precise activities or tasks carried out by a job holder.
    Worker   Concentrates on the underlying skill, aptitudes and other attributes of people.
Quantification
    High   Produces numerical or quantitative data.
    Low   Produces qualitative or subjective data.
Structure
    High   Method is highly detailed in a checklist form.
    Low   Content is very much dependent upon on the analyst, i.e. the applier of the method.

Table 2.2 A comparison of job analysis methods and approaches (based on Pearn & Kandola (1988); Johannsen (1988); McCormick (1979); Hackman & Oldham (1975))

Method/approach	Orientation[1]	Quantification[2]	Structure[3]	Packaging[4]	Sophistication[5]	Proximity to jobs[6]	Applicability[7]	Sensitivity[8]
1 Observation	Task	High	Moderate	Low	Low	High	Moderate	Low
2 Self-description/diaries/logs	Task	Low	Low	Low	Low	High	High	Low
3 Job analysis interviews	Task or Worker	Low	Moderate	Low	Low	Moderate	High	High
4 Critical incident technique	Worker	High or Low	Low	Low	Moderate	Moderate	High	High
5 Repertory grid	Worker	High or Low	Low	Low	High	Moderate	High	High
6 Checklist/inventories	Task	High	High	High	Low to High	Low	Moderate	Low
7 Hierarchical task analysis	Task	Low	Low	Low	Moderate	High	Moderate	High
8 Job-learning analysis	Worker	Low	High	High	Moderate	Moderate	High	High
9 Job components inventory	Worker	High	High	High	Moderate	Moderate	Moderate	Moderate
10 Position analysis questionnaire	Worker	High	High	High	High	Moderate	High	Low
11 Participant observation	Worker	High	High	High	Moderate	Moderate	Moderate	Moderate
12 Content analysis	Task or Worker	High or Low	High or Low	Low	Low	High or Low	Low	Moderate
13 Expert conferences	Worker	Low	Low	Low	High	High	Low	Moderate
14 Work performance survey system	Task	High	High or Low	High	Low	High	High	Moderate
15 Combination job analysis method	Worker	Moderate	Moderate	Low	Low	Low	High	Moderate
16 Functional job analysis	Task or Worker	High	High	Low	High	Low	High	Moderate
17 Job element method	Worker	Moderate	Moderate	Low	High	Low	High	Moderate
18 Ability requirement scales	Worker	High	High	Moderate	High	Low	High	Low
19 Problem incident	Worker or Task	High or Low	Low	Low	Moderate	Moderate	High	High
20 Fault analysis	Task	High or Low	Low	Low	Low	Moderate	High	High
21 Activity/work sampling	Task or Worker	High	High	Low	Low	High	High	Moderate
22 Job diagnostic survey	Worker	High	High	Moderate	Moderate	High	Moderate	Moderate
23 Fault management matrix analysis	Task	High or Low	Low	Low	Low	Moderate	Moderate	High
24 Work measurement/time study	Task or Worker	High	Moderate	Low	Low	Moderate	Moderate	Low
25 Occupation analysis inventory	Worker	High	High	High	High	Moderate	High	Low
26 Job information matrix system	Task or Worker	High	High	Low	High	Low	High	Moderate

[1] Worker or task-orientated methods.
[2] Quantified (high) or qualitative (low) methods.
[3] Open-ended (low) or closed (high) methods.
[4] Packaged systems (high) or do-it-yourself (low).
[5] Sophisticated (high) or straightforward (low) techniques.
[6] Remote from (low) or close to (high) the jobs under study.
[7] Wide application (high) or narrow (low).
[8] Adaptable (high) or inflexible (low).

What do existing approaches offer?

Packaging
- High Highly detailed pre-packaged systems which cover the whole process from formulation of objectives to interpretation and presentation of results.
- Low Internally/self-generated checklists, methods etc.

Sophistication
- High Requires a high level of knowledge and understanding of statistical methods and of their application and interpretation.
- Low Easy to use with little or no additional knowledge or training other than that required to understand the method being applied.

Proximity to jobs:
- High Active observation of, and even participation in, the job under study.
- Low Reliance upon more remote methods of collecting job-related information.

Applicability:
- High Almost unrestricted in its application and can be used in most if not all situations.
- Low Limited to a particular job or type of work.

Sensitivity:
- High Able to detect and record the discretionary and less visible attributes of a job.
- Low A more structured and detailed approach, less likely to detect subtle but important aspects of a job.

If we apply to these eight categories the thirteen criteria that were generated from the discussion of the process of change, the result is:

Orientation	Task
Quantification	High
Structure	Medium
Packaging	Medium
Sophistication	Medium to low
Proximity to jobs	High
Applicability	High
Sensitivity	High

Of the methods listed in Table 2.2, none satisfies the above list, and only seven agree on five of the category descriptors; the methods are:

Job analysis.
Interview.

Content analysis.
Work performance survey system.
Problem incident.
Fault analysis.
Activity/work sampling,

However, this is not to say that other methods do not have a possible contribution to make in the development of a method.

The twenty-six methods listed in Table 2.2 are predominantly of two types: either they focus on work in terms of the worker, examining the nature of the work performed and the attributes of the workers, or they focus on the work itself, varying as to data collection, data categorization and/or the element of the work considered. For example, the various task analysis approaches (e.g. hierarchical task analysis) consider the whole range of tasks an individual or a group of individuals undertakes. Others focus on key elements of the work, such as problem incident and fault analysis. One of the design criteria emerging from Chapter 1 and from the discussion in the first part of this chapter is the need to be able to handle complex situations. For example, the method must be able to comprise:

1. The underlying beliefs of people.
   The development of people.
   The idea of error reduction.
   The development of jobs that will stretch and develop people.
   The notion of 'learning by doing' and continuous improvement.
   The development of employee commitment to change.
   A project focus and built-in evaluation criteria for the assessment of progress.
2. Mission, vision and value statements.
   Zero accidents as the only target safety index.
   Communications in the fullest sense of the term.
3. Alignment of business strategy formulation with the means for its implementation in terms of organization structure.
   Coping with external pressures reshaping the workforce,
4. A scanning process which can identify and clarify the problems, and which sorts and places in order causes and symptoms.

None of the methods listed in Table 2.2 can cope with all of these requirements. They are what can best be described as 'second-order techniques', i.e. they are not lead techniques or methods in the overall process of change. They can be applied only after some other method has identified a need for their application. This is not to say, however, that the methods listed cannot form a part of an overall method.

This discussion can be taken further forward by considering other design criteria for a method in terms of the mechanics of its application, and also in terms of its output, building upon the discussion in the first part of this chapter and the methods listed in Table 2.2.

Criteria for the mechanics and specific steps of the method

1 The underlying assumptions and innate biases of the method must be made explicit from the outset: does the method, once applied, automatically lead to one type of output?
2 While the method must aid in the structuring of problem definition, project focus, data collection and analysis, it must still retain choice/ discretion.
3 Depending upon the outcome of the problem definition stage, the method must be able to cope with the combined or separate orientations to raise plant utilization and availability via a reliability or maintainability centred approach. All efforts to change job content and organization structure are seeking to combine the abilities of people with a production technology of some description and a controlling system e.g. planning and scheduling, raw material ordering etc. Most organizations, even those operating on a 'not-for-profit' basis, are trying to raise the effectiveness and efficiency of their production system by raising its utilization and availability. There are only two main ways to achieve this objective: either by raising the reliability of the production system by the systematic removal of blocks and barriers to a good production run, or by investing in the organization to create an ability to handle errors – i.e. the efficiency of the production system is raised by improving the quality and speed of response to system failure. The method must not therefore just seek to rearrange the present range of activities, but be able to refocus and redirect effort to improve the current situation.
4 Too many methods focus on the performer and/or his/her work, or on the process or some specific aspect of it, which must result in only a partial analysis of the potential barriers to improvement. The method must not only cope with a 'blank sheet of paper' or 'greenfield' approach, but also, in the course of designing and developing jobs and organization structures, deal with the complementary design of the production process and support services.
5 A key assumption that underlies the normative change strategy is the primary and unique contributions that an individual can make to the improvement of an organization. Moreover, many of the talents of individuals lie dormant and undeveloped as a result of the almost repressive design of jobs and organizations. For example, the bulk of

activities in manufacturing and packaging facilities require less than a month to learn (56 per cent of the tasks, and 67 per cent of the work by volume – i.e. by frequency of occurrence × the duration of the the task) and only 20 per cent of the work requires six or more months to master. It is surprising how constant this profile is, irrespective of process considered (see Chapter 7).

6 Another weakness of many methods is their rigidity: they can only be applied in one way and often must be applied completely. It is important that a method that seeks to design and develop jobs and organization structures, which is a long-term process, can adapt to local needs and circumstances, produce useful products at each stage, and be applied both formally and informally.

7 Perhaps sometimes unwittingly, methods and techniques evolve a language of their own which has little or no relevance to everyday activities at work. Furthermore, those methods which rely upon relatively complex statistical techniques introduce a still further set of jargon. Different and difficult terminology distances the users of a method from those on whose behalf it is being applied. This must be avoided, otherwise a barrier to communication is established.

8 Good methods making use of inadequate information cannot be expected to produce useful results and sound recommendations for action. The information must be reliable and verifiable, draw upon everyday experiences and events, use existing data where applicable, draw upon all potential sources in order both to appear and to be comprehensive, and maximize involvement in the process. The data must clearly also relate to the trio of interrelated factors of production systems: availability, maintainability and reliability.

9 In collecting data on work it is necessary to establish a currency, i.e. a unit, which everyone can understand, and which can then be used in developing roles and jobs, organizations, team membership etc. The most basic unit of work, 'the task', can be defined as follows: 'A task is a unit of work, is performed by an individual employee or employees, has a definite beginning and end, and results in a product or service' (see McCormick 1979: 19) and Chapter 5). Working initially at the level of the task allows further refinements of analysis, e.g. complexity or difficulty of the task, significance or criticality of the task, assistance required in performing the task etc. The number of secondary rating factors required depends upon the situation under investigation. Working at the task level also allows complete freedom to manipulate, redistribute and delete work as and when necessary. It is also developed out of what most people know best – what they do each day expressed in a language that they can readily understand. Finally, it is possible by working at the task level to recognize such factors as fear in an individual performing a task (something may be both easy to do and

frightening – e.g. climbing inside a vessel to clear a jam), the geography of the tasks, the time-pressure on task performance etc.

10 One point that repeatedly emerges from discussions of the change process is the need to involve, to consult, to communicate, to listen and to feed back on a continuous basis. This calls for a 'consensus systems design' approach (Mumford, 1981), i.e. 'a form of participation in which attempts are made to involve all members of the user department continuously throughout the design process'. Adoption of this consensus approach helps to provide a social process in which a rational method can be applied (see Lupton & Tanner, 1987).

11 A new method is unlikely to be developed unless its roots are firmly embedded in many of the current methods and approaches, and unless it is built upon research into, for example, task complexity and work efficiency, the loading of jobs etc. There is thus a body of research and practical experience which should assist in the development of a method, and in the interpretation of the output of that method. Key recent research studies include *Knowledge, Skill and Artificial Intelligence* (Goranzon & Josefson, 1988), *The Meaning of Work and Technological Options* (de Keyser *et al.*, 1988), *New Work Patterns* (Leighton & Syrett, 1989) *Tasks, Errors and Mental Models* (Goodstein *et al.*, 1988) etc. and more general works such as *From Taylorism to Fordism. A Rational Madness* (Doray, 1988).

There is rapidly growing volume of research material that describes, and in a few cases explains, the changes in the shape, nature and distribution of work and offers important insights into the task, technology and employment interrelationship. Any method, to be up to date and relevant, must be open to the inclusion of the findings of appropriate research.

12 One of the immediate problems confronted by any method is the level or scale upon which it is applied, and its ability to handle interrelationships between the levels. For example, the Lostock model (Figure 2.1) distinguishes five levels which must be developed in order to create a high-performance organization. It is unlikely that a method which operates at only one of the five levels (e.g. 'raising capability' or 'maintenance') will result in an improved organization. The method must be able to cope with all aspects of the organization and to place in context the specific focus of a study of only one or two levels.

13 While it is not vital that every aspect of the method be understood fully by everyone involved in its use and application, it is important that the underlying concepts of the method are relatively easy to explain and understand, and that the application of the method and the interpretation of the findings are not expert-dependent.

14 Most, if not all, methods are effective – they achieve their objectives – but quite a number are inefficient, disruptive, time-consuming and

costly to apply. Often a method cannot be applied at all unless it is applied with full support. It is therefore important that the method is easy to integrate into day-to-day activities and does not require a large amount of resources. It should also be possible, when applying the method, to trim back the time and resources devoted to it and to spell out the attendant consequences. For example, if the study period is halved is the quality of the output also reduced by half?

15 Most of the methods and techniques listed in Table 2.2 do not focus on the improvement of the outputs of a job, but rather on the job itself. One consequence of this approach is that the existing pool of tasks is redistributed instead of being challenged. Should a certain task be undertaken? Can it be improved, or deleted, or substituted? The method must not just describe the current situation, it must seek to challenge and improve upon it.

16 Very few organizations wish to be the first ones to apply any new approach or method: they want the reassurance that others have gone before them. This is almost an impossible criterion to satisfy. Virtually identical methods can have widely differing results unless application is highly controlled, i.e. among a restricted number of senior managers rather than in a highly participative fashion.

These sixteen further criteria help to define in still greater detail an appropriate method for the design and development of job contents and organization structures. An additional ten criteria have been developed concerning the outputs of the method, and when taken with all of the other criteria will result in a very clear definition of an appropriate method.

Criteria for the outputs of the method

1 One of the key outputs of any approach is that by its very application it should raise the likelihood of a successful implementation. Its purpose, interim outputs, data collection etc. and the implementation of its recommendations must be explicitly recognized in the design of the method.

2 As with all processes, the greater the range of outputs that can be produced by it, the greater its value. The method must therefore be able to produce wide range of outputs and its database should also have lasting utility. The products it should be able to contribute include:

Organization structure.
Team membership.
Job content and roles.
Estimate of the resource required to implement the recommendations.

What do existing approaches offer?

    An input into the design of the pay system.
    Balance between the use of in-house and out-of-house resources (contractors, temporary staff etc.)
    Design of training material, both in terms of content of training modules and in particular in determining training objectives, trainability assessments and job competencies.
    Establishment of job anchors for an appraisal/performance management system.
    Academic debates on, for instance, the alleged deskilling effects of technology.

Thus, depending upon the method and, in particular, on the data collected, it should be possible to produce a whole series of interrelated outputs.

3 The steps involved in the analysis of the data must be easy to understand and, if possible, to display in simple graphic and diagrammatic form. The analysis should be reproducible via a readily available computer software package.
4 The structure of the method and the nature of the outputs at each stage should be capable of being supportive of existing initiatives and even of leading them if necessary.
5 In analysing the data collected and in developing job roles and organization structures, the method should be able to produce options which can be evaluated. No method that is concerned with jobs and organization structures can really produce only one single solution, given the range of factors involved. This should ideally mean that an initial cost–benefit analysis can be undertaken on the final options.
6 One of the problems of many methods is that their output is a once-and-for-all output: the output is difficult to update and revise. If many of the longer-term benefits of a significant investment in a job and organization structure design exercise are to be realized it is important that it can be reviewed and updated. The process of job and organizational development is a dynamic one, and the method's output should recognize this.
7 In relatively recent times information on the experiences of different companies has become more widely available. Much of this is charted in the various specialist personnel and industrial relations journals, and also in a large number of books and reports. It is also noticeable that an increasing number of companies are actively seeking opportunities to share experiences with other, non-competing companies. The method should be able to assist in this process.
8 All too often in a change process there is overemphasis on the selling–negotiation phase and too little upon the preceding preparation, and the succeeding implementation stages. A key part of implementation is

the recognition of improvements made rather than the charting of events and happenings. What are the costs and benefits to date from implementation? This should be an integral part of the implementation stage, and an output to which the method should at least contribute in its development. This is particularly important in those cases where improvement/change and pay have been linked in some way.
9 One of the prime objectives of the final output of any job and organization design exercise is to provide further evidence that will reassure some people, reinforce confidence in others etc. The evidence presented and its format are key aspects of the launch of the implementation stage, and the method should be able, through the information collected, to provide a full and convincing case.
10 In attempting to challenge existing practices it is very easy to substitute one bad and unsafe practice for another. The method should include, either in the analysis or the evaluation stage, some check on such errors.

This consideration of existing methods and further examination of the 'musts' of a job and organization design method has resulted in thirty additional criteria: four relating to its overall approach, sixteen to its detailed operation and structure, and ten to the outputs. The following section takes these thirty criteria and combines them with the thirteen developed from the brief consideration of the process of change to design the method's structure.

Criteria for a method to design and develop job content and organization structures

In all, forty-three design criteria have been developed in the preceding part of this chapter, and these can be reduced to twenty-five by the removal of duplicates etc. These twenty-five criteria are:

Comprehensiveness.
Maximum participation.
Handles uncertainty.
Facilitates change.
Comprehensible/understandable process and outputs.
Time-elastic.
Combines vision with reality.
Universal applicability.
Adaptable.
Communicable outputs.

What do existing approaches offer?

Combines business strategy with organization structure.
Assumptions explicit/bias-free.
Maximizes choice/discretion.
Production process/output/error-reduction orientation.
Maximizes people's capabilities/improves job satisfaction.
Jargon-free.
Data-efficient.
Works from lowest possible common denominator at work – the task.
Operates at all levels/scales.
Reliable/effective/efficient.
Multiple outputs.
Easily updated.
Structure reflects balance of effort in the process of change.
Evaluation of output a key stage.
Exhaustive.

Now, armed with this list of design criteria, we can ask whether there is any method that can satisfy some or all of them. One general approach, known as *socio-technical design* (other variants also exist, e.g. transformation analysis, work restructuring, socio-technical systems assessment survey, socio-technical systems redesign method, open systems analysis and high performance work systems design) seeks to study both the social and the technical systems and result in a jointly designed socio-technical system. It is an integrated approach which does not give priority either to people or to technology, but does recognize the unique ability of people. It also recognizes the fallacies of both 'the technology imperative' and 'the technology fix' which give almost total priority to technology, i.e. approaches that hold that all solutions are based in technology and that total reliability is both possible and desirable.

The socio-technical design approach for the development of jobs, organization and production systems grew out of work started in the 1940s and was developed by the Tavistock Institute for Human Relations. It is an approach that has been known for over forty years and has been quite widely applied (see Pasmore (1988) for a review of its uses in the USA). While detailed texts and articles exist describing its origins and application (Hill (1971), Heller (1989), Cherns (1987), Herbst (1972), Taylor (1971), Pasmore (1988) – the list is a very long one), they generally lack the detail to allow direct application. For example, both Hill (1971) and Pasmore (1988) describe the ten or so stages in the application of the socio-technical approach, but do not contain enough detail for operators to design their own jobs. The 'Job Design' teaching manual of the Department of Employment and Industrial Relations of the Australian Government (Commonwealth of Australia, no date) provides some very useful teaching exercises and checklists, but is primarily concerned with the quality of working life and job re-design. As a teaching manual it also brings together many useful articles by Taylor, Mumford and others.

A number of areas have been identified where the socio-technical approach as generally applied and described in the literature is weak. It should be stressed that it can be modified to overcome these weaknesses.

1 There is a tendency to portray socio-technical design as a method or technique, rather than a social process by means of which organizations can be developed and improved. For example Paul Hill (1971), in his book about the application of the socio-technical design approach in Shell UK, describes in an appendix the method applied to a bitumen operation. He presents it not as a 'change process' in its own right but more as the outcome of the new management philosophy of Shell. It is interesting to note that Shell are going through a similar process at the present time at their major UK refinery at Stanlow.

2 The very title 'socio-technical design approach' is sufficient to alienate many people before they have learnt about the power and relevance of the approach. Similarly, some of the language used in applying it can act as a barrier to its use – e.g. 'transformation analysis', 'socio-technical systems assessment survey', 'variance analysis' etc. It is important that all of the terms can be easily interpreted and, preferably, are based on those already used within the company, department etc. where the method is to be applied.

3 While Pasmore (1988:104 Figure 5.2) shows that the socio-technical design approach has been used widely (he reports 134 cases with 18 different applications) there is a tendency to see the approach as only having relevance if a new site is being established, or a whole new department is being set up. The reality is that the socio-technical design approach has wide applicability and can produce a wide range of products.

4 A significant part of the philosophy that underlies the socio-technical design approach is that it seeks not only to aid in development of more appropriate and better jobs and organization structures, but also over a period of time to create a high-performance organization. Thus, its application should result not in a static, but in a dynamic solution. A number of the case studies reported in the literature give the distinct impression that the approach is just another technique which is best used to design an autonomous working group, or the transfer of tasks between maintenance and operations, or the design of a pay system. Yes, the approach can be used to produce such products, but many of the full benefits would be lost if its application were not extended further.

5 In applying the socio-technical design approach there is a tendency to report 'the solution' resulting from its application, and not the range of

options. There is also a tendency almost to hide the subjective and judgmental input behind the quasi-scientific and quantitative elements. The whole basis of the socio-technical design approach – one which seeks to challenge 'the technological imperative' and 'the technological fix' and prove that there is a choice in jobs and organization structures – is reflected in its output. In the experience of the author it is often possible to produce a range of structure options (usually three or four main ones) and a very wide range of job content/role options, and the choice between them all can be as well decided by employee preference as by anything else.
6 One of the findings to emerge from the research work undertaken by the Tavistock Institute which underpins the socio-technical design approach is the huge capacity of human beings. Yet the approach in its application is often described in managerial terms. Surely an approach that seeks to build upon and to develop the abilities of people is almost necessarily employee-centred in its launch and application and in the implementation of the resulting output. Again, the *process* of change needs to be combined with the method of deciding on the *direction* of change.
7 Finally, one aspect of the change process which the socio-technical design approach tends not to mention in any great detail is communications. It is vital, as was stated earlier, to ensure a consistent and constant stream of communicable material which can assist in the application of the approach and the implementation of its output.

These seven potentially weak areas are minor and can all be removed with careful thought in the design and application of the socio-technical approach. They represent still further design criteria for the method or approach which is able to combine the process (the 'how'), the method (the 'what' and the 'how') and the objective (the 'output'). It is also apparent from this brief discussion of socio-technical design that it offers an approach likely to satisfy the design criteria listed in this chapter.

What else can this approach offer? Taking just two descriptions of the socio-technical design approach (Hill, 1971; Pasmore, 1988), it is clear that the approach offers a systematic multi-stage method for job and organization structure design. Tables 2.3 and 2.4 are examples of Hill's and Pasmore's interpretations and practical applications of the socio-technical analysis approach. Both provide a series of logical steps across which the approach can be applied. Pasmore takes the approach and places it within an overall 'change model'. Both tables present a framework upon which to build, and which can be modified to incorporate the twenty-five design criteria developed earlier. This combination of the socio-technical approach framework and design criteria forms the basis of Chapter 3, which describes an eight-stage approach for job and organization structure design.

Table 2.3 *Method of socio-technical analysis (Hill, 1971)*

Step 1	Obtaining a brief over-view of the production system and its environment
Step 2	Identification of unit operations
Step 3	Identification of key process variances and their relationships
Step 4	Analysis of the social system
Step 5	Job-holders' perception of their roles
Step 6	Maintenance system
Step 7	Supply and user system
Step 8	Company environment and development plans
Step 9	Proposals for change

Table 2.4 *Socio-technical systems change model (Pasmore, 1988)*

Step 1	Define scope of system to be redesigned
Step 2	Determine environmental demands
Step 3	Create vision statement
Step 4	Educate organizational members
Step 5	Create change structure
Step 6	Conduct socio-technical analysis
Step 7	Formulate redesign proposals
Step 8	Implement recommended changes
Step 9	Evaluate changes/redesign

Summary

In developing any new method or procedure it is necessary to learn from experience in the application of existing methods. A review of existing methods and also a consideration of four robust 'change models' yielded forty-three design criteria. This initial list of design criteria was then summarized and reduced to a more manageable twenty-five. The general approach offered by socio-technical analysis satisfied a large number of the criteria and provided a tried and tested framework. It is this framework which will be combined with the design criteria in Chapter 3 to produce a method which can be applied to design, develop and change job content and organization structures.

3
The structure of the approach

Introduction

Any change method or process comprises a number of key components: orientation, capability, output, application and structure. Each of the twenty-five design criteria developed in Chapter 2 can be slotted in under one or more of these five component headings. The result of this process, shown in Table 3.1, can then be combined with the models offered by Hill, Pasmore (see Tables 2.3 and 2.4), Foster (1967) and Cummings (1976). It is the purpose of this chapter to outline the output of this 'combination' exercise and the describe briefly the content of each of the resulting stages.

The first requirement is to consider the overall orientation and structure of the approach. The approach must not assume from the outset that the need for and benefit of change are either recognized or understood. The approach itself must either achieve this awareness or be embarked upon after a commitment to change has been achieved. There is therefore a need to ensure a 'high level of education', probably through direct experience and the development of individual perceptions, in the first phase. This 'education/winning commitment to change' can be brought about by means of explicit educational inputs (as in the rational approach to change) and/or by means such as the raising of awareness of dissatisfaction with the current situation and of 'what could be'. Considerable time and a number of interventions are needed in moving through the various stages of gaining commitment to change. The approach should devote sufficient time and effort to achieving just this: a commitment to change and the realization of its benefits. It should also be added that it is unrealistic to expect the approach to be the only way to change attitudes and to gain commitment. It must be envisaged as a part of a vehicle for change that will provide the focus for a particular set of changes, and will be complemented by other change processes.

Another key step is 'evaluation'. Evaluation in this context includes the evaluation of the proposed job and organization options, a continuous monitoring and re-evaluation as the jobs and organization develop, and evaluation as an implicit process at each stage – for example, in the selection of a method, in the review of the implementation strategies, in the scoping

Table 3.1 Design criteria for a change process and organization design method

Key component	Design criteria
1 Application	Maximum participation Facilitates change Time-elastic Maximizes choice/discretion
2 Structure	Reflects balance of effort in the process of change Evaluation of output a key stage
3 Output	Comprehensible/understandable Communicable Multiple Easily updated
4 Orientation	Production process/output/error-reduction Maximizes people's capabilities Works from lowest possible common denominator of work – the task
5 Capability	Comprehensive Handles uncertainity Combines vision with reality Universally applicable Adaptable Combines business strategy with organization Assumptions explicit/bias-free Jargon-free Data-efficient Operates at all levels/scales Reliable/effective/efficient Exhaustive Comprehensible/understandable/ non expert-dependent

of the study area etc. If improvements are to result from the development of new jobs and a different organization, they must emerge from a rational process. And, as a result, decisions and the choice of options become increasingly visible, open and participative.

The approach requires a twofold orientation: it must seek to achieve a significant improvement in the performance of a specific production process or administrative system; it must also seek to provide meaningful jobs which build upon and stretch people's capabilities so that they can realize their potential. These may appear to be mutually exclusive orientations, but they do not need to be so. Let us take an existing production process and represent it as a single line. In reality this is probably a discontinuous line, moreover a discontinuous, wavy line, i.e. the production process is made up of a series of sub-processes: the process is neither continuous nor focused. The objective of re-designing the process and of examining ways of improving its performance is to raise the level of continuity and to provide a more limited focus. Discontinuities in the process may arise from out-of-line quality checks and inspections, specialist modifications to the product, changeovers, breakdowns in the equipment etc. Some of these events can be integrated into roles which are currently in existence, others can be resolved by the redesign of the line. The exact balance between a capital solution and an organizational solution depends upon the purpose of the production process and the factors that limit its utilization. The approach must therefore seek to develop an understanding of the process and provide a data set which can then result in 'capital' and 'organization/people' solutions. One unit of data which can meet this requirement is the 'task'. The task can represent both a stage or event in the production process and a unit of work (see Chapter 5 for a definition).

With regard to application, the approach must involve people in as many ways as possible, and in sufficient depth, in:

Problem scoping.
Data collection.
The making of key decisions, e.g. selection of options.
The implementation of the options.

This process of participation and involvement is integral to any change process, and thus satisfies the requirement, in the approach's structure, for integration of the 'change process'. However, the time available for the development and implementation of a change process by which new jobs and organizational structures are brought into being varies enormously. The method must therefore be able to be varied depending upon the time available and the precision and accuracy required. For example, a study examining the viability and benefits of introducing flexible working and multi-skilling across a series of manufacturing sites does not require the same detail as one in which potential job-holders are examining their own roles. These 'time' and 'degree of detail' factors affect not the structure of the approach, but its application.

Both the 'capability' and 'output' components relate to specific stages of the approach. For example, 'comprehensive', 'combines vision and reality', 'combines business strategy with organization' and 'operates at all levels/scales' all relate to the method itself and the breadth of information used in scoping the issues before developing the terms of reference. For 'output' the criteria are concerned with the utility of the output.

The overall structure of the approach

The overall structure (Table 3.2) has been designed both to design new jobs and organization structures and also to bring them into being. As indicated in Table 3.2, there are eight major stages. Each of them is described briefly and then followed in subsequent chapters by a more complete explanation.

Table 3.2 *Overall structure of the approach to change job and organization structure*

Stage 1	Detailed preparation for initial launch of a change initiative
Stage 2	Development of the terms of reference/rules for the proposed change
Stage 3	Definition/scoping of the problem/issues to be tackled
Stage 4	Selection of the appropriate method
Stage 5	Data and information collection
Stage 6	Data analysis
Stage 7	Selecting the 'best option'
Stage 8	Implementation

Note: This is not a simple linear process; there are feedback loops at all stages.

Stage 1. Detailed preparation for initial launch of a change initiative

Before embarking upon a detailed and rigorous examination of a particular job or organization, it is necessary first to gain acceptance that there is a need to make improvements and that areas of weaknesses are recognized. This process creates a level of dissatisfaction with the current situation, and can be positively produced by focusing on a 'desired future' and by developing a company/site mission or charter. The net result of this stage is to achieve a realization of the need to change and an acceptance of the broad direction in which change should proceed.

Stage 2. Development of the terms of reference/rules for the proposed changes

One of the most important steps, both in a change process and in a study of jobs and organization structures, is the identification and clarification of the key issues. This stage allows the surfacing and testing of the assumptions of individuals with regards to the current situation, and it then encourages the joint development and acceptance of the final terms of reference. In simple management terms, the more loosely defined the terms of reference are, the more difficult it is to manage the study and to know whether it is complete. It is at this stage that a design team or study group can be formed.

Stage 3. Definition/scoping of the problem/issues to be tackled

While the careful drafting of the terms of reference can include the scoping of the study, it is useful to draft the terms of reference and then challenge them. It is often necessary to modify the terms of reference as new information comes to light. Moreover, terms of reference might be specific with regard to the output of their completion, but more vague as to the exact focus of the study – as to what is worth considering in detail in order to improve performance. It is also necessary to be able to have, as far as possible, a 'greenfield' start in the design of jobs and organization structures, so there must be a stage at which there is some agreed reduction of the possible scope of the study to manageable proportions.

Stage 4. Selection of the appropriate method

Chaper 2 indicated the wide range of factors which go to shape the content and structure of a possible method. It is important that those applying a particular method understand how and why the method was selected and the benefits of the method chosen.

Most of the emphasis in the above four stages is laid on the preparation of people for change, and in particular of the group of representatives who are undertaking a study of what to change. This group invariably consists of enthusiastic volunteers holding a few preconceptions. Stages 1–4 help them to consider their current situation in some detail, and to challenge their own thinking. They also provide them with the opportunity to develop as a team, which takes time and practice.

Stage 5. Data and information collection

Most organizations have a wealth of information which can be used for more than one purpose, and which needs to be identified before any new data is collected. If is also necessary to assess the time and resources available to collect the information, which will affect the detail and method of data collection. When it has been decided that new data is required, it should be collected with the purpose of the study in mind at all times, and also the efficiency with which it can collected – i.e., it must not become an imposition upon everyday activities. This stage also shows how, with the minimal amount of detail, an assessment can be made of job and organization structure options: a picture is built up from the minimum data requirements and it is shown how this can be augmented to raise the sophistication, accuracy and precision of the study.

Stage 6. Data analysis

Development of a data set based upon 'the task' means that it can be manipulated in a whole series of ways. This manipulation can be achieved by means of the application of a few broad rules, and can be further refined by detailed reference to each task in the design of individual jobs. Several other sets of information can be brought into play during this stage, and these might relate to the experience of other organizations, the implications for plant and equipment design etc. This stage results in developing a series of job and organization options: it rarely, if ever results in a single option.

Stage 7. Selecting the 'best option'

This stage is devoted to the selection of a particular option based on a series of evaluation criteria, and then a costs and benefits analysis of the selected option. These two evaluation steps might then require the option to be changed in some way, and/or have some implications for the option's implementation. Again, this stage should be as open as possible, and be a key part of the change process.

Stage 8. Implementation

In this stage the specific issue of the various ways in which new jobs and organization structures can be implemented is tackled. The discussion is also concerned with providing a more general perspective on the process of change, based on the lessons learnt from developments in over 140 companies. It is a stage which requires detailed planning and can make use of the data and analysis of Stages 5 and 6.

Summary

An eight-stage approach to the creation of the climate for change, identification of what to change and the implementation of change has been described briefly in this chapter. The structure and content of the approach are based directly upon the discussion in Chapter 2 about possible methods and approaches.

Readers interested in the process of initiating change should read Chapter 4, while those interested in the collection of data and its analysis should read Chapters 5 to 7 inclusive. Other readers interested in specific aspects of the method are referred to the contents list and the index.

4
Establishing a start point

Introduction

Before a decision can be made as to which job to change or what team structure (if any) is appropriate, it is necessary to create a shared view that change is necessary and worth while. The purpose of this chapter is to describe how a common purpose and view on the need for change can be engendered, and then built upon to create a focused examination of jobs, roles and organization structures. It consists of four sections, each of which deals with one aspect of ground preparation: the detailed preparation for the initial launch of a change initiative; the development of the terms of reference/rules for the proposed change; the definition/scoping of the problem/issues to be tackled; the selection of the appropriate method.

Detailed preparation for the initial launch of a change initiative

The purpose of this stage is to develop as full a picture as possible of the future requirements of the organization, which can be used to develop a shared perception of the need to change and a description of the desired future organization.

There are a number of ways in which a vision can be generated, and the methods selected depend upon the purpose to which the vision is going to be put. For example, it can be used as a step in the study method which can be subsequently used to assist in the evaluation of the job and organization options developed. It is also possible to develop a vision which highlights the style and cultural aspects of the new organization. Often this second approach results in a management charter which is developed at the top of an organization or site and is then cascaded down the organization for further refinement and development.

We deal first with the generation of a vision and then with the possible processes involved. A vision of the future organization structure and content is a collection of interrelated statements based on an assessment of

Establishing a start point

future products, markets, production system technologies, changes in society etc. These foreseen future states are then used to derive statements about jobs, organization, values etc. which paint a picture of the desirable and most likely future state of the organizaton. Development of a vision of the future requires:

An understanding of the current organization's strengths and weaknesses.
An awareness of the principles that underlie high-performance organizations.
Individual/personal views of the desired future organization state.
Appreciation of the shortcomings of many organizations.
Clear understanding of customer requirements.

Use of the 'vision' step in different circumstances is illustrated here by four examples, each of which describes actions and outcomes in a major company. The words used are drawn directly from the notes and discussions arising during the 'vision' stage in the case-study companies. After all four of the examples have been described, a summary section details the lessons learnt from the examples and the key action points.

Example 1. Pay strategy

In 1987 the manufacturing director and his senior production, technical, quality and personnel colleagues of a UK subsidiary of a US parent company met to produce the beginnings of a manufacturing strategy. In 1986 the UK turnover had reached £662 million of which £257 million were derived from exports, and a gross profitability of 26 per cent was achieved. Since 1982 the number of UK employees had declined from 9209 to 7247, i.e. by 21 per cent. In order to improve upon this level of profitability and to ensure secure employment the manufacturing director's team produced a manufacturing strategy which stressed the need for quality improvement and for the involvement of people. The manufacturing strategy called for 'a well motivated and flexible workforce led by a well motivated and effective management team'. In order to achieve this 'people objective', two key actions were identified: first, to design a pay structure better suited to the future of manufacturing; second, 'because team working is so central to the way we plan to operate, we intend to devote more resources to the training and development of those who are charged with leading teams'.

Following the formulation of the manufacturing strategy, a study group of senior and middle managers was established to define a manufacturing view on the pay structures and related policies which would be consistent with meeting manufacturing and business needs over the next five years and beyond. Rather than following any structured approach to the formulation of a picture of the environment within manufacturing, the study group relied upon unstructured brainstorming and external visits to UK-based sites known to be making significant 'people changes.' Many of the external views came from their involvement in a productivity group of companies which included Courtaulds, British Steel, BP, Unilever, Lever Brothers, Pilkington Brothers, Nissan etc. The net result of these exercises was a listing of points under seven headings as follows:

1 Products
 Products will be similar to current products.
 Product range may proliferate to match market needs.
2 Capital
 Investment will be linked to improving product quality and reducing manufacturing costs.
3 Process
 Facilities will be similar to current facilities and a state of TQC will exist in many areas using SPC and JIT techniques.
 Greater use of electronic/computer control and measuring equipment.
 Further automation of storage and handling.
 Greater volume flexibility.
4 Organization
 No radical change in organization.
 Fewer levels of management.
5 Management style
 Greater freedom for groups to operate with different styles.
 More emphasis on team working.
 First level of 'management' recognized as a key role.
 More constructive relationship with the unions by greater participation and involvement of all employees.
 Visible strategic direction regularly reviewed, updated and communicated.
 Regular, frank and open discussions on objectives and results.
 Less tolerance of substandard performance and/or performance management and positive reinforcement techniques that encourage good performance.
 Greater accountability at the lowest possible level.
 Encouragement of experimentation and risk-taking.
 'Man' managers in management positions.
6 Job design
 Machine operation and setting will be to specifications, with less being left to discretion; more prescribed guidelines for decisions and actions.
 Operators and craftsmen expected to make greater contribution towards improving job and product/process quality.
 Quality integration – self-inspection.

Some operator jobs to be enhanced to incorporate machine-setting skills.

Further integration of craft, technical, clerical and secretarial functions with operator activity.

Greater flexibility.

7 People

Single-status workforce to be accommodated in a common grade structure.

Acceptance and participation in change.

A flexible approach to work.

Committed and therefore more productive.

Act as ambassadors for the company.

More control over the quality and output of the process.

Craftsmen and operators will require a much better understanding of process.

This very broad picture of the environment within manufacturing was then used to guide the design of a new payments system which had one main objective – to increase employee involvement in manufacturing aims. However, it is interesting to note that even this limited vision represented a political compromise within the study group and the recipients of its report.

In this example the vision was developed in an ad hoc fashion and used in a very limited way, but it was still useful to the study group.

Example 2. Organizing for manufacturing excellence

A study group was established in November 1987 to develop the most effective and efficient means for the manning and organizing of manufacturing at three UK production sites. The group consisted of production, personnel, engineering, work study/industrial engineering managers and a consultant. In all, 2400 people were employed on the three sites producing pharmaceutical products in the form of liquids, tablets, inhalants etc. As one step in meeting the study's objectives the group developed a vision for the future manufacturing organization by means of three distinct steps:

1 A review of the strengths and weaknesses of the company.
2 Identification of the principles of an effective organization.
3 Preparation of personal vision statements.

The vision resulting from this process was then used to guide the analysis of task data and the design of the organization. First, the strengths and weaknesses of the company were reviewed.

Company strengths

> Technical competence on sites.
> Experience/know-how.
> Commitment/loyalty.
> Staff cover/many levels in the hierarchy.
> Ability to respond.
> Product quality progress.
> Computer systems.
> Under-utilized capacity.
> Fire-fighting ability.
> Communication media.
> Awareness of need for change among specific groups.
> Attractive pay structures.
> Improving facilities.
> Capital available for effecting change.
> High company profile in the industry.
> Enthusiasm from shop floor for quality circles etc.
> Inter-site cohesion.
> Caring company.
> Technical awareness.
> Customer service progress.

As part of the examination of weaknesses, a model of the organization was developed to help to classify them and provide a logical structure for the vision statement. This was scheduled at this stage to help members of the group to gain a broader concept of the elements that make up an organization and the way they fit together. The model found to be most appropriate to meet this requirement is based on the organization design concepts advanced by Jay Galbraith (1973).

Six categories of weakness were identified: organization, control/information, resource, people, culture and external relations. These categories were further subdivided by company, site and environment:

Company weaknesses

(a) Organization
    Imbalance of accountabilities/responsibilities.
    Method of process management.
    Management of small projects.
    Cost control.
(b) Control/information
    Pay structures.

Establishing a start point 41

      Industrial relations structures.
      Imbalance of accountabilities/responsibilities.
      Job evaluation.
      Lack of incentives.
(c) Resource
      Inventory management.
      Manpower planning (senior management continuity).
(d) People
      Job design.
(e) Culture
      'Not a learning organization'.
(f) External relations
      Industrial relations structures.
      Bargaining structures.
      Remoteness of marketing and research.
      Site/centre relationship.
      Product rationalization.
      Pack proliferation.
      'Too many fingers in the pie'.

Site weaknesses

(a) Organization
      Technical support remoteness.
      Inertia.
      Communications.
      Organization structure.
      Imbalance of accountability/responsibility.
      Technical skill v. management skill.
      Method of process improvement.
      Management of small projects.
      Under-utilization of 'shop floor' knowledge.
      Too many interactions/interruptions.
      Demarcations.
      Problem solvers divorced from problem areas.
      Unpredictable outputs.
(b) Control/information
      Cost information.
      Performance information.
      Imbalance of accountability/responsibility.
      Budgeting.
      In-process control v. product testing.
(c) Resource
      Inventory management.

Labour management
Manpower planning (senior management continuity).
New blood on the shop floor.
(d) People
Managerial competence.
Training and development.
'Have we got the right people?'
(e) Culture
Inertia.
Business awareness.
Cost consciousness.
Managerial competence.
Demarcation.
Safety.
(f) External relations
Site/centre relationship.
Safety.

Environment

(a) Organization
Introduction of new products and processes.
(b) Control/information
Industrial structure.
Bargaining structure.
(c) Culture
Culture/value system.
Safety.
(d) External relations
Industrial relations structure.
Bargaining structure.
Safety.

The personal visions of the study group members were built upon these lists of strengths and weaknesses; in all, five were produced. The following is a summary of these personal vision statements.

Vision 1

(a) Performance
Customer service.
Service level: export greater than 90%.
home greater than 98%.

Quality
- Continually improving quality index.
- Satisfy external regulatory authorities.
- Continually enhance the company's reputation in terms of actual and perceived product quality.

Cost
- Set meaningful budgets which are met.
- Reduce unit costs.

(b) Organization/structure
- Fewer levels of management.
- At sites, organization centred around product groups.
- More skills under the direct control of each level of management.
- Accountability matched with necessary training, resources and responsibilities.
- Individual responsibilities related to routine production not to be confused with long-term improvements, i.e. greater clarity of role avoiding mixed/diffuse responsibilities.
- Pay/reward system which reflects the responsibilities of individuals in the modified structure.
- A flexible system of working hours, working week, shift patterns etc. which can be matched to particular business needs.
- Technical specialists used only where high levels of expertise required and not in routine situations.

(c) Characteristics of the organization
- Business awareness at each level in the organization.
- Improved management skills at each level.
- Closer to the customer.
- Listens to customer and reacts.
- Flexibility to deal with unforecasted and unforeseen customer requirements.
- Information is transmitted easily and consistently up and down the management structure.
- Deals with new ideas; changes with enthusiasm and in a timely manner.
- Listens to staff suggestions and reacts.
- Adapts easily to current and future business needs.
- Technical, managerial and business skills continually improved.
- Provides sufficient incentives and rewards.
- Considers all aspects of safety.
- All individuals take responsibility for all of the performance objectives – quality, customer service, cost and safety.
- Union/industrial relations situation which enables performance objectives to be achieved and supports the structure and characteristics of the organization.

Greater management stability.
(d) Information/control systems/resources
Performance/cost information available on a daily basis and related to understood and accepted standards.
Quality information supplied on a daily basis.
Cost information which enables management decisions to be made at each level, to ensure good cost control.
More emphasis on control of material usage and overhead costs.
New or modified processes/systems/equipment introduced on time and without a disruptive effect on customer service, quality and cost performance.
End product testing reduced and replaced by more in-process control.
Production operators with greater responsibility for in-process control, basic engineering maintenance and equipment change-overs.
Labour planning system which enables fluctuations in workload to be handled cost-effectively.
Stock control/inventory management systems which reduce costs while improving customer service.
Control systems that do not divert management responsibility from other key tasks.
Greater emphasis on the role of industrial engineers in improving day-to-day performance.

Vision 2

The most effective and efficient means of manning and organizing manufacture is to restructure the factory operations into a series of product-orientated business centres on each site. A business centre is a closely integrated self-contained unit with short chains of command and clear open communications, operating as a single well-coordinated team with shared objectives and working towards the achievement of a clearly identified common goal. The key characteristics of a business centre are as follows:
(a) Close integration
The unit should be sufficiently small to be free from internal divisions and achieve total acceptance of common ideals and shared output.
(b) Self-containment
The unit must contain and control all the major resources required for effective and efficient manufacture.
(c) Short chains of command
There should be minimal layers of hierarchy in the organization – ideally only two intermediaries between the lowest operator and the business centre manager.

(d) Clear open communications
Communications both vertically and horizontally should be open and clear, with a high level of staff information and awareness; also open discussion of business centre issues and performance could be encouraged at all levels.
(e) Single well-coordinated team
All staff recognize their interdependence and commonality of purpose in striving towards a common goal.
(f) Shared objectives
Unlike the functional factory organization, all objectives within the business centre structure should be mutually compatible.
(g) Clearly identified common goal
All staff should be well aware of the single shared objective for all members of the business unit. Each staff member should be able to identify his/her contribution towards the common goal, thereby maximizing commitment and achieving high morale.

Vision 3

(a) Design principles
Development activities are separated from 'core business' activities, which are housed in the manufacturing centre.
Core business activities should utilize only robust manufacturing systems.
Process 'engineering' (technology-based activities) should be divorced from management activities.
Sufficient resources should be allocated to each core business area to allow its objectives to be met. This will include control over relevant support services.
Organisation structures should be designed to achieve and maintain 'a high rate of evolutionary change'. This suggests a move to tightly-knit operational teams and support teams within a flatter hierarchy, i.e. a move from a 'role' to a 'task' culture.
Authority and responsibility levels should be matched.
The staffing strategy should be one of keeping a core staff supplemented by temporary staff and contractors as appropriate (dictated by business needs).
(b) What the new organization might look like
On larger sites there should be more than one business or manufacturing centre.
There should be no more than four levels or layers in the organization.
Support functions are integrated into the business centre structure.
Teams abound (designed around 'chunks' of work).

The management style is 'open' and democratic but also very commercially aware.

Vision 4

The object is to create the most efficient factory units structured on the basis of self-contained business centres operating towards shared common goals. The units will optimize the performance of all their operations by ensuring that all staff are working towards the achievement of clearly defined objectives designed to maximize and coordinate all the activities in the factory unit.

(a) Implicit assumptions of the vision

Maximize profit potential.

Achieve maximum production efficiency while maintaining the highest quality standards.

Reduce unit costs.

Employ well-motivated and well-rewarded staff.

Provide funds for future investment.

(b) Organization roles

Factory manager. Responsible for the overall 'year-to-year' direction of the factory unit. Must be clearly identified as the sole controller/coordinator of factory operation, answerable only to the board.

Business centre manager. Responsible for the total 'month-to-year' activities of the business centre. Will ensure that all the objectives within the centre dovetail with the objectives of the supporting services in order to achieve the goals of the centre.

Section manager. Responsible for the 'week-to-month' activities of the centre. Will be involved with the detail of the operations within his/her section and will ensure that the activities of the specialist technicians are coordinated and effective.

Team leader. Responsible for the 'day-to-day' activities of the centre. He/she will be responsible for ensuring that all the day-to-day operational targets are achieved through the management of his/her team which will include specialist technicians. Ideally, the team should not be more than 20. Each member of the team must be aware of his/her responsibilities and accountabilities.

Operators/craftsmen. Responsible for the minute-to-minute functions within their specific area of operation. There will be differing levels of skill for both operators and craftsmen, dependent on job requirements and individual capabilities. The objective, of course, will be to maximize the individual capabilities of every employee in order to achieve job enrichment by giving as much accountability and responsibility as is practicable.

Specialist technicians. These will be the recognized experts within their field of operation. They will provide day-to-day support by linking

Establishing a start point

with the operators and craftsmen and the team leaders and they will also report to the section manager on projects and outstanding long-term problems of a technical nature.

Support services. The support services outlined above must be lean and functional, comprising specialists whose goal is primarily the provision of a first class service to the business centres. Any internal goals must be secondary to the goal of supporting the business centres.

(c) Control/information

In order to establish operational control over the factory unit it is necessary to be 'crystal clear' about what is actually to be achieved. These objectives must then be 'rolled down' through the factory in order that:

Each employee is aware of the overall goal of the factory/centre and what part he/she can play towards that goal.

Every operation within the factory can be critically examined in terms of its contribution to factory objectives.

Examples of some key objectives are as follows:

Output	Produce x million units in a year.
Performance	Achieve 75 per cent utilization on all lines.
Costs	Achieve x unit cost on a product A.
	Reduce material wastage by 10 per cent
Quality	Reduce rework stock by 10 per cent.
People	Achieve targeted number of x employees.
Customer service	Achieve service levels of 98 per cent.

From the above objectives, targets can then be set for each level within the organization, which in turn should then generate:

Clear lines of responsibility/accountability.
Clear reporting relationships.
Clear lines of communication.
An open system.
Any shortfalls within the system which could lead to the objectives not being met.
The type and format of the information required to measure whether objectives are being achieved.
The timescale by which each piece of information is required, e.g. daily, weekly, monthly.

(d) Information

As much relevant information as possible must be made available to the team leader and the team on a weekly/daily basis in order for the team to be fully aware of the effectiveness of their actions.

The key critical decisions of the business centre must be posted on special notice boards or screens and also made known by means of weekly team briefings.

(e) Resources

Manpower requirements, i.e. permanent employees, temporary staff, part-time staff, must be linked directly to production requirements in order to achieve optimum performance and reduce unit costs. This will require a detailed knowledge of likely production levels over the next five years.

Stock control/inventory control systems should be easily understandable and result in reduced wastage, reduced costs and improved customer service.

Specialist external resources, e.g. product development, should operate with as little impact as possible on day-to-day operations and should be answerable to the business centre/factory manager for any interruptions to production.

(f) People

It is necessary to obtain and retain the right quantity and quality of people to achieve the corporate objective of 'the best people with the strongest motivation in the right jobs'. The company must achieve the highest standards of recruitment and selection, training and development, appraisal/performance review/objective setting, succession planning and rewards systems. All of these factors must be harmonized into a total concerted approach that matches the needs of the factory, the business centre and each individual.

The organizational structure outlined previously and the personnel policies above should lead, by careful and consistent management, to employees who are:

Well motivated, i.e. interested in their job because they have accountability and responsibility and are pushed to the edges of their competence.

Part of a team, and know how the team knits together.

More flexible (fewer lines of demarcation).

Aware of the consequences of their actions i.e. aware of the effect of poor performance on target levels.

Well paid – and feel relatively well paid in terms of the team/centre/factory/industry, given the scope of their job.

Responsive to change and contribute through their team to change initiatives/opportunities.

(g) Culture

The organization should generate a culture which allows:

Decisions to be made at as low a level as is possible/practical.

The team leader and team to act with confidence in the knowledge that they have the authority to make decisions.

Establishing a start point

An open system where mistakes are discussed and dissected without subsequent effect on morale and performance – the findings of such investigations should be kept for future reference.

All information to be readily available in order that sound decisions can be made.

Commitment to change as a way of life.

Recognition that continual improvements to efficient working practices and manning levels will be a continuing part of future life in the centre/factory.

An environment where all staff are clear about the consequences of continued poor performance/mismanagement.

(h) External relations

The factors that operate within the factory/centre environment but are controlled from outside must be managed in such a way that they support the central objectives of the new organization. The following are some examples:

Site/centre relationships

Better understanding of the centre's role and the elements within the centre.

More information about the impact each department within the centre can have on factory performance.

Improved lines of information.

Industrial relations structures.

Fewer bargaining groups.

An industrial relations structure that reflects the proposed organizational structure.

Clear recognition rights (trade union membership etc.) that reflect roles/skills of employees within the centres.

Product rationalization

Factory-centre to have an input into decisions about where products are manufactured.

Products handed to factory only after being commissioned at a given line utilization for a given period.

Clear lines of responsibility for progressing products to final production stage.

Vision 5

(a) The company mission

To develop and manufacture products to the highest standards of quality, service and efficiency through the excellence of our operations.

(b) Proposed manufacturing site mission

To create the most efficient and effective manufacturing organization in our business through the maximizing of career and employment opportunities for all employees.

(c)

Existing organization	Desired organization
Technically driven	Business driven
Sub-optimal task breakdown, few narrow skills	Optimum task groups, many broad skills
External controls (supervisors, technical specialists, inspection systems etc.)	Internal controls (self-regulation of individuals and teams)
Tall organization chart/structure	Flat organization chart/structure
Discrete functions	Multi-functional teams
Restricted decision-making	Devolved decision-making
Restricted knowledge-holding and usage	Dispersed/open knowledge-holding and usage
Values implicit, imposed and technical/professional	Values explicit, joint and shared
Learning formalized and not promoted	Learning a way of life
Improvement through imposition	Continuous improvement through day-to-day actions
Quality of product and service paramount	Total quality in all areas of operation
Rewards biased to managerial rank, not to quality or relevance of contribution	Rewards promote quality and enhancement of contribution
Roles lack clarity and distinctiveness, and tend to overlap	Roles clearly defined, distinct and understood by all
Little challenge, opportunity and job satisfaction for the bulk of employees	'Culture' and job structures provide challenge and interest/motivation to improve
Inter-functional blinds spots	Multi-functional groupings reduce blind spots (must avoid an over-emphasis on the here and now at the expense of the future)

(d) Business/manufacturing centre – a working definition
   A business/market-orientated organization commanding the functional resources required to think about performance in terms of its commercial/competitive impact.

Establishing a start point 51

Task-centred, business/manufacturing-focused groups/teams thinking about decisions which cover both inputs to and outputs from their production process, through to the final market.

Individuals loyal to business/manufacturing teams and through them to the objectives of the site and company, thinking about implementation in terms of managing the interface at each stage of the product stream from procurement to customer.

A structure with a developing integrated conceptual base with distinctive roles for each level, thinking about things from the perspective of the ends that need to be achieved and what has to be created/undertaken to achieve them.

An organization that will improve the efficiency and effectiveness of manufacturing by creating a human environment that encourages the full utilization of individual and group capabilities, developing a shared commitment to a common set of goals and standards of excellence, and building a structure with the minimum number of levels/layers, short lines of communication and a rapid response time.

(e) Some key principles which will be promoted by the desired organization:

All people in the organization have many talents and are capable of (and enjoy) learning and using a variety of skills.

People are trustworthy and will be respected and dealt with as individuals.

People want to be involved and want to contribute.

People should participate in the decisions that affect them and their work groups.

People are results-orientated and will strive to meet tough goals, particularly if they help to set them.

People are motivated by work content. Jobs should provide some variety and challenge the individuals assigned.

High performance is expected – poor performance will not be tolerated.

Authority and responsibility should be delegated to the level in the organization where knowledge and talent/skill exist to make the appropriate decisions.

Every employee should be a manager and a business person. To this end, business information/strategies should be communicated to the people performing the work. Given the same information as management, they will make similar (if not better) decisions.

Employees should receive timely feedback on their performance.

Overt site team management will be used where there is a high degree of interdependency and common goals.

Conflict should be brought to the surface and dealt with openly, recognizing that conflict can lead to improvements.

Communications should be open and meaningful. Direct and free communication across departmental and team boundaries, without going through intermediaries, is considered necessary for an effective organization.

Management should be accessible to everyone. There is a strong need for management presence on the plant.

Employees are expected to be responsible for their own safety and be dedicated to having a safe workplace.

People should be flexible and adaptable in meeting the changing demands of the work schedules, business volumes and the working environment.

Decisions should reflect what is good for the business/manufacturing centre, plant and site as a whole rather than what is good for only a part of any one of them.

These five visions, the strengths and weaknesses analysis and the published company mission statement were pulled together to create a joint vision for the future manufacturing organization. In the words of the study team: 'The vision of the future is a set of principles which underpin the formulation and application of policy and the management and operation at each of the sites. Wide exposure of this vision will raise awareness and acceptance of the need for change and provide guidance towards the preferred operational structure.' The principles underlying the vision are made up of five components:

Organization

> Multi-functional roles.
> Contribution to a team limited only by a person's competence.
> Flexible in terms of skills, working time and the introduction of new products and processes.
> Few layers in the structure.
> Concentration on core tasks in a manufacturing operation.
> Self-contained in terms of resources.
> Team-based.

People

> Adaptable and seeking to develop their potential.
> Self-starters with high personal standards.
> Versatile in terms of work skills and (social) behaviour.
> Perceptive to the needs of colleagues and the organization.

Well balanced.
Able to play a team role.
Able to participate in decisions.
Concerned for implications of their actions.
Competent in core skills.

Culture

Effective leadership.
Business understanding.
Consistency of management style.
High performance the norm.
Change regarded as a way of life.
Commitment to continual improvement.
Encourages staff development.
Team synergy.
Recognises needs of the individual.

Control and systems

Clear, open communications.
Clear standards and goals.
Continual feedback of information on performance.
Accountability and responsibility equated.
Authority and decision-making delegated to lowest appropriate level.
Supportive total reward system.

External relations

Close contact with and response to all customers.
A supportive industrial relations structure.
Build and maintain a high reputation,

This final vision then formed the basis of a detailed study of three different manufacturing processes on three sites. The actual visioning process took 3–4 weeks (about 20 per cent of the whole study time) and it provided a means of exposing initial preconceptions of the existing organization and of sharing thoughts about 'where next?'. The fact that the visions, while differing in detail, were in agreement on virtually all issues helped to bring the study team together at a very early stage. The cohesiveness of the team's thinking and understanding of why a 'new' organization must be achieved proved to be very important in the selling of the vision and its detailed implementation over the following 12–18 months.

Example 3. Creating a mission and vision for materials control

Within all manufacturing companies, and especially those which operate on a Europe-wide basis, there is a continual 'battle' between service, inventory and cost variables within materials control. Moreover, what is sound materials management for one business may be wholly inappropriate for another. There is therefore a need for a robust means of balancing the three variables of service, inventory and cost with conflicting business requirements. This example charts the developments in one North American multi-national with major businesses across Europe (including The Netherlands, Denmark, UK, West Germany, France, Italy, Spain, Portugal, Belgium and Greece). It operates in 49 countries and employs 82,000 people who invent, produce and sell a wide variety of 'added value products' resulting from over 100 identifiable company technologies. The company currently has 50,000 listed products and is divided on into four business sectors: industrial and electronic; information and imaging technologies; life sciences; and commercial and consumer. These four business sectors serve ten major markets: communication arts; construction and maintenance; consumer; electronics/electrical manufacturing; health care; industrial production; office, training and business; safety and security; transportation equipment manufacturing and maintenance; and voice, video and data communications.

As part of the push to improve the efficiency of the European materials control operation a number of initiatives were undertaken: for instance, in materials management the objective for distribution was 'to become the best service company in Europe' via new inventory control techniques, changes in warehousing network and a new organization for finished goods inventory management. There were also changes in other areas, e.g. in customer service where improvements were introduced by means of closer interface with marketing, strengthening of key account involvement, customer service programmes and a new order management system. Yet in the UK operation there was no formal strategy for materials control. As a result of this there had been no 'conceptual education' of senior management on the real conflicts involved in materials control and the necessity for a positive compromise. The senior people involved in materials control knew what their objectives were within their own businesses; it was just that no collective strategy had been developed.

The importance of service, inventory control, cycle times and just-in-time was appreciated by senior management. Their interrelationship and the different compromises that had to be made for the different businesses were not well understood. It was for this reason that the overall business requirements (of the total company) were translated into specific programmes, such as inventory reduction targets, that were applied to all the

Establishing a start point 55

businesses without proper consideration of their individual needs. There is a tendency for materials control to become reactive to such company programmes rather than proactive towards meeting business needs.

There was therefore a need to develop a strategy for the materials control function within the distribution, engineering and manufacturing organization to meet the requirements of the UK company. To meet this objective the following steps were taken:

Define a mission statement.
Stakeholder analysis for materials control.
SWOT/5P analysis of materials control.
Identify the products of materials control.
Identify a vision for materials control.
Develop a strategy.
Picture the mission.

What follows is a shortened version of the above process. First, it was necessary to establish who were the customers and the key stakeholders in materials control, to ensure that the debate would not be restricted to the internal workings of materials control. (Stakeholders are all those interest groups, parties, actors, claimants and institutions – both internal and external to the corporation – that exert a hold on it: that is, stakeholders are those parties who either affect or are affected by a corporation's or department's actions, behaviour and policies – see Mitroff (1983:4).) This served to illustrate that virtually all departments/activities interfaced in some way with materials control, in particular the following stakeholders:

Materials control itself.
Purchasing.
Sales and marketing.
Distribution.
Production.
Technical.
Customer.
Financial group.
Project engineering.
Senior management.

Having established the 'market' for materials control and the interdependencies which exist, it was necessary to create a picture of the current materials control organization and of where it might move in the future. To achieve this a 'SWOT/5P' analysis was undertaken by a small group. In essence, this analytical tool seeks to generate information on the strengths, weaknesses, opportunities and threats facing materials across five categories (the 5 Ps):

(a) Product
   The output of the materials control department. Consider here the fulfilment of customer/stakeholder needs and the ability of materials control to meet them to agreed standards, e.g. quality, quantity, price, delivery dates etc.
(b) Plant
   The tools and equipment used by materials control in the development and supply of its product.
(c) Processes
   How the product is delivered, including consideration of available capacity, equipment (reliability and maintainability) etc.
(d) Programmes
   Timetables for delivery, purchasing, scheduling, inventory/storage levels etc.
(e) People
   The materials control workforce. Consider skills, training, organization, wages structure, communication, recruitment etc.

This exercise generated the following information.

Product

Strengths
   The job gets done.
   Low inventories.
   Useful rapid information.
   Overall quality.
Weaknesses
   Allowing materials control to be wholly responsible for service.
   Information systems.
   Alternative sources of materials.
   Product line rationalization.
Opportunities
   Teamwork approach to service.
   Open systems.
Threats
   Complacency.
   Incompatible goals.
   Alternative sources of materials.

Plant

Strengths
   Equipment/computer systems.
   Quality.

Weaknesses
  Ageing software.
  Inflexible.
  Expensive and difficult to change.
  Too complex to understand.
  Capacity constraints.
  Contingency plan.
Opportunities
  Decentralize.
  Distributed processing.
  Inventory.
Threats
  Cost of change.
  Information systems and data processing 'empire'.
  Capacity.
  Contingency plans.

Processes

Strengths
  Common systems.
  Sophistication of systems.
  Satisfying requirements.
  Distribution.
Weaknesses
  Over-reliant on systems.
  Planning systems.
  Forecast.
  Defining requirements.
Opportunities
  Move towards just-in-time/optimized operations.
  Communication, accountability and ownership.
  Purchasing.
Threats
  Lose control.

Programmes

Strengths
  Procedures well documented and followed.
  Systems.
  Plans.
Weaknesses
  Not widely known outside.

Well-intentioned edicts.
Operating procedures.
Execution.
Information systems and data processing justification.
Opportunities
Extend use of facilities.
Promote knowledge of systems.
Objectives set.
Just-in-time.

People

Strengths
Knowledge – operations, processes, procedures.
How to get things done.
Movement.
High stability.
Weaknesses
Calibre of people – educational, intellectual.
Incapacity for creative thinking.
'Turfiness.'
Lack of expertise.
Lack of right people.
Lack of specialists.
Low rate of introduction of new people.
Training.
Operating procedures.
Outsider understanding.
Qualifications.
Resource of systems people.
Opportunities
Recruit better people.
Operate with fewer.
Training.
Reduce headcount.
Improve intellect.
Threats
Union.
Fear of change.
Outsider understanding.

The sharing of the picture created by this composite SWOT/5P analysis (the product of the collation of the work of three separate syndicate groups) provided a means of establishing agreement on the current situation. It also provided a means of getting the materials control group (a mix of head-office and plant-based managers) to appreciate the different perceptions across the sites, businesses and from head office, i.e. it provided a team-building process. The 'opportunities' and 'threats' elements of the analysis identified areas crucial to planning for the future.

Having established an agreed picture of materials control across the UK operation, two particular strands were followed: first, identification of the product supplied by materials control; second, a vision for the future. Again these tasks were undertaken by three syndicate groups. The 'product' output of the SWOT/5P was taken and defined in greater detail, and also 'success' for the product was defined in quantitative terms. This step was particularly relevant to clarifying the purpose of the materials control activity, and hence providing information upon which the mission statement could be based.

Product outputs

Product (1). Develop and maintain manufacturing plan by dealing with two key aspects:

Market	Product	Measures
1 Materials control	Purchasing	Stock turnover
	Customer order	Stockout
	Forecast	Service
	Inventory control	Department cost
	Capacity planning	
2 Production control	Issue schedules (short and long term)	Schedule conformance
	Conformance	Productivity/waste
	Adjust	Accuracy

Also provided to both 'markets' are data, record update and analysis/advice.

Product (2).

Main Product	Measures
Forecast demand	Forecast accuracy
MPS	Output v. MPS-schedule
Department plans	Deliveries of materials
Vendor plans	Customer service
Inventory forecast	Cycle time – performance v. forecast
	Advise customer of exceptions

Product (3).

Markets	Products	Measures
Purchasing	Schedule	Amendments
	Orders	Expedites
		Stockouts
Customer service	Promise dates	Number of redates
	Inventory level	PI checks
	Shipping	Reporting errors
	Key account performance	Back orders
Senior management	Performance data	Audits
		Performance long-term
Production	I/C forecast	Change to plan
	Production forecast	Schedule adherence
	Production schedule	Customer service
Warehouse	Orders	
Sales/marketing	Key accounts	
Accounts	Inventory level	
	Production data	

From this 'product data' a first attempt was made to define the mission of materials control which encompassed the product, the customer and the overall process involved. This was done by listing words and phrases that summarized the above output. The first attempt to devise a mission statement for materials control was:

'To provide the right quality information to internal and external customers which optimizes the efficiency and effectiveness of the materials transformation process.'

This then became:

'To provide the right quality information to internal and external customers which actively assists in raising the company's overall efficiency and effectiveness in the managing and controlling of the whole materials conversion/transformation process.'

And finally it became:

'To provide effective and efficient information to control and manage the material conversion process, thereby adding value and meeting internal and external customer requirements.'

Establishing a start point

The next issue to be tackled was to develop a joint 'vision' of the desired and required organization to deliver the mission. To assist this stage the 7-S model of McKinsey (Waterman et al., 1980) was used to provide a series of headings under which initial ideas could be collated. Once the vision had been established, the appropriate strategy bridging the present situation to the future could be developed. The initial vision that was developed (in part building upon the SWOT/5P exercise, especially on the strengths and opportunities of the existing organization) was as follows:

(a) Systems
    Order management.
    Bar coding.
    Hazardous goods movements.
    Total management system – materials.
    Shop floor data collection.
    Personalized.
    Flexible, simpler.
    Full on-line availability with internal and external networks.
(b) Skills
    Numeracy.
    Product knowledge.
    Knowledge of customer area.
    Interface.
    Communication.
    Influence/persuasiveness.
    Leadership ability.
    Communication.
    Computer literacy.
    Just-in-time/latest techniques.
(c) Shared values
    Team spirit.
    Commitment.
    Accountability.
    Ownership.
    Trust and confidence (from results).
    Shared goals.
    Common, visible, accurate data plus systems understanding.
(d) Staff
    Balance 'movers' and 'stayers'.
    Interchange with others.
    Qualified.
    Flexibility – cover.
    Adequate training.
    Rewards and recognition.

Job evaluation.
Supervision of system, not 'people'.
High calibre.
Opportunities.
Few high-intellect people.
System designers.
Users – customer orientated/business managers.
(e) Style
Not confrontational.
Receptive to change (instigators).
Flexible.
Manage, not react.
Catalyst.
Positive approach.
Synergistic.
Resilient diplomacy.
Highly professional – be seen to be progressive.
Proactive.
Good information for business decisions.
Eliminate low value-added clerical work.
(f) Structure:
Horizontal, linking customer service, production planning, warehousing, traffic, purchasing-coordinators and systems group.

This vision was then summarized, ranked in terms of impact on the materials control mission and scored (existing organization compared with the vision – how well did it match what was required?). The result (Table 4.1) indicates that the materials control group considered three key items to be critical to the success of the mission: people, goals and systems. Each of these three items also scored poorly when assessed in the existing organization. It was these three items that received the initial effort in devising the future strategy for materials control.

It is not appropriate here to go into the detail of the strategy developed by the materials group. Suffice it to say that the resulting strategy went on to be accepted and implemented by the group with the support of the manufacturing director.

Example 4. Creating a future for engineering on site

An engineering steering group (made up of fitters, electricians, instrument technicians, managers etc.) was formed in May 1988 on a fine chemicals processing and packaging site where about 160 people are involved in engineering work. This multidisciplinary study team was given the

Table 4.1 *Strategy criteria rated on a scale 1 (low) to 10 (high)*

Key word	Impact on mission	Assessment of current organization against vision (average)
1 Goals	9	4.6
2 Structure	5	5.7
3 Image	3	4.9
4 Systems	9	5.2
5 Skills	5	4.6
6 People	10	4.1
7 Justification	2	3.5
8 Customer interface	6	5.3
9 Measures	2	6.3
10 Forecasting	1	4.9
11 Flexibility	3	4.5

opportunity to investigate the effectiveness of the engineering department. Specific terms of reference, developed by the site management team and the senior stewards, were adopted by the engineering steering group when it began structured investigations in mid-July 1988.

The first stage of the engineering steering group's work was to diagnose the 'problems' within the existing engineering organization. In order to do this the group used a wide range of information sources which identified five main categories of 'problem': organization, culture, control and systems, people and external relations. In all, five sources of information were used: 'problems list' (problems/weaknesses associated with the current engineering department); a survey of the clients of the engineering department; personal visions; views of production managers; and specific survey of the instrument and electrical sections of the engineering department where a number of specific problems existed. The output from these five sources of information were then summarized to produce the design criteria upon which the future engineering structure would be based.

Taking each of these sources in turn, it can be hown how the engineering steering group came to its joint design criteria, i.e. the design principles of its future organization. First the engineering steering group asked a simple question of its customers in production: 'Are you satisfied with the service that engineering provides?'. The answers fall into two groups:

'Yes'
   Adequate service.

Work done is good.
Service OK, but . . .
Good relationship with mechanical supervisor.
Fitters willing to be flexible with production.
Resource is satisfactory.
Politics getting better.
Good resource.
Instrument technicians are motivated and give a good service.
Better now than before.
Good mechanically.
Totally happy, but . . .
Good resource.
Generally OK, but . . .
Mechanical resource good due to dedication.
Acceptable.

'No'
Poor communications between electricians and their supervisors.
Do not call for help soon enough when problem is beyond them.
Poor dialogue between engineer and line supervisor.
Only does job requested, does not follow up.
Waiting individuals do not cooperate.
Varying levels of skill within disciplines leads to a variable quality of service.
Attitude problem.
Lack of interest and pride.
Fitters and electricians do not give good service.
Poor modifications.
Lack of urgency (when responding to requests for assistance).
More dedication required.
Bad communications.
Bad housekeeping.
More integration between engineering and production is required.
Poor diagnosis of problems (lack of specialized knowledge).
Tend to do the job then leave it.
Do not understand reconciliation problems.
Poor housekeeping.
Line dedication is required.
Break times differ.
Struggle on without calling for help.
Seem to be doing nothing between breakdowns.
Demarcation and infighting causes problems.
Problems with inexperienced staff.
Waiting for a long time.
Attitude – may be due to production always giving problems.

Establishing a start point 65

Unhappy with instrument department.
Avoid use because of excess waiting time.
Hierarchy is slow and frustrating, with poor access.
Attitude – could not care less.
Top level of engineers remote from production.
No unanimity between disciplines.
Do not understand production's problems.
Engineering play one off against each other via production.
Equipment does not appear to do the job.
Long time to wait.
Unsure of who to call for help.
Poor feasibility of hierarchy.
Requisition system too slow, therefore use indirect method.
Poor communication with electrical staff.
Very poor communication with instrument staff.
Resent taking instructions from line supervisors.
Poor feedback to supervisor.
Do not ask for help soon enough.
Resentment in taking over somebody else's work.
Lack of line identity, i.e. fix-and-forget attitude.
Resource wasted on menial tasks.
Lack of dedication.
Too much red tape for projects.
Slow progress on new work.
Traditional demarcation does not help.
Too much polarization regarding the way the jobs are done.

These lists of 16 and 53 items respectively represent the views of production managers and supervisors which predominantly identified a series of attitude, communication, skill level, structure, demarcation and resource issues. Do people in the engineering department hold similar views? Broadly the answer is 'yes', with the following items identified:

Denies/inhibits opportunity for advancement/improvement.
Squanders our resources (people).
Fails to keep us in touch with the actual situation.
Poor lines of communication.
Top-heavy organization.
Restricts chances for variety/improvement in skills.
Fails to give clear directives.
Does not generate team spirit.
Leads to wasted/misused resources.
Pay differentials within own department.
Time wasted.

Pay anomalies do not make sense in organization.
Status differentials/barriers among us.
Slow-moving (inert) systems.
Lack of cooperation between trades.
People potential cannot be used.
System encourages/makes people moan
Does not discourage bad/tense atmosphere.
Mistrust is rife.
People disappointed with lack of opportunity.
Does little to break down barriers between us and other departments.
Does not foster supervisor interest in people.
Fails to negate 'fear'.
Encourages/does not tackle/people's lack of security.
Allows double standards to be imposed.
Decision-makers not seen to be involved/informed people.
Trade union barriers rife.
Trade union representation/representative of people.
People with closed/singular views tolerated/accepted.
Does not give good guidelines.
No clear accountability and responsibility.
Not geared up to accept/use our ideas.
Unable to give/use flexibility.
Unfair increment system both in use and availability.
Decisions not well enough presented to earn respect even if warranted.
Leads to suspect production processes being forced on us.
Are we best structured, and do we really know what resources we need to do our job?
Lack of technical engineers (specialists), trouble-shooters and expert back-up.
We do not plan and use our resources too well.
Failure to understand the need to reassure our people about the use of and number of contractors.
Poor reporting/passing-on of information/facts enabling distortion/misinterpretation.
Do not see the support when we take decisions which are questioned/wrong.
Has not identified our role and contribution to the company (or sold it) so company does not know our role.
Petty unofficial industrial action creates bad image to outsiders as being a militant lot.
Department management unable to use potential.
Insufficient information given to enable engineers to understand implications of engineering decisions on process.

Establishing a start point 67

Systems are not in place to keep us informed of new machinery/technology use, maintenance and training.

Skill level does not meet requirements; are we doing the right things, or is there a recruitment problem?

Do we know what our customer 'wants' and are we providing it? (Customer care).

System has allowed us to be seen as second class citizens.

Lack of integration with engineers in other (customer) departments.

Selection methods ill-defined and seen as unfair, resulting in the 'wrong' people in jobs.

Impersonal organization, does not seem to care/recognize us.

Demarcation lines have been drawn which are artificial and are not seen to be sensible and some are unknown until unwittingly transgressed.

Standards by which we are judged to be competent are inconsistent and changing.

Engineering managers are out of touch with what goes on at the 'coalface' – or are perceived to be, as rarely seen walking the job, particularly in isolated/small work stations.

Management appears to be unaware of the number and speed of changes on shop floor.

There is no continuity of policy seen to be directing us because of frequent management changes; new manager, new direction.

We have no/low professional profile as it has not been defined/demonstrated.

Our job structure has been built up over years of in-fighting and anarchy reigns.

Rewards do not reflect the company image portrayed, i.e. 'first in country' etc.

Engineering standards are inconsistent, leading to confusion by us and others.

Because of production's specialist needs many of our processes are not tried and tested, but are experimental. Our role is one of experimental engineers rather than maintenance men on machines which need longer periods of run-up/growth curves than is allowed.

We do not have a system that learns from mistakes.

This list of 67 comments formed the next key input into the Engineering Steering Group's thinking and was added to by the input of one single production manager who had canvassed opinion among his colleagues. In summary his 'vision' for engineering included the following seven elements:

Engineering should be a partnership with production in a joint team, or at least joint teamwork.

Engineering should have high standards and image as they are pharmaceutical engineers.

Engineering should be innovative and improvement-orientated, and not locked into low-skilled work.

Engineering should be competitive and help move the business forward.

Engineering should play key roles in commissioning and validation work.

Engineering should have as simple a structure as possible to make it easy to deal with.

Engineering should adopt a 'whole machine' approach to maintenance.

The individual vision statements prepared by the members provided a view very similar to that held by production managers, in summary:

Engineering should be multi-disciplinary, at least at the team level if not the individual level.

Engineering should be made up of joint teams.

Engineering should seek to help production to develop operator mechanics.

Engineering and production should be a partnership.

Engineering should be primarily concerned with engineering standards.

Within any new engineering structure the contributions of individuals and their development should be limited only by their competence.

Engineering should be a 'flat' organization.

The final input into the development of the design criteria came from a survey of 38 instrument technicians, electrical technicians and electrical craftsmen. Historically, all three of these trades had operated in isolation with their own pay scales. However, a number of factors were contributing to a need to change the existing structure – changes in technology, changes in the nature of apprenticeships, changes in the use of contractors on traditional electrical work, the recent influx of electricians and instrument technicians with a variety of experiences from other companies etc. Basically, there were a series of pressures which challenged the existing demarcation lines between these three groups of craftsmen/technicians. The survey itself, conducted in February 1988, attempted to map out current opinions, feelings and attitudes rather than provide solutions. It served to highlight the specific problems faced in this part of the engineering department.

The five sources of information (survey of customers, production management viewpoint, personal visions of steering group members, survey of instrument–electrical sections, problems/weaknesses identified within the current engineering organization) were then brought together and the duplicate entries removed. This resulted in an initial list of ten items that all of the five inputs suggested should characterize any future engineering organization:

- Flat structure.
- Multi-skilled individuals/teams.
- Production–maintenance partnership, i.e. leading to a sharing of skills.
- Focus on improvement/making best use of skills.
- Minimal demarcation.
- Both individuals and team development operating to 'time, ability and safety' principles.
- Production/manufacturing orientation.
- Minimal (direct) supervision.
- Maintenance of high skill base/standards.
- Prevention of wasted talent and time.

This list, while not totally accepted by some steering group members, went on to be developed further and refined to form the design criteria which were used to design and evaluate the new engineering organization.

Detailed design criteria

1. Flat structure
   Department team, product-based.
   Team has authority to act/react to the day-to-day situation.
   Holds and develops own budget.
   Information available directly at individual/team level.
2. Multi-skilled individuals/teams
   Team has the ability to handle most day-to-day decisions/actions.
   Acquisition of skills and knowledge through evolutionary means.
   Resources within the team to allow training to proceed successfully.
   Competence of existing people/achievable with existing people.
   Individuals are accountable for their actions.
   Consistent with company and national safety standards.
   Training to national standards where possible and appropriate.
3. Production–maintenance partnership
   Integrated/joint management structure.
   Common targets/purposes.
   Equal opportunities for career progression and rewards.
4. Focus on improvement
   Skills and knowledge in team relevant to improving day-to-day activities at least to specification level, with a budget to support them.

Provides time for increased resources to be devoted to improvement work.
5 Workable demarcation/jobs and teams operate to TAS principles
Individuals work to TAS (time, ability and safety) principles irrespective of current job or role.
6 Production/manufacturing centre orientation
Project skills and knowledge integrated into manufacturing centre team.
Mobility between teams (between manufacturing centres) for cover within a manufacturing centre and on a planned basis (collective learning).
7 Minimal direct supervision
Ownership of clear goals and objectives.
Clearly defined and understood team and individual roles.
8 Maintenance of high level of skills, standards and motivation
Retention of specialists.
Retention and transfer of learning between teams to maintain engineering standards.
9 Prevention of wasted time and talent
Mechanism/structure to avoid the duplication of work.
All changes in role and structure can be achieved broadly within existing numbers.
10 Supportive reward structure
Fair and consistent application of any rewards system across and within teams.

These criteria were then used to assist in the design of the new engineering organization which was built up from a task base.

Summary of the examples

These four examples illustrate in four different settings the initial steps taken to establish agreement among a group of managers and, in two cases, whole departments about 'where to change to'. Table 4.2 summarizes a number of the points described in the case studies. Perhaps one important point to note is the high degree of commonality across all four examples with regard to their 'visions'. Even though the scale and focus of the exercises described in the case studies varied, they all agreed on the type of organization that they would like to bring into being and that was needed for the future. In all four cases, also, the various teams and groups found it useful to develop pictures of both the present and the future in order to get some idea of the scale of change required.

The steps gone through in the various one-day and two-day sessions also

Table 4.2 Summary of the case studies

Factor	Example 1	Example 2	Example 3	Example 4
Physical scope	3 sites	4 sites	5 sites	1 site
Key issue	Pay	Manufacturing	Manufacturing	Engineering
Who directly involved?	Snr management	Snr + middle management	Snr + middle management	All levels
Who consulted?	Snr management	Snr + middle management	Snr + middle management	All levels
No. involved	30–40	50–60	25–30	250+
No. directly affected by outcome	2000	2200	50–80	160 (direct) 1200 (indirect)
Timescale	1 month 3–4 one-day sessions	1 month 3–4 one-day sessions	2 months 1 two-day and 3–4 one-day sessions	2 months 6–8 one-day sessions
Resources used	Internal facilitator	External facilitator	External and internal facilitators	External facilitator
Sponsor	Manufacturing Director	Technical Director	Manufacturing Director	Factory Manager
Vision publicized?	No	Very restricted	Very restricted	Yes
Led to other initiatives?	No	Yes	No	Yes

provided a means of raising understanding and awareness within the teams of the starting positions of other team members. This is useful in team-building terms, and also in identifying at a very early stage areas of divergence and disagreement.

Lessons learnt – process

1 The need to develop a common understanding of the starting position and agreement on the sort of future state worth working towards, which will remove or help to overcome existing barriers to improvement.
2 The need to identify within the organization, at team, individual and departmental levels, why change is necessary and where improvements are needed most urgently.

3 The need to provide a means of bringing existing assumptions and perceptions to the surface.
4 The need to allow time for people to think through for themselves the type of organization that is required for success in the future: very few people will find it possible to defend inefficient practices.
5 The need to provide a series of formal steps for the generation of information, to allow a joint diagnosis and start position to be established.
6 The need to share current perceptions and thoughts for the future as the basis for developing products that can be used in a wide range of environments.
7 The need to provide a learning process through which a picture of the future can be established and shared with others, so starting the communication process.

Lessons learnt – key steps

The four examples used a range of simple methods to generate information which would help to develop two maps: one of the exisiting situation, one of the future. The main objectives of the four example studies were:

1 To identify the weakness of, and threats to, the existing situation.
2 To identify the strengths of, and opportunities for, the existing situation.
3 To identify the customers and stakeholders who had an interest in both the existing and any future situation of the organization.
4 To develop personal views on the desired and needed future state.
5 To clarify the product/purpose of the organization.
6 To collate information from the experience of other companies and the latest thinking on organization structures and individual roles.

A key part of the process is first to agree the overall process, and then, using a specific series of methods, to realize the outcome of the process. The key steps are therefore:

1 Establish a map in which the current situation and the desired and required future state are linked (Figure 4.1).
2 Identify the sources and types of information required.
3 Diagnose the issues constraining, and the weaknesses of, the current situation.
4 Derive a scheme for the future state which will remove the weaknesses and problems of the existing situation and be able to handle the foreseen future environment/developments.

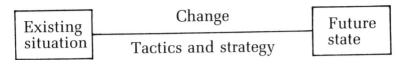

Figure 4.1 *Relationship of the existing situation and the required future state*

It is on the basis of an agreed future state that the detail of what to change, how and when, can now be considered. This is the purpose of the following two sections.

Developing the terms of reference and rules for the proposed change

Definition stage

The definition stage forms the foundation upon which the remainder of a study is built. Without knowing what your target is, the end result is unlikely to be anything but poor. The chances of providing solutions which cannot be implemented to solve a particular problem are high if constraints are not considered. The definition should include:

1 A statement of 'what makes the present situation unsatisfactory', which could include such items as low yield, low quality, jobs providing little or no satisfaction, poor training, a need to improve working conditions or the general environment.
2 Objectives – which can be classified as 'musts' and 'wants'; for example, 'musts' would include:

   (a) The lines must be available 75 per cent of production time.
   (b) Must produce at a quality at least equal to specifications.

   'Wants' might include:

   (a) Minimum capital expenditure.
   (b) Maximum operating efficiencies.
   (c) Technical input met from own resources.
   (d) Meaningful and satisfying jobs.
   (e) Best use made of the abilities of all in the department.

   Any solution failing to meet a 'must' objective is no solution. The solution that best meets the 'want' objectives is the solution to be chosen.

'Wants' can be ranked in order of priority, and some will conflict. There should be an agreed method for measuring objectives.

3 Criterion of completion: what is the end point of the study – is it a proposal and/or an implementation plan? The study team should know the end point of the study.
4 Constraints: what constraints exist, technical, financial, organizational, social etc? What are the boundaries of the problem? Objectives and constraints are related, e.g. the objective 'maximize line availability' and the constraint 'the availability of plant must be at 75 per cent'. The constraints are often expressed as 'base' levels.
5 People – the most important is the responsible person (the one to implement, the one to seek assistance from in case of difficulty), followed by the study team and its leader. Consider who else and what else will be affected by the investigation and the implementation of the solution.

Remember that the drafting of terms of reference is not necessarily the beginning of the basic procedure sequence; data collection may precede it. The terms of reference are not fixed, since with good reason they can be changed. Preferably they are drawn up jointly by, for example, the study team and the site executive.

Completion of terms of reference

1 Subject of study (brief heading for reference and filing purposes).
   Date started.
   'Client' for the study.
2 The problem
   Reasons for changing the present situation:
   (a) What makes the present situation appear to be unsatisfactory?
   (b) What is informed opinion and what is fact?
   (c) What other documents/events should be referred to?
   (d) Is any data unavailable?
3 Objectives to be achieved
   (a) Answers need to be specific and quantitative.
   (b) List objectives in terms of 'musts' and 'wants'.
   (c) Consider relative strengths of wants.
4 Action plan
   (a) What are the steps to be taken to solve the problem?
   (b) What will be the sequence?
   (c) What areas should be examined in order to produce the solution?
   (d) What are the time targets for various parts of the plan?

5 Criteria of completion
   (a) What is to be the end-product of the formal study?
   (b) How far is the study to be taken?
   (c) What is the form of the final report?
      A list of proposals for decision and action?
      Fully evaluated proposals for decision and action?
      An agreed course of action, fully implemented?
6 Constraints
   (a) Time. When must the solution be implemented?
      When must the report be submitted?
      Are there deadlines for particular stages in the study?
   (b) Technical, financial, organizational limitations
   (c) What may not be changed?
   (d) What prior decisions must be respected?
   (e) What areas may not be explored?
   (f) Are the limitations absolute or relative to cost involved?
7 To whom is the study team responsible for progress and final reporting?
8 Which person or group will be responsible for implementing the accepted conclusions?

By following these eight steps it should be possible to develop an initial brief to examine the current situation and improve upon it. It is also useful to use a checklist which was developed to help in fully fleshing out the terms of reference:

1 How has the project arisen?
   Originators – what did they envisage?
   Has a formal proposal been made to the appropriate authority?
   Is it part of an existing project?
   Does a similar brief exist or has another group covered this area before?
   Who is responsible for the project?
2 What about cost/benefits of the project?
   Can Finance and Administration help in the evaluation?
   Has any other company/department tried this before?
   What information can be got from libraries, universities, specialists, advisory boards, colleagues, management?
3 What is the real problem?
   Can we define it ourselves?
   Do we need to talk to functional line managers, production staff, maintenance experts, technical experts?
   Do we need to talk to other company functions?
   Do we need to talk to suppliers or external specialists?

4 What are the constraints?
    Who are the *final* decision-makers?
    How much time do we have and can it be extended?
    What are the financial/budget constraints?
    What expertise, knowledge or resources are needed/available?
    What are the political and environmental constraints?
    What are the legal constraints?
    What impact will the project have on the workload of the whole group, now and in the future (i.e. maintenance)?
5 In view of the constraints, do we have to redefine the problem?
    Are there any technical reasons for redefinition?
    Are there any financial/political/legal/environmental reasons?
    Are there any ambiguities in the problem?
6 What are the sub-objectives?
    What does the team think the project *must* do?
    What does the team *want* the project to do?
    What are the relative priorities of the 'wants'?
    Are any other criteria to be used for assessing the project?
7 How can we generate our alternative approaches to the project
    Has anyone solved this or a similar problem before?
    Can we use a logical method for generating approaches?
    Do we need a creative approach?
8 How shall we screen possible approaches?
    Is the best approach self-evident?
    Can we provisionally select from the most likely approach?
    Can we produce a short-list of possible approaches?
    Are there any serious drawbacks to any of the approaches?
    Do we need a detailed decision analysis?
9 What potential problems exist in the chosen approach?
    What is the seriousness of each problem?
    What is the likelihood of each problem arising?
    Can we avoid serious problems or make contingency plans?
    Are there problems we cannot avoid or can do nothing about?
    Is the chosen approach feasible or should we reconsider?
10 What detailed planning should we do?
    To what level and detail should we plan?
    What planning approach should we use?
        Planning diagrams?
        Networks?
        Bar charts?
    How does our project relate to others?
    Will we have cost, time or resource problems?
    Do we have to replan the project to avoid these?
    When should we next review the project?

Establishing a start point

The application of these principles in drawing up terms of reference is not as straightforward as is sometimes suggested. An example will illustrate this point.

Example. 'Being in front' – developing the most competitive means of manufacturing

On a site of 365 people in North West England the site management team had been developing an awareness of the need to change. Their general method was to develop a site management team 'charter' describing the organization, culture etc. they thought would best secure their site's future. This charter was then shared and developed with their colleagues and, over time, with all site personnel. In all, this process lasted from November 1987 to October/November 1988. It was made up of eight distinct steps:

1 Development of the site objectives and management charter/philosophy ... November 1987–January 1988
2 Team-building for the site management team .... November 1987–January 1988
  and for the rest of the management on site .... began February 1988
3 Objective programme covering the overall manufacturing function of the company .... February 1988–March 1988
  and then applied to individual departments .... March 1988–May 1988
4 Follow-up on the company mission with the factory manager, department managers and their deputies .... initially December 1987–January 1988
  and then monthly .... from May 1988
5 'Organizational effectiveness workshops' for department managers and their deputies .... March 1988
  and for all supervisors .... June 1988–July 1988
6 Development of site training plan via a survey/needs analysis among the department managers and their deputies .... November 1987 and preparation over December 1987
  among supervisors .... April 1988
  followed by main implementation, i.e. team-building, listening, giving feedback etc. courses .... beginning April 1988

7 Workshop with trade unions on site ....July 1988 and follow-ups
8 Development of 'shop floor' plan ......July 1988–September 1988
   leading to a major series of workshops
   with the themes 'working together'
   and 'towards a common goal' ....November 1988

The 'shop floor' workshops had two objectives:

1 To promote understanding and support for the future business challenges facing the site (including product rationalization).
2 To promote understanding of how people needed to work together to ensure continual competitiveness and success.

During the one-day workshops a series of questions was posed, which the staff addressed in syndicates. The most important questions were:

What do we want to change?
What do we need to preserve?
Where are we now?
Which are the key areas to address?

Of the many issues raised in attempting to answer these questions, a main issue was 'involvement'. In addition to 'lack of involvement', a whole range of weaknesses was identified, e.g. lack of training, poor communications, poor management etc. The response of the site management team to these answers was to establish a study group to examine its part of the factory and to put forward proposals as to how it could be improved. The terms of reference tabled by the site management team via the personnel manager were as follows:

> The scope of the study is to develop the most competitive means of manufacture to meet business needs without constraint by existing methods, rules and activities.
>
> The conclusions of the study will meet the following criteria:
>
> 1 Be acceptable to statutory bodies.
> 2 Be able to adapt to future changes in inventory, volume, product, pack type etc.
> 3 Meet and improve upon existing standards.
> 4 Any training required to be readily identifiable.
> 5 Be within the culture in which continuous improvement is the norm.
> 6 Improve communications.

Establishing a start point

7 Provide sufficient benefits to the company to make the changes attractive and to provide meaningful and rewarding jobs.
8 Maximize existing abilities of individuals.
9 To conclude the study and present the conclusions within six months of starting.
10 Throughout the study, the group will actively communicate its activities to staff at all levels in the study area and to other interested individuals or groups of staff.

The study group will not be responsible for negotiating the changes recommended, e.g. the group may recommend appropriate grading structure/s, but would not recommend pay levels.
The study group will be made up of the following members:

Leader/chairman	1
Operators (manufacturing and filling, packaging, and collation)	5
Production supervisor	1
Production fitter	1
Production electrical	1
QA/labs	2

In addition the group will have internal administrative support (especially computing) and an external adviser.

Volunteers were sought to fill the eleven posts in February 1989. The study group underwent team training (two days) in mid-March 1989 and then went about examining the terms of reference. The group first posed a series of questions and reservations concerning the initial terms of reference to the site personnel manager in order to clarify their understanding. Their questions, and the answers they received are as follows:

Question: What are the existing thoughts/plans on the implementation of changes in the department/across the site, e.g. pay systems?

Answer: As regards pay, there is the intention to apply the principles as set out in our mission statement. We must therefore move to a pay system which allows people to develop and progress. Currently both development and progression are hampered by the relatively restrictive, rigid and narrow 'boxes' of the current pay system. I would be surprised therefore if the study group did not come up with a proposal based on new jobs, roles and an organization structure which calls for a reduction in the number of grades, and for scope for development within grades. The detail of such a proposal, e.g. how it would be introduced, the placing of people in new grades, the rate of pay per grade etc., would be dealt with via the usual routes with the unions on site.

More broadly, there are no detailed change plans for a particular department or the site as a whole; what we are clear about is the broad direction we should be going in: see our mission statement and charter. We are also clear about the business strategy and key actions. We are clear that we need to develop and change roles in order to maintain jobs, and we have taken opportunities as they have arisen, e.g. the truck drivers and fork-lift truck drivers. But these types of changes have been opportunist and have only changed the way we do things at the margin. This study group has a clean sheet of paper, and so can do a very detailed, thorough and fundamental study of how we could and should be doing things. This study can therefore consider all of the inputs that are relevant to the manufacture, filling and packaging of our main product. It can challenge existing methods, consider how best to handle the increase in volumes etc. There are very few constraints on the study, and it can examine the boundaries/interfaces with other departments inside and outside the manufacturing centre.

Question: Is this study group expected to consider implementation, and to develop a plan and timetable?

Answer: 'Yes' is the simple answer. The implementation plan will need to cover the possible approaches, the overall timetable, the phases of implementation etc. To some extent the difficulty of the problem and the solution proposed will determine the timescale, e.g. training people for new roles which are radically different would take much longer than if only modest changes to roles were proposed. We do not expect a plan, though, which spells out the minute detail.

Question: How is this study group different from others we have had in the past?

Answer: Many of the previous working parties have only tackled relatively small issues. This one is being fully resourced with a room, as much time to meet and work as is needed etc. The size of the issues being tackled is much larger and it will need to come up with some radical proposals if the 20–30 per cent productivity gain is to be achieved. One thing we have learnt from previous study groups is the importance of communication – this study group must communicate as it goes along, sharing the steps it is going through, explaining its approach and its initial findings etc. The final proposals will therefore come as a shock to no one. We must all listen to and learn from this study group not only as regards the proposals but also as regards implementation. Remember, this is the first study group we have set up since we developed the charter – how the study group works, develops its proposals, and shares them with us all is a test of our charter.

Question: What guarantees will the company/the site executive give as regards the implementation of the study group findings, e.g. in terms of job security, income security, shift working etc?

Answer: The company has already said that the numbers were broadly right across all three sites. Here we have the right numbers, and with the current volumes and those in the business plan we should be all right. The key is having the right volume of work.

Income security is very much a personal issue. We want to achieve a situation in which people who want to progress and contribute can do so (and get greater rewards) and those who don't won't be forced to do so or be threatened in any way. Thus, if people are asked to change to roles which might threaten their grade, we will seek to offer them comparable jobs elsewhere in the factory, and with the move to a new pay system which recognizes individual contribution this should be easier to achieve. And again, our mission and our charter set out the principles by which we intend to work. Income will only be 'insecure' for someone if they choose not to progress, or not to take up a comparable role.

Shift working very much depends on volumes and the cost of the equipment we use. If, for business reasons and for the good of the site, we did need to move to shifts then we would attempt to accommodate individual circumstances and needs. We managed to achieve the move to shifts at our site in the North East with 317 (of a possible 1000 in production) being retrained because they did not want to work shifts. We would go down the same route.

Question: Does 'culture' mean our charter in the draft remit?

Answer: Yes, it is also an extension of the mission statement, and it includes changes in society and among our competitors. It represents the combination of how we do things (our charter) and the needs of the market (our customers) and we must be sure we are successful in bringing the two together.

Question: What is the measure for improvement?

Answer: We have a series of 'givens' in our business which includes cost, quality, customer service levels, rewards, job satisfaction etc. These must be taken together, and anything that the study group proposes *must* improve upon them. Also, if you go through the strategic goals of the business, our charter etc., you can develop a list of the key measures. Of course, in the 'soft' areas like communication, job satisfaction etc. you will need to go on your own judgement and experience of the site.

Question: What does 'sufficient benefits' mean? How much benefit? How is it measured?

Answer: This study group is designing a new way of manufacturing for tomorrow, and one which *must* be capable of achieving a 30 per cent improvement in productivity. It must also be an adaptable and responsive approach to manufacturing which can cope with changes in volume, inventory etc.

Question: Is it expected that the study group will do a full costs and benefits evaluation of the options developed?

Answer: Yes, but not in great detail. It must be shown, however, that any proposals developed by the study group do make economic sense, and that they move the site forward. So you will need to call on the accountants for the facts and figures and help. You will need to indicate where the costs and benefits will arise from.

Question: Does the scope of the study also include systems and plant as well as jobs and organization?

Answer: While the detailed work on systems will be done by a major computer equipment supplier (on site to meet the site executive on 3 and 4 April 1989) it will be necessary to provide them with an input on information requirements. They will not be telling us who should be using the information. Likewise, on the plant and equipment side the study group can help in the specification. The core of the project is roles and organization relevant to manufacturing, e.g. covering installation, commissioning, operating etc. Our new systems manager can help act as the bridge between this project and the activities of the study group.

Question: This study group is restricted to one production department; what about the other areas/departments on site, e.g. the movement of people between departments?

Answer: The study had to begin somewhere. Your department is well documented and we have a lot of information on it. Also, the importance of it to the site is growing with volumes increasing by 70 per cent over the next few years. This study group will need to consider the interfaces with other departments which are relevant.

Question: Are there plans to set up other study groups for other departments or will they have to accept our solutions/proposals?

Answer: It is not the intention for this study group to design the whole site organization, and in time other study groups will be set up to examine their own departments. It would be surprising, though, if the method developed by this study group were not applicable elsewhere on site. Similarly, some of the findings might be applicable elsewhere also. When other study groups will be set up is not clear at the moment.

Question: Already changes are being introduced informally at department and line level; if we make them formal (possibly without any extra pay) we might lose what we have already got. Do you think this will be the case?

Answer: Here there are two key points. First, we must develop a way of dealing with those people who want to progress and those who don't, for whatever reason. And second, we must make sure that the study group communicates at all times so that nothing comes as a surprise to anyone, least of all the management. Again, we must seek to line up to our mission and charter.

Question: Is the 31 July 1989 the only end date, or can it be changed?

Answer: When the study was set up we had to make some estimate both of the time to be spent on it per week (about two days per person per week) and how long it would take (about six months). But if necessary the date can be changed. Please note, though, the amount of time being made available; it means that the study group is tackling a large and complex issue.

Question: What happens if the majority of people in the department don't accept the proposals, but the management do, or vice versa?

Answer: It is clear to everyone that we must improve from where we are, e.g. 30 per cent improvement in productivity. Many of the necessary improvements will be identified by the study group and will be shared with everyone on site throughout the study. So nothing will come as a surprise. Also, no one is being forced to do anything, we will need to cater for those who do want to progress, and those who don't. Finally, if both or one side reject the proposals then we've all failed, and what would that say about the long-term future of the site?

Question: The company's track record on 'delivering the goods' in the past has been poor, e.g. payment for the 'role of craftsmen agreement', stand-in supervisor, temporary moves in to the labs etc. Will it be different in the future?

Answer: We all must recognize the need for change, especially among management. In fact it is often more difficult to get managers to see the need for change. Externally, we can see the competition reshaping, the emergence of Europe post-1992, new technologies, new products, erratic and fast-changing financial/trading environments, e.g. high inflation in the Third World. All of these elements make up our 'trading world' which is constantly changing, and which we are likewise constantly changing to meet. Our determination to improve and lead changes is all the greater, which is evident in the latest company video.

This video was shown and revealed the broad external changes and the internal responses within the company to these changes. In particular the Government's recent White Paper on the National Health Service (NHS) was picked out, which will influence the prescribing practices of doctors in the NHS: rather than the current priorities, when prescribing a drug, of (1) Does it work? (2) Is it safe? (3) What does it cost? – it is proposed that all three factors should be considered together, though never to the detriment of the treatment of the patient. Even though we, as a company, might disagree with this shift in the NHS, a major customer, it will affect both the prescription of current products and the acceptance of new products.

In response to this and other changes we have also been changing along a clear strategic direction which has resulted in the reshaping of the commercial/selling arm, the development of manufacturing centres at the three manufacturing sites, the drawing-up of a joint site charter etc.

Already our changing and improving organization is showing encouraging signs of success. In the first quarter of 1989 profits are up by 16 per cent, sales are up 21 per cent, we hit a turnover of £145 million – a 20 per cent increase. Currently we hold 13.6 per cent of the general practitioner market, and 12.5 per cent of the UK market. Our main product hit £50 millions of sales, and our number two sales were up by 14 per cent. On the cost/productivity side we are on target to achieve the 30 per cent improvement over a five year period.

Further changes will be necessary and might include the dual promotion of products through the various business divisions. We must also strive for a greater alignment of our values and beliefs to ensure an exciting and successful future.

The video gives me confidence that we are determined to change and are serious about recognizing the effort that will be required to achieve and maintain the necessary improvements.

Just taking this study group, this is part of the overall process of improvement outlined in the video. It shows that the site and the company are serious about improving in line with the charter. And while the study group develops your department for the future, we are beginning to pull threads together on training and development for the company so it can deliver our 'people development' strategy.

Question: Performance-related pay (PRP) – is it coming here?

Answer: Already we have a form of PRP at one site and for the commercial people. You may have seen a booklet describing it. PRP can take on various forms, e.g. commission-based on the levels of sales achieved, payment-based on the number of units produced (piece rate) etc. In some environments PRP can work. It is not appropriate to manufacturing. In manufacturing we rely on a team effort so PRP, which is generally focused on the individual, would not be helpful.

What we must do, though, is move towards an integrated system which would bring together the existing fragmented and functional payment systems. We have to remember what business we are in. Here we are in the 'conversion' business yet we have job structures and payment systems which tend to encourage some of the better people to leave direct manufacturing jobs, and to move into the labs. At present it is almost exclusively in the labs that has evolved a set career paths where individuals can gain skills, knowledge and formal educational qualifications. We need to develop similar paths for other jobs and parts of the factory, and if possible offer careers to all who want to progress on an individual basis.

Also, we must find a way which allows and encourages individuals to develop, acquire and use additional skills and knowledge and which does not rely on 'establishment numbers', i.e. a fixed number of jobs in a particular grade. If we could achieve this we would avoid the problems of stand-in payments for supervisors (and so avoid 'payment is never today, all based on pay tomorrow – yet tomorrow never seems to come for most of us'). The same can be said of the 'Role of Craftsman' agreement and payments – we paid a little for a principle, and in real terms got little. Both sides were frustrated. Again we must find a way to avoid these problems in the future.

However, it must be remembered that part of the problem with the 'Role of Craftsman' discussion was caused by the 'fitter is a fitter is a fitter' syndrome. Because of this approach adopted by the AEU at the full-time official level there was a great reluctance to move away from a common craft rate.

In summary, we must find a way of training, developing and rewarding people which allows individuals to acquire and use new skills, and gets the right skills in the right place at the right time.

Question: How will we decide which option we should pursue?

Answer: I'm sure the study group will come up with a range of options, and that they will not be all equally attractive and meet the terms of reference. A clear favourite will probably emerge. So in the interim report I would expect you to be able to spell out the strengths and weaknesses of a range of options, and to come down and support one of them in particular.

While the selected option might be quite different from what we have now, we can work towards it in time through training and development on a joint contract basis – with the individual and the company making a contribution and gaining the benefits.

The option you select and describe in the interim report will not be 'voted on' – the real debate will be how we will implement the option.

Question: Why aren't we meeting with the unions?

Answer: The unions are 'pro' the study group but don't want to compromise their position in any way. Members of the site union committee are already keeping themselves informed of what the study group is doing by coming down to the study group's room, and by talking with individual study group members.

As soon as the interim report is out I will start talking with the unions to 'scope out' the implications of where the study group's work is leading us.

Question: There is a feeling among staff that study group members will get preferential treatment for jobs in the future. This could work both ways. Would the managers be tempted to apply positive discrimination against members of the study group? And how will the study group members fit back into the department if there is ill-feeling among staff?

Answer: People who take opportunities and 'put themselves about' by joining quality circles, volunteering for the study group, etc. are generally those who want to get on in some way. They will tend to perform well at interviews and have a wider range of experiences to offer when applying for a different job or promotion. So the answer is 'no', study group members will be treated exactly the same as anyone else.

This question-and-answer approach with the personnel manager, which took place over two sessions, helped to reassure the group with regard to job security and to clarify their understanding of many of the criteria. This then led to the development of a revised set of terms of reference.

Terms of reference

1 The scope of the study will cover those tasks related to the operation of the 'lines' in the department.
2 The objective of the study is to develop the most competitive means of manufacture to meet business needs without constraint by existing methods, roles and activities.
3 The conclusions of the study will meet the following criteria:

>Be acceptable to statutory bodies.
>Be able to adapt to future changes in inventory, volume, product, pack type etc.
>Meet and improve upon existing quality standards.
>Any training required to be readily identifiable.
>Be within the culture in which continuous improvement is the norm.
>Improve communications.
>Provide sufficient benefits to the company to make the changes attractive and to provide meaningful and rewarding jobs for employees.

Establishing a start point

Maximize existing abilities of individuals.
To conclude the study and present the conclusions by September

4 Throughout the study, the group will actively communicate its activities to staff at all levels in the study area and to other interested individuals or groups of staff.
5 The study group will not be responsible for negotiating the changes recommended, e.g. the group may recommend appropriate grading structure/s but would not recommend pay levels.

This was modified one week later to the following version.

Terms of reference

1 The scope of the study will cover those tasks (including systems, jobs, organization and plant) related to the study group's department.
2 The objective of the study is to develop the most competitive means for organizing manufacturing to meet business needs without constraint of existing methods, traditions, roles and activities.
3 The recommendations of the study group will meet the following criteria:

> Be acceptable to statutory bodies, e.g. Medicines Inspectorate, HSE, FDA.
> Be able to adapt to future changes in inventory, volume, product, pack type etc., e.g. volume up by 70 per cent by 1992–93.
> Meet and improve upon existing quality standards.
> Be within the culture (combination of Site Charter and external competitive environment) in which continuous improvement is the norm.
> Improve communications.
> Provide sufficient benefits to the company and for employees to make the changes attractive and to provide meaningful and rewarding jobs.
> Develop and build upon existing abilities and needs of individuals.
> To conclude the study and present the conclusions within six months

4 Throughout the study, the group will actively communicate its activities to staff at all levels in the study area and to other interested individuals or groups of staff.
5 Will provide a broad implementation plan and timetable with associated costs and benefits.
6 The study will also consider those aspects of other departments with impact on manufacturing. In time other departments will have their own study which will consider the detail relevant to their own operation.

7 The study group will not be responsible for negotiating the changes recommended, e.g. the group may recommend appropriate grading structure/s but would not recommend pay levels.

The final version of the terms of reference was not developed until the exact focus of the study had been established. This process is described in the next section.

Summary

In this example the terms of reference were drawn up with no detailed examination of the issues concerned. The key items which were decided at the 'development of the terms of reference' stage were the objective of the study, some of the study 'success criteria' and aspects of the study approach. It allowed a period of time for the study group to settle in and begin to understand their terms of reference and their 'power and influence base'. The detail of the terms of reference, e.g. what issues would be tackled, did not come until they had scoped the study and identified where it would be most profitable to concentrate their efforts.

Definition and scoping of the problems and issues to be tackled

Here the approach is to move beyond the very broad terms of reference and to examine what issues are worth tackling, and what the study can tackle in six months. In all, three actions can be taken here:

1 A general sweep of the issues via a SWOT/5P analysis – what are the general issues?
2 An examination of existing sources of information – what do we know already?
3 Mapping of the existing production process – what prevents us from having a good run?

Each of these steps will now be illustrated by a single example which continues the previous one used to illustrate the first steps in developing the terms of reference.

Example 1. 'Being in front' – developing the most competitive means of manufacturing

First, a 'SWOT/5P analysis' was undertaken using the following brief.

1 The purpose

This exercise is to provide the study group with a means for describing individual views and thoughts of the department. The presentation which you will make, along with those of others, will provide us with a framework for a general discussion to enable the study group to begin the definition of the areas worthy of investigation.

2 Presentation format

Present an analysis of the department supported by visual aids (overhead, flipchart etc.) in not more than 5/6 minutes with a further 4/5 minutes given for discussion and questions.

With the knowledge of the operation supplemented wherever possible by quantitative data (e.g. productivity measures, capital employed, skills used, efficiency measures etc.) use the matrix shown below to the extent that it is appropriate. Use of the matrix provides a commonality of approach for comparison purposes. If the matrix appears inappropriate, please devise your own matrix.

	Strengths	Weaknesses	Opportunities	Threats
Products				
Plant				
Processes				
Programmes				
People				

3 Further considerations

(a) Try to draw out how the department fits in with the whole site operation. Is there total compatibility or some apparent divergence?
(b) In the context of this exercise:
  (i) Product: the output of the operation. Consider the fulfilment of customer need and the ability to make the product to agreed standards, e.g. quality, quantity, price, delivery dates etc.
  (ii) Plant: the buildings and equipment (the fixed assets).

(iii) Processes: how the product is 'made', i.e. how the final product is produced. It includes consideration of available capacity, plant availability (reliability and maintainability), layout, safety, maintenance requirements etc.
(iv) Programmes: covers timetables for delivery, purchasing, scheduling, inventory levels etc.
(v) People: the workforce. Consider skills, training, organization, wages structure, trade union involvement etc.

This exercise resulted in the following output:

1 Products

Strengths
  Established.
  One of the top sellers.
  Widely used.
  Reliable.
  Quality of use/operation.
  Good profit.
  Well presented.
  Respected by end user.
  Well marketed.
  Lower cost than competitors.
Weaknesses
  Off patent.
  Getting old.
  Newer products coming onto market.
Opportunities
  Market growing (external).
  '1992'.
  'Airlink'.
  Line extensions.
  Start from strong position.
  Packaging form/presentation.
  Output growth (internal).
Threats
  Introduction of new drugs.
  CFC ban.
  Competitors with similar drugs, (internal and external).
  Different forms of administering the drug.
  Parallel importing.
  NHS reforms.
  Counterfeit products.

2 Plant

Strengths
  The plant is paid for.
  The site is clean.
  Room for expansion.
  The cost of refurbishment is low, compared to other sites.
  User friendly.
  Cost recovery high.

Weaknesses
  Output doesn't meet customer demand (tamper evident pack is required for the UK market).
  High rates.
  Open to all comers.
  Faulty components with packaging.
  Noisy atmosphere/poor environment.
  Isolation, e.g. no windows.
  Machinery old/unreliable, spares availability.
  Unreliable control equipment.
  Short on line monitoring.
  Position of lines in factory.
  Tolerance too fine.

Opportunities
  Money available.
  New department/building.
  Refurbish equipment and new layout.
  New machines more reliable leading to higher output.

Threats
  Capacity available elsewhere in company (e.g. Italy).
  Money not authorized.
  Limited plant adaptable.
  Total exhaustion of plant capability.

3 Processes

Strengths
  Easy process to operate.
  Tried and tested process.
  Good safety level.
  Good component reliability – manufacturing only.
  Good contact with component suppliers.

Weaknesses
  Double handling of labels, leaflets etc.

Time-wasting.
Double-checking results.
Complexity of testing procedures.
Qualifications needed by tester/releaser.
Batch waste (can it stand overnight?).
Planning/scheduling dependency (especially in packaging).

Opportunities
Computer-based systems.
Reduce lead times and inventory.
Upskilling for operators.
Developing roles across the whole of the manufacturing centre.

Threats
People reluctant to take on more responsibility.
Higher cost of raw materials.
Quality standards.
External regulations/internal QA.
Rigid company procedures (standards committee).
Non-availability of plant when required.

4 Programmes

Strengths
High service levels (e.g. exports 99 per cent).
Planning.
Well established home service levels.
Responsive.
Service support/cooperation high.

Weaknesses
Home service levels (especially to warehouse).
Poor scheduling on packaging side.
Batch size/component support changeover.
Packaging development liaison.
Batch scheduling for packaging.

Opportunities
Combination/overlapping of production and planning roles.
Development of scheduling/planning/customer services role.
Current consideration of planning organization/computer.

Threats
Loss of orders.
Inefficiency waiting for information.
Loss of key suppliers.
Insular nature of systems.
System failure.

5 *People*

  Strengths
    Committed/cooperative/loyal.
    Willing to learn.
    Skilled people.
    Openminded.
    Objective.
    Hard-working.
    Confident.
    Open to change.
  Weaknesses.
    Two populations.
    Insufficient training.
    Communication.
    Career development.
    Promotion within/overly related to qualifications.
    Too many channels.
    No incentives.
    High absence level/counselling system.
    Boredom.
    Friction.
    Organization.
  Opportunities
    Promotion/development.
    Recognition.
    Company commitment and cash.
    Rewards.
    Greater role/part in the operation.
    Meet people.
    Greater job satisfaction.
    Better working environment.
  Threats
    Reluctant to change.
    Might not get the rewards.
    Down-grading.
    Job losses.
    Disinterest.
    Pressured in too short a time to change.
    Too much responsibility in the wrong places.
    Trained people leave.

This was the first analysis of the possible issues which could be examined in depth by the study group. It was then necessary to see who was already handling these issues (if anyone), and what the study group could contribute. It was soon established that three of the areas were already the subject of significant study, i.e. new products (by the company's research and development department), all systems were being reviewed, and the department on which the study was based had a project team seeking monies for new plant, equipment and facilities. In the last two cases it is desirable for the study group to have an input to assist in the design of the new systems and new plant and equipment (see Figure 4.2). It was then logical to focus on the 'people' component of the department and to consider which issues should be tackled.

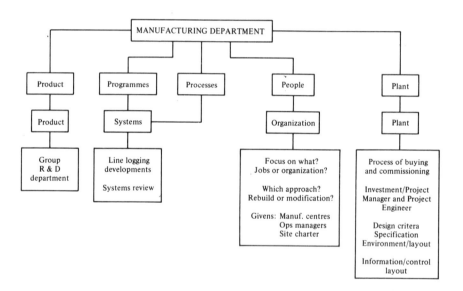

Figure 4.2 *Areas of review and analysis*

A list of possible information sources was developed to help direct the enquiry to what was already known.

Possible data sources

Line logs/diary.
Job descriptions.
Standard operating procedures.
Technical guide.
Validation protocol.
Planned preventative maintenance routines.
Monthly accounts (line utilization, labour, materials, batch yield).
Monthly reports (outputs, problems).
Goods received notes.
Works study line reports.
Complaints.
Near miss forms.
Department safety audit.
Safety meeting minutes.
Lab. results.
Business plan.
Filling log book.
Engineering work request sheets.
Labour transfers.
Personnel records – absence, overtime, length of service etc.
Fixed asset list.
Proposal for equipment purchases.
Purchase orders.
Mop and bucket record.
Board paper for new department.
Capital budget data – historical.
Service records on equipment.
Inventory policy.
Stock write-offs.
Service levels.
Current and past job-holders.
Training records – departmental and personnel.
Training modules.
Other sites' data.
Other company data.
Manufacturing documents.
Job pack.
Job evaluation data.

These possible data sources were then examined to identify those that would help initially to refine the focus of the study. The SWOT/5P analysis helped to suggest that the 'people' would be the most appropriate focus for the study group, and this analysis needed refinement to include the specific issues of their department. The first step in this part of the further scoping of the study required the charting of the production process from the receiving of an order through to the despatch of the order. This charting of the production process was conducted in the following way:

1 Assume a 'good run' with no hold-ups due to equipment, out-of-specification materials etc.
2 Concentrate on the separate main steps which must be undertaken in order to move the production process forward.
3 Once the whole production process has been charted, add in all the main support tasks which must also occur in order for the production process to flow, e.g. in the warehouse, quality assurance, planning/scheduling etc.

An example of this three-step approach is presented in Figure 4.3 for the manufacture, filling and packaging of an aerosol can. Of the 36 sequential steps linking receipt of order to despatch, seventeen are support activities: if any of these does not occur, the whole production process stops. In many cases the support task involves only a check on the product and the process e.g. steps 21, 23, 26, 28 and 30 – while in others it concerns the ordering of material and components and their testing – e.g. steps 4, 7 and 19. The other support tasks relate to quality assurance sampling and testing and to the changing of the equipment to accommodate different pack types.

This chart of the production process can now be used as a framework in which the current barriers to improving performance can be identified. The identification of the barriers to improvement, or aspect of a 'bad run', forms the second stage of this step. So once the 'production process running well' has been described, those actions and events which cause it not to run well can be allocated to one of the 36 main steps. It is these weaknesses of the current system which need to be identified, and which any new department should not inherit if at all possible.

The second step was also undertaken to validate the first scoping of the terms of reference through the SWOT/5P approach. Do, for example, people/organization issues really account for hold-ups in production? Are they the most important area for the study group to examine? The study groups therefore went through each of the 36 steps in the production process in order to identify the factors which resulted in 'bad runs'. This resulted in the identification of 251 items. These are listed in Table 4.4 and each has been allocated to one of four categories (people; systems; equipment; materials) or to some combination of these categories. The results are summarized in Table 4.5.

Establishing a start point 97

(1) Order received
(2) Long-term planning schedule
(3) Suggestion of product mix and volume for filling
(4) Firm order for a full batch of filled cans
(5) Filling schedule
(6) Allocate batch number
(7) Order components and raw materials
(8) Dispense raw materials
(9) Manufacture and mix batch
(10) Transfer to filling line
(11) Load cans on to line
(12) Air blower
(13) Pamasol (can cleaning and filling equipment)
(14) Checkweigher
(15) Batch codes
(16) Load cans on to trays
(17) Reconcile batch
(18) Transfer to bond store
(19) Order packaging components from store
(20) Collate order
(21) Transfer to packaging line
(22) Load turntable
(23) Checkweigh
(24) Primer
(25) Spray test
(26) Label and batch code
(27) Put can into actuator
(28) Carton and leaflet
(29) Security label
(30) Scan pack
(31) Pack case
(32) Load pallet
(33) Reconcile materials
(34) Check job pack
(35) Collate documents and release order
(36) Despatch order

Figure 4.3 *Chart of the production process*

Table 4.4 *States of bad run (P = people; S = systems; E = equipment; M = materials)*

Production Step	Fault	Category
1 Manufacturing		
Issue manufacturing documents	Incorrect batch number	P
	Incorrect batch size	P
	Product	P
Order components and raw materials	Wrong components	P/S
	Components not passed	P/S
	Components failed test	S
	Raw material variation	
	Wrong version	P/S
	Late issue	P
	Late delivery	S
	Damage on receipt	P
Dispense raw materials	Dispense wrong drug	P
	Insular system	S
Manufacture and mix	Balance and computer disputes	S
	Operator/supervisor error	P
	Wrong item added	P
	Contaminated equipment	P
	Poor equipment assembly	P
Pamasol	Star wheels	E/M
	Valve feed	E/M
	Can feed	M
	Sensor not working	E
	Cans falling over	E/M
	Valve debris	M/P
	Filling problem	P/E
	Gassing problem	P/E
	Crimping problem	E
	Damaged pipework	E/P
	Propellant 12 pressure fluctuations	E
Batch coder	Air pressure	E
	Poor print	E/P
	No print	E/P
	Greasy cans	M
	Ink spraying	E
	No ink	P
	Make-up	P

Establishing a start point

Checkweigher	Wrong batch or item code	P/E
	Going off during a run	E
	Not noticed by operator	P
	Incorrectly set, e.g. reference weight, tolerances	P
	Belts jamming	E/P
	Accuracy	E
Loading cans into tray	Cans jamming at 'take-off' point	E
	Tray packer jamming	E/P
	Rogue cans in/under 'Auto Packer'	P
	Dents etc. not noticed when being loaded	P
	'Auto Packer' not releasing filled trays	E
	Incorrect number of cans in trays	E/P
	Wrong tray number used	P
	Stop system system not working correctly	E
	Trays not available	P/S
	Dirty trays	P
	Rogue cans from previous batches in empty trays	P
Reconciliation of batch	Batch count not double-checked	P
	Trays incorrectly labelled	P
	Incorrect no. of cans in trays	P/E
Check documents	Signatures missing	P
	Transcription errors	P
	In-process checks missing	P
	Illegible writing	P
	Dispensary labels missing	S/E/P
Transfer to bond store	Mixed batch numbers products	P
	Stacks falling over	P

2 Filling

Transfer to filling line	Wrong vessel	P
	Vessel incorrectly set up	P
	Vessel refrigeration failure	E
	Vessel alarm system not working	E
	Vessel motor/pump failure	E

Table 4.4 (*cont.*):

Production Step	Fault	Category
Loading cans/valves	Vessel pipework leaking	E
	Vessel filters blocked	E/P
	Rondo	
	Belts cutting out (moving sideways)	E
	Vibrator plate cutting out	E
	Cans jam at falling point	M
	Turntable running out	P
	Cans falling over on turntable	E
	Wrong type of valve	P
	Insufficient components	M/P/S
	Damaged components	M/P
	Foreign bodies	M
	Rogue cans/valves	M/P/E
	Disassembled valves	M/P
Air blower	Cans jamming	M/E

3 Packaging

Production Step	Fault	Category
Components	Wrong components/version	P/S
	Not enough components	P
	Damaged/soiled components	M
	Components not released	P/S
	Overprinting – wrong information/not ready	P
	Labels reeled wrong way	P
	Artwork on label	P
	Components go to wrong department	P
	Absence	P
	Not up from stores	P/S
	Components not on site	P
	Components not ordered on time	P
Collation	Absence	P
	Human error	P
	Wrong information/no information	P/S
	Wrong count	P
	Batch in quarantine	P/S

Establishing a start point 101

	Not off test	P/S
	No components	P/S
	Stereo ordered from main overprint	P/S
	Part overprinted on-line/ off-line	E/S E/S
	Overprint done on same day batch is to be out	S/P
Packaging line (transfer)	Batch going on wrong line	P
	Wrong job pack	P
	Not enough room for batch on line (mix-up with other line)	P
	Stack falling	P/E
	Count not right	P
	Receiving order too late	P/S/M
	Job pack does not match manual	S/P
	Design of components wrong	P/S
	Preprint does not match job pack	P/S
Load turntable	Cans falling	E
	Labels running out	P
	Print running out	P
	No components	P/S
	Cans jamming on sessions	E
	Too many on the turntable (cans fall over)	P
	When relieving, turntable can run out	S/P S/P
	Timing out	E
	Machine breakdown	E
	Rogue and dirty valves	P/M
Checkweigh	Not working	E
	Under weight	E/P
	Cans fall coming off turntable	E
Primer	Cans jam	E
	Not set or setting has been changed	E/P E/P
	Cans need priming twice	E/M
	Jetting prime needs cleaning	P
	Bottle needs filling	E/P
	Damaged valves	P/E
	Different-sized valves	E/P

Table 4.4 (cont.):

Production Step	Fault	Category
Spray test	Build-up of drug	E/P
	Rejects	E/M
	Cans jamming (damaged)	E/P
	Machine breakdown	E
	Reset	E/P
	Timing out	E
	Sensor	E
Label and batch code	Wrong information on job pack	P/S
	Human error (fitter with batch/girls let print run out)	P
	Black tape run out	P
	Print difficult because of artwork on label	S/P
	High and low labels	E/M
	Turned-in labels	E
	Double labels	E
	Missing print, all or part	E/P
	Dirty labels	E/M/P
	Not enough labels for the batch	S/P
		S/P
	No black tape in stock	P
	Bad labels	M/P
	Sellotape joins	M/P
	Labels run through	P
	Wrong width black tape	P/M
	Bad crimps	E/P
Security label	Machine breakdown	E
	Wrong position on pack	P/E
	Miss pack altogether	E
	Fly off and stick to belt/floor	E
	Reel runs out/wrong way	P
	Too many rejects (time-wasting)	E
	Dibs not in stock	P
	Cartons pile up and miss dibs	E
Scan pack	Not working	E
	Cartons pile up and go through together	E

Establishing a start point 103

	Not adjusted/too sensitive	E
	Blows carton off unnecessary/ does not blow off	E
	Bins get full	P/E
	Cartons fall off belt and get stuck inside	E
	Cartons get jammed at the beginning of scan pack	E
Pack case	Cartons go in wrong way	E
	Cartons fall through onto bottom ledge	E
	Out of sequence	E
	Cartons build up on belt	E/P
	Not putting box on arm/not putting arm up	P
	Flaps out on cartons	E/P
	Build-up of boxes on rollers	P
	Outers too tight	M
	Outers stuck together	M
	Outers seams open up	M
	Outers too sharp	M
	Outers out of shape	M
	Outers artwork missed	M
	Cartons missed out of box	E/P
Load pallet	Pallet loaded wrongly	P
	No labels/wrong labels	P
	Labels not showing on pallet	P
	Labels upside down on boxes	P
	Wrong outers	P
	Pallets packed too high/too low	P
	Pallets not packed neatly	P
	Wrong count on pallet	P
	No note on pallet	P
Put can into actuator	No actuators	S/P
	Machine breakdown	E
	Wrong actuators	P
	Damaged actuators	E/M
	Actuator with no caps on	M/P
	Cans jamming going into actuators by pusher	E
	Human error (not filling pockets or placing in pockets properly)	P

Table 4.4 (cont.):

Production Step	Fault	Category
	Damaged actuators/damaged cans	E
	Cans not going in actuators/cans going without actuator	E/P
	Caps and elastic bands inside actuators causing jams	M
	Hopper running out	P
	Wrong actuators in hopper	P
	Can not adequately rinsed in arcton	P
	Actuators not tested	P/S
Carton and leaflet	Human error (cartons/leaflets in wrong way)	P
	Wrong batch change	P
	Waiting for batch change	P
	Not taking block out for overprinted cartons	P
	Code reader not working (dirty eye)	E/P
	Leaflet guide wrong width and length	P
	Cartons slipping	E/M
	No suction	E
	Machine too fast	E/P
	Jams	E/P
	Machine breakdown	E
	Wrong cartons/leaflets	P
	Flaps out	E/P
	Damaged cartons/cans	E
	Different-sized cartons	M
	Position of print differs	S/P
	Print blocked in	E/P
	Leaflets folded in together	P
	Leaflets folded different ways	P
	Pinchers not opening up	E
	Blank leaflets	M
Load to pallet	No 'awaiting labels' notes placed on pallets awaiting outer labels	P
	Damp and dirty pallets	M

Establishing a start point 105

	Waiting for pallets	P
	No truck to take pallets away	E
	Not enough outer labels for batch	P/E
	Not enough despatch notes	S
	Forgetting to put outer labels on boxes (if more than one)	P P
	Not putting part box tape on part box	P
	Wrong amount on part box	P
	Not putting amount on outer label on part box	P
	Labels stick together	M
Reconcile materials	Leaving components on line	P
	Count wrong	P
	Rogue cans left on line	P/S/E
	Cans over/under	P
	Takes time	S
Check job pack	Writing not legible	P
	Wrong job pack to wrong batch	P
	Filled in wrong	P
	Not signed for	P
	Does not add up	P
	Lost paperwork	P

This more detailed analysis of the study group's department confirmed the impact of 'people' upon the current production process and its deviation from an optimum performance. It was therefore clear that the study should focus upon 'people' (including organization structure etc.), but should also recognize the impacts of equipment, materials and system on the production process. To accommodate these factors two sub-groups were established to ensure that appropriate modifications could be made to the existing equipment, and that the specification of the new equipment would avoid incorporating these problems. In pursuing these inputs into the design of the equipment it must also be recognized that there is direct feedback to the content of the work to be done, i.e. existing work will probably be removed, or at least modified, and new items of work will be added.

By this stage of the study it was also very clear to the study group members that a whole range of areas needed to be changed, and that improvements were required urgently. It should be noted that over half the members of this study group had worked in quality circles, and had

Table 4.5 *Summary of 'states of bad run' categories*

Category	Occurrences (No.)	(%)
People	95	38
Systems	6	2
Materials	16	6
Equipment	51	20
People and systems	25	10
People and materials	8	3
People and equipment	34	14
People and equipment and systems	2	1
People and systems and materials	2	1
People and equipment and materials	2	1
Equipment and materials	9	4
Equipment and systems	1	0.5
Total	251	

therefore learnt many of the basic analytical techniques, e.g. surveys, statistical charting techniques (Pareto, fishbone, flow, run, histograms), 'imagineering' and some the principles of work through industrial engineering methods. It was this initial understanding and use of analytical tools which would be built upon in deciding which method to use, and how to collect and analyse the relevant information.

Selection of an appropriate method

Here there are two main steps. First, decide what is expected and required of the study method. Second, decide which of the available methods can meet these requirements. To progress the first step a series of questions was posed:

> What is the focus of the study?
> What are the boundaries of the study?
> What inputs/areas need to be covered?
> Who is going to use the method?
> How much time and money do we have?
> Who is going to provide the information?
> Who is going to conduct the analysis?
> Who is going to explain the output?

Who is going to receive the output?
What is required of the outputs?

It was the answer to these questions which helped to develop the criteria for the selection of the study method (see Chapter 2) and resulted in the following list.

1 Output – diagrammatic form.
2 Not expert-dependent.
3 Can handle qualitative and quantitative outputs.
4 Data readily available and/or can be collected without too much effort.
5 Must work – has been used elsewhere.
6 Output is comparable with other sites/companies.
7 Method efficient and effective.
8 Data reliable/high validity.
9 Understandable by study group and rest of the site.
10 Software available.
11 Data collection open and participative.
12 Comprehensive – can cover plant, systems and people.
13 Thorough at the detail level and logical/relevant to all.
14 Method usable in other departments/areas of the site.
15 Output can be translated into costs and benefits (both cash and non-cash).
16 Reflects site charter.
17 Challenges existing approaches.
18 Can be updated easily.
19 Output can be used to produce many products.

It was now possible to consider the available methods which might satisfy these criteria. The biggest stumbling block was the need for a method that reflected their site charter (Figure 4.4) and covered such areas as systems, plant and people. Immediately this meant the rejection of wholly people/worker-centred approaches, and also classic work study/scientific management approaches which treat people as an appendage of the machine. This left only one tried and tested approach, the socio-technical analytical approach, which could meet all of the criteria. Those critera relating to data requirements, analytical methods and the range of the inputs depend very much upon the detailed application of the socio-technical analytical approach.

Site Charter

We are committed to achieving excellent results through people, through effective teamwork and positive attitudes.

We will maintain a safe working environment. We will encourage open, honest two-way communications and support initiative and commitment to change beneficial to our business.

We are determined to adopt a management approach that leads by example and is fair, enthusiastic and consistent.

This will be achieved with:

Objectives
Committing ourselves to realistic objectives consistent with our customer needs, that will retain our competitive edge.

Involvement
Encouraging participation, innovation, delegation and decision-making by allowing individuals the freedom to act within their area of responsibility.

Development
Training and coaching all our staff and encouraging them with regular constructive feedback, enabling them to maximize their potential to develop within the business.

Recognition
Recognize individual and team contribution by praise, respect for the individual and providing development opportunities.

Figure 4.4 *The site charter*

Summary

This chapter has detailed, and then described through a series of case studies drawn from a range of backgrounds, the following points:

1 Process

If long-term change is to be achieved it is necessary to enter into a process that ensures the following:

(a) Both the need to change, and specifically what to change, are identified.
(b) It is a joint and shared process leading to a joint and shared output. Joint ownership of the output is important in that it provides one of the initial steps in moving beyond the awareness of the need to change to a state where a larger group of individuals want to change themselves, and increasingly realize how the most appropriate changes might occur.
(c) The basis is provided for developing an understanding and agreement not only within the specific group of individuals involved in the study itself, but also throughout the department and site. The process provides a series of 'products', and steps in preparing the products, e.g. the SWOT/5P analysis, the visions etc., where a wider group of individuals can be involved.
(d) All misconceptions and assumptions can be brought to the surface and either rejected or accepted and built upon.
(e) The process is an overt example of participative, open decision-making consistent with a shift in management style.
(f) Both time and means are provided for the 'ownership' of the content and idea of the study to become that of the people on site, not just of one group such as 'management'.

2 Material

It is too easy to confuse and obscure the subject of a study by over-complex and even irrelevant information. The steps detailed in this chapter and the examples demonstrate quite clearly the ease with which 'new' information can be generated and categorized to challenge the existing situation. Again, this is all part of the openness and jointness of the approach. It is clear how the move is made from the initial remit through to the selection of a study method. The information used by the group is also in everyday language which is understandable by all concerned. Finally, members of the group are allowed to function on an equal basis with regard to input. It is quite possible to deluge a group with existing information ('management information') which may reduce some group members to a passive role, and so challenge the functioning of the group.

3 Output

The whole purpose of embarking on these first four steps is not purely to ensure that the terms of reference are 'correct', or that the 'right' method is selected, but rather to indicate the style and general approach to change. Both the breadth and depth of the first stage, here divided into four steps, provide the basis of the beginnings of a more significant long-term change, and through the processes employed win supporters to the cause.

The remaining chapters of the book build upon this base and again ensure maximum involvement and as a high a level of understanding as possible through data collection, analysis, option development and evaluation, and subsequent implementation.

5
Data and information collection

Introduction

Before any information is collected it is necessary to ask three questions: What is the output of the exercise going to be used for? What resources and time are available? Who is to be involved in data collection and other aspects of the study? The answers to these three questions, and in particular to the first two, largely determine the method and nature of data and information to be collected. Table 5.1 summarizes the possible sets of answers to these questions.

Taking 'Situation A' first, it is evident that the data collection must be restricted in terms of the people consulted and in the detail required. It is likely in this case that the study group would use as much existing

Table 5.1 *Selection of data and information collection methods*

	Question	Situation A	Situation B
1	What is the output going to be used for?	Develop broad structure of organization and jobs	Develop detailed specification of organization and jobs
2(a)	What resources are available?	Minimal, only the study group	Any that can be justified
2(b)	What time is available?	Minimal, fixed timetable	Adjustable to suit the needs of the study in meeting its objectives
3	Who is to be involved in data collection?	As few as possible – study is 'strictly confidential'.	Anyone who needs to be – study is an 'open book'

information as possible and rely on their own knowledge to supplement it along with that of a limited number of 'experts'. The output in this case does not require the individual inputs of data and information to be either precise or exhaustive, but it must have overall validity.

'Situation B' is just the reverse of the above case. Here the concern is for the quality of the output rather than any constraint of time, resources and confidentiality. This means that the numbers of people consulted and the detail of the study can be much greater.

It does not follow, however, that fundamentally different sets of data need to be collected. In both cases the same type of data can be collected and used, but in 'Situation B' it will be accurate, precise and collected from a wide range of inputs.

The remainder of this chapter tackles the issues of the form of the data to be collected and the possible methods to use. First, though, it is necessary to settle on an appropriate unit or currency of work in which the data can be collected and expressed.

Measurement of work

It is a telling comment upon the regard in which organization structure and job designers are held that many people will read the title of this section as 'work measurement'. Work measurement is a work study term which is solely concerned with the establishment of the time required for a qualified worker to carry out a task at a defined level of working (Whitmore, 1987:6) (see Figure 5.1). In 'measurement of work' the measurement of the duration of task is important but is only one factor to consider. The proposed approach to the measurement of work goes beyond work measurement as a simple measure of labour input, though the focus on the task or a derivative of it is common to both approaches.

Work can be considered in terms of the inputs, the nature of the work conducted, and also its outputs. It is suggested that in order to obtain as full a measure as possible of work it is necessary to consider many of the following factors:

1 Complexity of the work or its component parts.
2 Working environment/conditions where work is undertaken.
3 Duration of the work or its component parts.
4 Frequency with which work or its component parts are undertaken.
5 Skills and knowledge required to undertake the work.
6 Absolute number of tasks.
7 Work allocation and control procedures.
8 Method(s) of progressing interlinked tasks.

Data and information collection

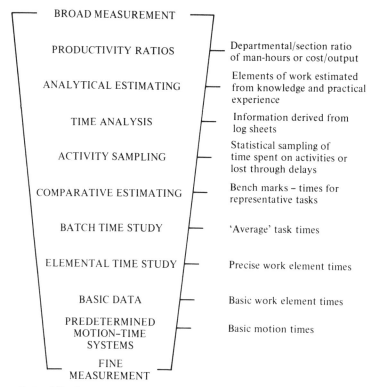

Figure 5.1 *Work measurement – in perspective*

9 Required speed of response to tasks arising, in order for them to be done.
10 Human resources (number of people and their roles) required to undertake work.
11 Variety/range of work arising.
12 Additional resources required to undertake work.
13 Health and safety regulations/restrictions.
14 Physical size of the plant/equipment on which tasks arise.
15 Accuracy and precision with which work must be undertaken.
16 Speed with which work must be undertaken.
17 Impact of incomplete and/or poorly undertaken work.
18 Frequency with which technical advice and assistance are required to undertake the work (see: Cross, 1986:24).

Taking these factors together, a full description of 'work' is almost possible but it is necessary to break down the general term 'work' into manageable elements or components such as 'task', 'operation' and 'element'. A task is a unit of work which is performed by an individual or group of individuals, has a definite beginning and end, and results in a product or service. A task will be made up of a number of smaller activities. For example, if the task is to erect a chain block to a beam, the activities could include:

Climb with a handline to anchorage point.
Uncoil handline and lower to floor.
Attach handline to chain sling at floor.
Hoist chain sling to anchorage.
Detach handline and lower to floor.
Attach chain sling to steel beam (over hessian bag). etc.

These small activities within a task are known as 'elements'. The British Standards Institution (BSI) definition of an element is: 'A distinct part of an operation selected for convenience of observation, measurement and analysis'. Elements of work may occur in groups rather than singly; such a group of elements may be called an 'operation'. For example, in the case of erecting a chain block to a beam, one operation could be 'Lift chain sling to anchorage point and attach to beam'. The BSI definition of an operation is: 'The smallest unit of work used for planning or control purposes . . . a combination of elements'.

In most cases the level of detail required is the task, which can then be aggregated into roles and groups of roles. It is possible to split tasks, where appropriate, into elements and operations. Elemental and operational data is at such a fine level of detail and is so voluminous that it is difficult to know to what use it could be put. There is also a greater likelihood of mistakes being made in the collection of such detailed information and, of course, more resources are required for its collection and validation.

If the task is the appropriate level at which to collect information on the type and nature of the work undertaken, what other variables should also be collected? If information on the type and nature of the work is to be collected at task level with the minimum expenditure of resources, experience suggests that data is required on the following aspects of the task:

1 Description of task – what is done?
2 Location of the task – where is it undertaken?
3 Performer – who undertakes the task?
4 Frequency – how often is the task undertaken?
5 Duration – how long does the task take to perform?
6 Complexity – how difficult is the task?
7 Volume – how much work is undertaken?

This information can then be enhanced by taking into account the following factors:

1 *Batch type.*
   Specific circumstances determining a different production condition.
2 *Performer.*
   Is the task undertaken by a single individual or a group? If a group, who is involved?
3 *Support.*
   Is any support resource required? Is it information? Is it equipment?
4 *Impact.*
   If a task is not undertaken, or is undertaken poorly, where is the impact felt?
5 *Type of work.*
   What general category of work does the task fall into?

Accepting that these are the appropriate variables to collect to 'measure' work, how can they be further defined and then collected? First it is necessary to consider the writing of a task statement.

The task statement

Establishing the level of task definition

The purpose of this step is to establish at what level of detail the task statements should be written. The first step is to map the process under study. This might be a manufacturing, an administrative or a support process. For example, in a food factory there is a series of major steps in the manufacturing process consisting of raw materials intake, manufacture of the product (involving mixing, blending, cooking etc.), the filling of a container, possibly some secondary processing, and then packaging and despatch. Each of these major steps in the manufacturing process can be further subdivided into the steps that make up manufacturing, filling etc. This subdivision procedure needs to be undertaken several times (usually three or four) until the level is reached that represents the work activity undertaken by an individual or a group of individuals.

Rather than go through this step-by-step procedure, it is possible to start immediately at the appropriate task level. One reason for not always going directly to the task level deemed appropriate is the need to establish a consistent level of detail to be worked to by all involved in collecting, providing and analysing the task data.

A second reason for adopting this hierarchical approach to task level definition is that it allows the manufacturing (or other) process to be mapped, and this can then be extended. First, the stages directly relevant to progressing the process are established and recorded; the activities which support this first series of stages of the process are then established and recorded; finally, all other support activities provided in-house or by some third party are established and recorded. As a part of the identification of these three groups of activities it is important to record them in two process states: 'good running' and 'bad running'. This provides a list of those activities required to return the process from a 'bad' to a 'good' state.

Together, these three steps provide a map of the full range of activities which allow a process to function on a day-to-day basis. It can be further extended by considering those activities involved in the design, installation and commissioning of the process in the first place, and any subsequent input required for the development of the process.

An alternative approach is described later under 'Development of the task listing'.

Once the level of detail has been established and agreed, the formal task statements can be written.

Writing the task statement (based on Gael, 1983)

It is easy to compose well-written task statements, and the knack of writing them can be acquired with just a little study and practice. All that is required is that a few simple rules are understood and followed. The following paragraphs describe how task statements should be structured, and present guidelines for writing effective, easily understood task statements.

Why is the way task statements are written so important? The task statement is the basic building block of the method of analysis, and the task statements constitute the basis for the results obtained.

Definition of a task

A task – is a unit of work;
  – is performed by an individual or individuals;
  – has a definite beginning and end;
  – results in a product or service.

Given this definition, the likelihood is that a task will be accomplished in a relatively short period of time. As a work activity comes to require more and more time, the possibility increases that the activity is a work unit larger than a task. Further, if a product or service cannot be identified, the activity is not considered a task. For example, 'Request information from another department' is not considered a task because the description of the actual work is too vague and does not sufficiently identify the output of the activity – what 'information' from what 'department'? In contrast,

'Request customer billing information from Accounts to verify receipt of customer payment' identifies specifically what is to be accomplished and why. Even in the second case, however, the task statement would probably be more specific in practice, naming a particular billing information form or the type of billing information desired, and perhaps giving the job title of the accounts department clerk contacted.

Components of a task statement

Task statements should be written in a manner that clearly distinguishes them from other work activity descriptions, such as descriptions of functions and sub-tasks. The standard form for a task statement is the simple sentence with a subject, a verb and an immediate object, but the subject, the 'I', is omitted from the task statement. The verb is an action verb and the object of the task statement is, of course, the object of the verb. The general practice is to omit articles from task statements, thereby making the statements somewhat choppy, as well as shorter and less well structured than complete sentences.

Task statements can be written rather routinely as long as the question of what is done to what is covered. Some qualifying information almost always is included in task statements to make them more complete and meaningful: for instance, a task statement may include information about the purpose that the task is supposed to serve – in other words, why it is performed. In the task statement mentioned earlier, for example, billing information was requested by the accounts department to verify that a customer had made a payment. How a task is performed is usually not included in a task statement unless it is necessary, for instance when a task can be accomplished in several ways. The task of digging trenches, for example, might be accomplished with hand tools or with heavy equipment depending on the situation, and the appropriate method should be made absolutely clear in the task statement. Brevity is the watchword. A customer contact task can be written so that the 'how' is contained in the action verb – for example, 'Call customers to . . .' or 'Write customers to . . .'. If the means used to contact customers is not important, the task statement could be written: 'Notify customers of . . .'.

When writing task statements:

1 Begin with an appropriate action verb in the present tense – *what is done*.
2 Include the object of that verb – *what is being acted upon*.
3 Include qualifying information as needed.

Four task statements are analysed below according to these three components.

	What is done (Action)	*To what* (Object)	*Qualifier* (when necessary)
1	Send	purchase requests	to the purchasing department
2	Type	legal affidavits	
3	Call	customers	to extend installation date
4	Transmit	data	to other offices using data phone

Qualifying information is needed to round out task statements under the following conditions:

1 HOW
   For tasks that can be accomplished in more than one way.
   Example: Identify component failure patterns using automatic trouble analysis reports.
2 WHY
   For tasks that can have multiple purposes.
   Example: Call repair service to expedite an order.
3 WHERE or WHEN
   For tasks that have multiple situations or conditions.
   Examples: Send erroneous service order back to originator.
   Set automatic trouble analysis equipment to day configuration at start of shift.
4 HOW MUCH OF
   For tasks in which the range of what is acted upon is involved.
   Example: Determine charges for complex service orders.

Guidelines for writing task statements

Specific verbs and nouns

Task statements should be sufficiently specific that the work accomplished is clearly defined and the task statement is concise and unambiguous. Explicit action verbs should be used to specify each task performed. Passive verbs or verbs that describe processes – for example, 'assure', 'determine', 'evaluate', 'indicate', 'ensure', 'supervise', and 'verify' – should ideally not be used to express task statements. The task statement, 'Ensure that customer service requests are accomplished on a timely basis', does not really specify a particular activity accomplished by the job incumbent; verbs that describe processes are open ended and subject to various interpretations.

Nouns used in task statements should also be as specific as possible. The task statement, 'Repair fuel system components', could be made more specific by naming the particular fuel system component that is to be repaired – for example, 'Repair fuel pumps'. Likewise, the task statement 'Clean work area' may be too general.

One action, one object

As a rule, a task can be performed independently of other tasks, and only one action and one object should be included in a task statement. If a description of work covers more than one independent activity, it is not a single task. The task statement, 'Review and prepare cost estimates' should be separated into two statements, 'Review cost estimates' and 'Prepare cost estimates'. In the same way, the statement 'Review files, reports, and correspondence' should be separated into three task statements, since three separate activities are covered. A job-holder might perform only one of the activities and not the others and therefore would not be able to answer questions about the tasks appropriately. In some cases, however, actions or objects may be so closely related that they form a unit of work or a single work activity, e.g. 'Locate and repair short in wiring'; 'Address letters and packages'.

Stand-alone content

Each task statement should be intelligible when standing apart from other task statements. 'Perform other kinds of equipment checks' is not a well-written task statement, but it might make sense if it followed a series of task statements concerning specific equipment checks.

Familiar words

Task statements should be expressed in language that is familiar to everyone on site. Only the most common abbreviations and acronyms should be used. The first time an acronym appears in a task statement it should be spelled out in full; in subsequent statements the acronym can stand alone.

Consistent use of words

The same actions or objects should be described by the same verbs or nouns to avoid confusion. Synonyms should not be interchanged. Verbs frequently used in writing task statement are listed in Table 5.2.

Compatibility with rating scales

A task statement should be written in a manner that enables job-holders to answer questions about task attributes, such as 'How important is each task to your job?', 'How difficult/complex is each task?'. It is relatively simple to test whether a task statement is compatible with the various possible rating scales. The job-holders should be able to rate how much time they devote to performing the task and how frequently they perform it. If the job-holders cannot answer those questions with regard to a task statement, or if the answers would not make sense, then the task statement probably needs some improvement.

Table 5.2 *Lists of possible task verbs*

ACCUMULATE	BLEND	COLLECT	DELETE
ACT	BOOK	COMMUNICATE	DELIVER
ADD	BREAK	COMPARE	DEMONSTRATE
ADHERE	BRIEF	COMPILE	DESCRIBE
ADJUST	BRUSH	COMPLAIN	DESIGN
ADMINISTER	BUDGET	COMPLETE	DESUSPEND
ADVISE	BUFF	COMPUTE	DETECT
AGREE	BUILD	CONDUCT	DEVELOP
AID	BUY	CONFIRM	DIAGNOSE
ALIGN		CONNECT	DIRECT
ALLOCATE	CALCULATE	CONSULT	DISCHARGE
AMEND	CALIBRATE	CONTACT	DISCIPLINE
ANALYSE	CANCEL	CONTRACT	DISCONNECT
ANSWER	CARRY	CONTRIBUTE	DISCRIMINATE
APPLY	CERTIFY	CONTROL	DISPATCH
APPRAISE	CHALLENGE	CONVEY	DISPENSE
APPROVE	CHANGE	COOL	DISPLACE
ARRANGE	CHARGE	COORDINATE	DISPOSE
ASSEMBLE	CHASE	COPY	DISSOLVE
ASSESS	CHECK	CORRECT	DIVIDE
ASSIGN	CHOOSE	COUNSEL	DOCUMENT
ASSIST	CIRCULATE	COUNT	DOWNDATE
ATTEND	CITE	CREATE	DRAW
ATTRIBUTE	CLASSIFY	CURE	DRIVE
AUDIT	CLEAN		DRY
AUTHORIZE	CLEAR	DATE	DRY RUN
	COACH	DEBRIEF	
BALANCE	CODE	DEBURR	EDIT
BATCH	COLLATE	DECIDE	EMPTY

Table 5.2 (*cont.*):

ENCODE	INPUT	OBSERVE	READY
ENCOURAGE	INSERT	OBTAIN	REASON
ENTER	INSPECT	OPEN	REASSEMBLE
ERECT	INSTALL	OPERATE	RECALL
ESTIMATE	INSTRUCT	ORDER	RECEIVE
EVALUATE	INTERVIEW	ORGANIZE	RECOGNIZE
EXAMINE	INVEST	OVERHAUL	RECOMMEND
EXPLAIN	ISOLATE		RECONCILE
EXTINGUISH	ISSUE	PACK	RECONDITION
EXTRACT		PAINT	RECORD
	JOIN	PASS	RECTIFY
FABRICATE	JUDGE	PATCH	REDUCE
FAULT FIND		PAY	REFER
FEED		PERMIT	REFILL
FIGURE	LABEL	PHONE	REFIT
FILE	LEAD	PHOTOCOPY	REGISTER
FILL	LIAISE	PICK	REGULATE
FLUSH	LINK	PLACE	REJECT
FOLD	LIST	PLAN	RELAY
FORMULATE	LOAD	POLISH	RELEASE
FREE	LOAN	POSITION	RELIEVE
	LOCATE	POST	REMOVE
GATHER	LOG	POUR	RENEW
GAUGE	LUBRICATE	PREPARE	REPAIR
GIVE		PRESCRIBE	REPLACE
GREASE	MAINTAIN	PRESENT	REPLENISH
GROUP	MAKE	PRIME	REPLY
GUARD	MAKE UP	PROBE	REPORT
GUIDE	MARK	PROBLEM-SOLVE	REPRODUCE
	MATCH	PROCESS	REQUEST
HANDLE	MEASURE	PROGRAMME	REQUISITION
HELP	MEET	PROPOSE	RESAMPLE
HIGHLIGHT	MICROFILM	PULL	RETRIEVE
HIRE	MODIFY	PUMP	RETURN
HOLD	MONITOR	PURCHASE	REVIEW
HOOVER	MOP		REVISE
	MOVE	QUALIFY	REWEIGH
IDENTIFY		QUOTE	REWIND
IMPROVE	NAME		REWIRE
INDICATE	NEGOTIATE	RACK	REWORK
INFORM	NEUTRALIZE	RAISE	ROUTE
INITIATE	NOTIFY	READ	

122 *Changing Job Structures*

SAMPLE	SOAK	SUPERVISE	TREAT
SCAN	SOLDER	SUPPLY	TROUBLESHOOT
SCHEDULE	SORT	SURVEY	TUNE
SCRAP	SOURCE	SUSPEND	TURN
SCRUB	SPECIFY	SWITCH	TYPE
SCRUTINIZE	SPLICE		
SEAL	SPLIT	TABULATE	UNDERSTAND
SECURE	SPRAY	TAKE	UNSTRAP
SELECT	STACK	TAP	UPDATE
SENTENCE	STAMP	TAPE	USE
SERVICE	STAND	TENDER	UTILIZE
SET	STAND-IN	TEST	VALIDATE
SET UP	START	THREAD	VENTILATE
SHAKE	STOCK	TIME	VERIFY
SHARPEN	STOCKTAKE	TRACE	VISIT
SIGN	STOP	TRAIN	
SIGNAL	STORE	TRANSCRIBE	WASH
SIMULATE	STRAP	TRANSFER	WEIGH
SLIT	STRIP	TRANSMIT	WRITE

Types of information that should *not* form the basis for a task statement

1 Worker or job qualifications, such as intelligence, aptitudes, knowledge, or experience – for example, 'Requires knowledge of computer operations and three months of experience to advise Marketing of customer needs'.
2 Participation in any directly non-productive activities, such as attending training courses and receiving instructions – for example, 'Attend clerical skills training'.
3 Organization policies, responsibilities, and practices – for example, 'Observe safety procedures', 'Treat customers courteously', 'Wear hardhat in the new plant area'.
4 Working conditions – for example, 'Work in a well-lighted room with ample room for movement'.
5 Imprecise or ambiguous terms, such as and/or and etc. – for example, 'Call Accounts for billing adjustment information etc.'

Level of task statement detail

Task statements can be written very narrowly or very broadly and at varying levels of detail or specificity. Before beginning preparation of task statements, the study group or compiler should determine the level of detail that will be expressed to describe the work undertaken to complete 'good' runs (see above). If every minute detail involved in performing the task were to be recorded, several volumes would be needed to describe the simplest job. Levels of detail can relate to individual task statements and to the number of task statements used to describe a particular work activity. If a large number of statements is used to describe a work activity, survey results usually will have to be combined and summarized to represent broader work activities; otherwise, the information will not be meaningful, since it is difficult to concentrate on and interpret data obtained for each of several hundred tasks and to develop meaningful conclusions about a job, or range of interrelated jobs, from so much data. The same is true if too few, general statements are used to describe job activities – for most purposes it will not be possible to draw meaningful conclusions. It is, of course, better to obtain a large number of task statements and then deal with the problem of extracting useful information than to obtain too little information.

A distinction should be drawn at this point between tasks and sub-tasks, since it may not be possible to tell them apart when they are viewed out of context. We know what a task is. A sub-task is simply a step performed to accomplish a task. Sub-tasks do not have a purpose or output distinct from the purpose or output of the task, and they cannot stand by themselves, whereas adequately written task statements can stand alone and be interpreted.

Task attributes

Task location

Task location relates to where the task is performed and its range of reference is from a whole department to a specific piece of equipment. It is therefore possible to have a hierarchy of location codes/categories (Figure 5.2).

Each of the levels and areas within a level has its own identifying code, and for each piece of equipment or grouping of equipment there is a sub-code placing it within one of the general areas. So, for example, if we take the aerosol filling area and give it the code 0404 (it is often useful and easier to use the existing cost allocation coding system or asset register coding system for this purpose: these lists are normally held either by the engineering department or by finance), line 1 in filling would be 0404 (the code for filling) 03 (the code for line 1). Then taking an individual piece of equipment on line 1, e.g. the filling heads, the code would now read 0404–03–04. This type of specific location code makes it possible to

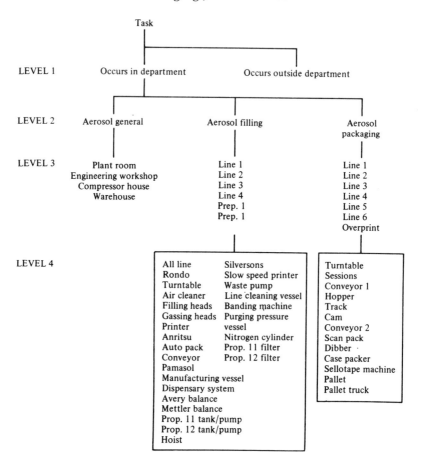

Figure 5.2 *Location coding of tasks applied to aerosol manufacture*

manipulate the resulting task database at any level from general departmental level right down to a specified piece of equipment on one line.

In collecting and coding the task data it is important to decide what the output is going to be used for. If the aim is broadly to design a whole site within a company, the departmental level of detail can be sufficient. If it is the aim to design specific jobs and roles and, say, some form of team structure, then it is necessary to go to the equipment, i.e. the level 4, degree of detail.

The task performer

Identifying the task performer is usually straightforward in that the task owner or owners are in a particular job, e.g. packaging operator. It is possible for the same task to be undertaken by a range of different performers, and/or undertaken by a group of performers. In the latter case the group might be made up of individuals in the same job or in different jobs. No matter what the nature of the output, it is important to ensure that the predominant ownership of a task is established, i.e. who it is that undertakes the task most of the time, and how many people are involved in undertaking the task, i.e. the volume of labour required.

This level of detail is adequate for most examinations of work. If the task data is to be used to design and build up jobs, the input and direct involvement of others should be recorded. This additional input into the task might be required for a number of reasons, e.g. the task is of such a size that it requires two people to perform it or the task requires an additional input in terms of skills and knowledge, or it is a reflection of the control mechanisms in place, i.e. checking on the completion of a task. A compromise solution to this multiple involvement in the completion of a task is to record the involvement of one or of several individuals. Then, when it comes to the reallocation or the modification of the task, it is tacked with a record of multiple involvement which can be pursued with the relevant individuals.

As regards the degree of detail required in performer data, it is usually necessary to record only the performer and the number of performers where whole departments are being designed and a general direction in which jobs should be structured in the future is being established. Again, if jobs are to be designed and developed, the more comprehensive the initial database the better. It should also be considered that in the collection of the task data there is a limit both to people's memories and to their knowledge about a particular task, and the greater the detail collected the greater the resource expended on its collection, computer loading and validation. A balance must be struck between the effort put into collecting the task data and its subsequent use. If an attempt is made to be exhaustive in the measurement of work it is highly likely that most of the resulting data will not be used. Unused data is both a waste of time and effort and irritating for the people who provided the information. A test as to the degree of detail to collect on this and other variables is to ask: 'Why is it needed and how will it be used?'. If these questions cannot be answered by a clear statement, do not collect the data in the first place.

Task frequency

It is useful to collect data on the frequency of a task on the basis of a hierarchy of frequencies, e.g. once an hour, once a day, . . ., once a year etc. (see Table 5.3). Sometimes it is not possible to do this because the frequency relates directly to a machine speed, volume of throughput, number of changeovers etc. In such cases it is best to measure the task frequency on the basis of production throughput or volume, e.g. a machine needs charging with raw materials five or six times in a batch and the number of batches can vary: here the frequency data would be recorded in terms of the number of times per batch, then the production figures would be used to calculate the frequency of the task on a daily basis.

As with all of the variables it is necessary to validate the data by means of as many sources of information as possible. However, experience has shown that there is usually a high degree of accuracy in people's estimation of the frequency of a task: disagreements occur with regard to other variables where greater judgement is required.

Rather than expressing each frequency on a different time scale, it is necessary to convert the frequencies to a single unit of time. Usually the number of times a task is performed per day is the most useful way to express frequency of task performance. Table 5.3 gives a few examples of this conversion of absolute frequency rates into daily frequency rates.

Table 5.3 *Task frequency conversion*

Task frequency	Task frequency per day
1 per hour	7.5
1 per 2 hours	3.75
1 per day	1.00
1 per week	0.2
1 per 2 weeks	0.1
1 per month	0.04
1 per 3 months	0.015
1 per 6 months	0.0076
1 per year	0.0038

In expressing the frequency of tasks on a daily basis it is important to establish the length of the working day rather than take the hours worked per day (the standard day plus extended hours working). In shift operations it is best to relate the frequencies to the shift and divide daytime tasks on a pro-rata or an equivalent basis.

Task duration

The duration of a task is the measure of the time the task lasts. Table 5.4 lists the task duration times found in a study of one production department involving nearly 1400 tasks. At the outset of collecting the task data and allocating duration times it can be decided either to impose time bands, e.g. 0 to 1 minutes, 1 to 5 minutes etc., or to record absolute task durations. The time-bands method will give a broad picture, but it is preferable to record absolute task duration times and then impose bandings. A 'natural level' of detail as regards task duration is also imposed by the data collection method used. If, for example, only a small number of managers are consulted as to task duration, it is likely that they will identify most of the tasks but be vague as to their duration: in such a case it is best to use time bands. If the current task performers are consulted they will be able to be precise about the duration of specific tasks.

Table 5.4 *Range of possible task duration times*

Minutes	Seconds	Minutes	Seconds	Minutes	Seconds
0	1	11		150	
0	5	14		180	
0	10	15		200	
0	15	20		210	
0	20	25		230	
0	30	29		240	
0	45	30		260	
1		35		300	
1	30	36		340	
2		40		360	
3		45		400	
4		50		445	
4	30	55		460	
5		60		480	
6		67		500	
7		80		540	
7	30	90		620	
8		95		960	
9		100		1200	
9	30	120			
10		140			

Task complexity

While it is relatively easy to describe a task in terms of its location of performance, its frequency and duration, it is less easy to describe and measure a task's degree of difficulty or complexity. Here there is a need to establish some form of a start point which can be used as the basis of a complexity measurement system. The reason for creating a 'unit' of complexity which is then applied to all tasks in common is to remove personal bias.

The task attributes that should be considered include:

1. The amount of training and experience required before a job-holder can competently perform the task.
2. The amount of physical and/or mental effort required to perform the task competently.
3. The difficulty of the task as compared with other tasks performed.
4. The number of steps encompassed in a task sequence.
5. The difficulty of learning the task.

A job-holder can be asked to rate the individual tasks that make up his/her job as follows: 'Rate each task for difficulty on the basis of the amount of skill needed to do it satisfactorily and using the following categories of difficulty:

Very much below average	1
Below average	2
Slightly below average	3
About average	4
Slightly above average	5
Above average	6
Very much above average	7'

In the population of job-holders asked to use this type of rating system there may be some people new to the job, some who have been doing it for many years, and still others who have done a wide range of jobs. In this mixed population, which would not be untypical of many working environments, there would be a wide interpretation of the term 'average'. Average for whom? Average in what context? A simple task can become difficult if there is an undue time, social or physical pressure to complete it. Then, once the job-holders have rated the tasks, what does the 'average' represent? The introduction of a measure which assesses the performer of the task rather than the task itself would tend to defeat one of the purposes of designing the method, which is to provide an objective, task-orientated and output-orientated approach.

Another way of tackling the same issue is to rate the task according to the time it takes to learn how to perform it competently. The following is an example of such a rating system.

Scale of difficulty/complexity based on the time taken to learn a task

Less than 1 day	1
Between 1 day and 1 week	2
Between 1 week and 2 weeks	3
Between 2 weeks and 1 month	4
Between 1 month and 3 months	5
Between 3 months and 6 months	6
Between 6 months and 1 year	7
Greater than 1 year	8

This type of rating system is also open to individual bias, but this can be removed if the 'speed of learning for whom' can be defined. It is usually easiest if a new recruit is taken as the base case for training for a particular task. In one study of an engineering department a 17-year-old engineering apprentice with only the basic skills was taken as the baseline.

Even when using this baseline approach it is still necessary to arrive at a common interpretation of how quickly a new recruit or a 17-year-old can learn a particular job. This proves not to be a major problem once individuals have allocated a number of tasks to one of the complexity categories and so established a series of initial markers – for example, the following series of packing operator tasks scored according to the eight complexity levels listed above:

Task	Score on difficulty/complexity scale
Pull job onto line and charge batch number	1
Take tickets off trays and load turntable	2
Thread labels through machine	3
Get actuators from stores and put into hopper	1
Stack trays and white tubs and take out	1
Empty the cans from the reject bins	1
Put rejected can back onto turntable	1
When labels run out change reel over	2
Clean the drug from around the spray	1
Change the black tape when it runs out	3
Put badly labelled cans into arcton	2
Count definite rejects at end of batch	1

In this case most of the packaging operators helped in rating the full list of tasks according to the eight complexity levels, and there was minimal disagreement among the scores. It is worth noting that the rating of such detailed tasks is really only possible with the direct input of the current task performer. The more remote the person completing the task rating is from the undertaking of the task, the more likely it is that some degree of distortion (bias) will be introduced. This introduction of bias need not be a problem if the purpose of the data-collection exercise is to provide the basis for a broad analysis of jobs and roles, and not the detail of those jobs and roles.

Rating of task complexity is relatively easy for mechanical tasks where the period of practice required to master competency is minimal and the amount of knowledge required to perform the task is also minimal. It becomes more difficult and debatable where experience and knowledge are important factors in the task's competent completion. Let us consider the possible dividing lines between types of task so that we can understand the issues involved here.

To ensure that any production system can operate adequately, a series of prescribed tasks must be performed. In the completion of these tasks there is little discretion and the main purpose of the task performer is to adhere to the tasks as spelt out in the operating procedures. In this case the task performer is not expected to handle deviations from the prescribed tasks nor to change the tasks.

At a higher level is a set of tasks in which judgement and discretion are required. Not only is there the need to undertake a series of prescribed tasks, but also to handle deviations from set procedures, i.e. the task performer needs sufficient skill, knowledge and experience to handle both the routine work and problems encountered on a day-to-day basis.

In addition there is a yet higher level of tasks which require the ability to handle routine tasks, deviations from the prescribed operating conditions and also more deep-seated problems which may require a change in the operating procedures or a modification to the production system. This ability to handle this type of task depends upon experience, skill and knowledge of a different order from those required to follow a set operating procedure.

These different types of task (which are comparable to the levels specified in the UK National Council for Vocational Qualification system of qualifications equivalence) require different inputs from the individuals who are to perform them successfully.

Here the key lies in the relationship between a training input and the speed with which a task can then be competently performed. Thus, a simple task such as lifting a box on to a pallet can be successfully taught in a few minutes: the level of proficiency in performing the task will rise with practice. Handling an intermittent fault on a packaging line, which might arise from a number of sources – packaging materials, deposition of material on the production equipment and conveyor belt etc. – requires knowledge not only of the production process, the production equipment and packaging materials, but also of the operating procedures. In addition to this, there is a need for experience in logical fault-finding and in fault and cause recognition. While a specific training input to develop knowledge and skills in relation to each of these areas can raise the general level of proficiency, there is little or no substitute for practice and experience of fault-finding and correction in a working environment.

It is here that judgement really comes in to the use of the complexity rating system. How long does it take someone to acquire knowledge and skill which are dependent upon experience and upon the conditions arising in which those skills and knowledge can be used ? Remember also that the rating is made in isolation from all other tasks, i.e. it is not assumed that there is any proficiency in any other task, and so all of the supporting knowledge and experience required for one particular task (even though it may be required for a wide range of other tasks) is assumed to be 're-learnt'.

Again this problem can be overcome. First, there is a need to compare tasks with one another in order to create two baselines: one is set on the 'new recruit' basis and the other by the comparison of one task with another. Second, there is often documentation relating to training on specific pieces of equipment and the range of expertise gained from being trained. Third, when the analyses are undertaken using the task data described by complexity and other variables, the various subdivisions of complexity are merged to form three or four complexity bandings. (This issue will be returned to later in Chaper 6 when the task data are being cleaned and validated.) Together these three points simplify the problems which might be created by highly complex tasks.

Task volume

Volume is the measure of the total amount of time devoted to a task, i.e. the frequency of the task multiplied by the duration of the task multiplied by the number of performers. It does not necessarily follow, though, that all performers should be included in this calculation. It is best therefore, in the initial stages, to tie the number of performers to, say, the number of batches in a day or shift and then use this figure in the volume calculation. Allowance will also be required for number of duplicated production lines or plants.

One test to see if the 'volume' figure is correct for all tasks recorded in a particular department or line is to compare it with the number of people currently doing the tasks recorded. (This is discussed in more detail in Chapter 6 when the task data are being cleaned and validated.)

Batch type

Quite often a particular type of product, or a product going to an export market or specific customer, requires some modification to the normal production run. Here it is only necessary to cover those changes to the production process that deviate from the general production process conditions and procedures.

Task support

In addition to requiring the extra input of two or more people, many tasks require particular pieces of equipment, e.g. visual programming unit, special tools, lifting equipment. There is also a need to record those tasks which require specific information e.g. technical information, recipe/raw material mix information, etc. It is usually only necessary to record whether or not equipment and information are required; then, when designing and developing new roles, it is possible to check back to see what modification (if any) to information flows might be required (and can be the subject of a separate study) and what tools might also have to be made available.

Task impact

There are two main ways of considering the impact of a task. First, there is the simple recording of what impact the non-completion of a task might have on, say, output or quality. This can be recorded in a binary fashion, i.e. 1 = impact, 0 = no impact. Again, this is done purely to check the possible consequences of the moving of a particular task between performers. There is often a high correlation between the level of task complexity and task impact.

Second, it is possible to categorize tasks according to their impact and degree of discretion. The impact of a particular task and the consequences of its non-completion can be graded according to the scale:

Restricted to own work station/area or adjacent work area	1
Seriously affects unit or line,	2
Seriously affects whole department	3
Seriously affects whole site	4

Again this type of task rating also covers the assessment of the quality of decision made and to some extent its complexity. These categories also act as a means of checking for inconsistencies between task complexity and impact ratings, as they should be positively correlated.

Type of task

It is useful to allocate tasks to a particular category of activity. This is done to assist in the presentation of the task data when plotted and it offers another means of presenting the data. There are no hard-and-fast rules for the allocation of a task to a particular category other than that every attempt should be made to ensure consistency. Two examples are offered here, one from a study of an engineering department, and the other from a wide-ranging study of all functions involved in manufacturing on three sites.

General task categories – engineering study

1 Maintenance.
2 Repair.
3 Replacement.
4 Diagnosis.
5 Changeover.
6 Construction.
7 Installation.
8 Commissioning.
9 Calibration.
10 Miscellaneous.

General task categories – manufacturing study

1 Adjust.
2 Closedown.
3 Communication.
4 Diagnosis.
5 Engineering repair.
6 Inspection.
7 Engineering maintenance.
8 Material movements.
9 Operation.
10 Record.
11 Start-up.
12 Non-management.
13 Planning.
14 Technical.

The preceding pages have described how work can be measured without using a 'time and motion' approach. In all, twelve variables or factors have been identified which are relevant to the full measurement of work at the task level:

Description of the task.
Location of the task.
Performer of the task.
Frequency of the task.
Duration of the task.
Complexity of the task.
Volume of the task.
Batch type.
Additional task performer.
Support resources required.
Potential impact of the task.
Type of work undertaken.

The remainder of this chapter deals with the development of the task listing and the collection of task-related data.

Development of the task listing

There are three main steps in developing the task listing.

1 Identification of existing lists of tasks which may be useful as thought-starters in drafting the first task list. This can be supplemented by brainstorming in other areas as well.
2 Creation of the first full draft of lists which can then be used in informal interviews with those who know the tasks well (this might be possible within a study if it comprises a wide range of job-holders) and the current task performers.
3 This initial draft task list can then be more fully developed by the detailed consideration of a small sample of the job-holders whose jobs are included in the task listing.
(See: Establishing the level of task definition.)

Examples of the output of these three steps are given in Tables 5.5, 5.6 and 5.7. Table 5.5 lists a number of possible sources of information which can be used initially to identify a series of tasks. One way of identifying lists that might be available and useful is to work through the production process step by step and ask the question: what information exists that describes those tasks whose purpose is to move the production process forward?

Table 5.5 *Sources of information for task list*

Operating manuals/maintenance manuals
Job descriptions
Training records
Specialist skill of equipment manufacturers
Standard operating procedures
'Experts' on site
Shift logs
Batch logs/production logs
Line equipment logs
Work study data on lines
Accident/near miss reports
Commissioning data
Validation data
Safety data
Design/layout data
Deviation from Good Manufacturing Practice
Planned maintenance records
Specified maintenance work

Table 5.6 *First manufacturing task listing*

PLANNING	Planning/scheduling
	Logistics of materials
	Changeover stores
	Local stores of materials
	Holiday rota
	Acquisition of engineering and other materials
MAN-MANAGEMENT	People assessment/selection
	Discipline
	Absence control
	Overtime allocation/control
	Fitness for work
	Setting and improving standards of performance
	Job/role boundary knowledge
	Boundary management
	Knowledge of organization systems
	Man-management
HYGIENE	Cleaning
	Housekeeping
	Safety

Table 5.6 (*cont.*):

QUALITY	Changing routines Health and hygiene Identification of assistance Validation of resources processes Aseptic techniques Changing routines Monitoring of aseptic areas In-process control Pharmaceutical problems Line-up/down information Testing Sampling Inspection Calibration
PROCESS	Running equipment Product make/standard operating procedures Pharmaceutical problems Changeovers Inspection Calibration Aseptic techniques Changing routines Sterilization/disinfection Specific technical skills Computing skills Identification of assistance Packaging material knowledge Validation of resources/processes
MEASUREMENT OF PERFORMANCE	Budget/cost management Setting and improving standards of performance Knowledge of customer/products Labour recording Batch/product information Material usage Plant performance Progress monitoring
BEHAVIOURAL SKILLS	Training Communication Team working skills Learning for yourself Presentation skills Job design/redesign

EQUIPMENT SKILLS	Joint problem solving
	Use/liaise with experts
	Fork-lift truck driving
	Changeovers
	Settings
	Maintenance (breakdown and planned)
	Installation
	Tuning
	Adjusting
	Running equipment
	Machine-minding
COGNITIVE	Diagnostic
	Tuning
	Adjusting
	Pharmaceutical problems
	Learning for yourself
	Identification of assistance
TECHNICAL	Knowledge of customer/products
	Industrial engineering skills
	Modification
	Installation
	Tuning
	Adjusting

Table 5.7 *Second manufacturing task listing*

QUALITY	Understand and write standard operating procedures	Engineering
		Production
		Quality assurance
	Environmental monitoring:	
		Microbiological
		Particulate
		Dust
	Inspection:	
		Manual and Standards
		Automatic
	In-process standards:	
		Product
		Packaging
		Knowledge of specifications

Table 5.7 (*cont.*):

	Operate to Good Manufacturing Practice:	
		UK
		USA
		Sterile products
		Non-sterile products
		Raw materials
	Reconciliation	
		Documentation
		Limits
	Product quality routines:	
		Prepare
		Perform
	Calibration:	
		Equipment
		Manufacturing
		Testing
		Services
		Frequency
		Recording
	Diagnosis:	
		Process
		Equipment
		Services
		Raw materials
		Packaging components
	Analytical skills – laboratory:	
		Safety
		Technical
	Labelling and product packaging:	
		Security
	Process improvement	
	Documentation – recording:	
		Engineering
		Quality assurance
		Production and Warehouse
	Verification and validation:	
		Aseptic and non-aseptic
		Equipment
		Computers
		Processes
		People

Data and information collection 139

	Equipment specification – reliability/robustness	
	Aseptic techniques:	
		Sterilization and disinfection
		Regulatory requirements
		Training
		Testing techniques
		Monitoring
	Cleaning	
		Security
		Sterile
		Non-sterile
		Housekeeping
		Health and safety
	Product design:	
		Robust
		Validated
		Product knowledge
		Processing knowledge
	Changing routines:	
		Training
		Aseptic and controlled operations
PLANNING		
	Planning and scheduling	
		Line start-up time
		Line cleandown time
		Line changeover time
	Logistics of materials	
		Warehouse delivery patterns
	Changepart stores	
		Deployment during changeover
		Changepart replacement procedures
		Expenditure budgeting
	Acquisition of engineering and other materials	
		Requisition/recording system
		Linking with planned maintenance system
MAN MANAGEMENT	Motivation of others	
	Discipline	
	Training	

Table 5.7 (*cont.*):

	Team skills	
	Leadership	
	Appraisal	
	Decision-making	
	Counselling	
	Communication	
	Manning levels	
	Industrial relations	
	Maintenance and administration of group personnel policies	
	Recruitment, selection and development	
	Boundary – interaction	
	Suitability for work	
	Absence control	
		Record keeping
		Submission of data for personnel records
	Overtime allocation/control	
		Knowledge of priorities/ delivery deadlines
		Knowledge of capacity loadings
		Knowledge of staff circumstances
		Knowledge of skill requirements
	Learning for yourself	
	Knowledge of organization systems	
	Presentation skills	
	Job design/redesign	
	Joint problem solving	
PROCESS AND EQUIPMENT	Equipment skills:	
		Installation
		Tuning/setting
	Sterilization/disinfection	
Process	Machine attendants:	
		Sterilization
		Washing
	Adjustment of process:	
		Engineering

Data and information collection 141

	Waste disposal	
		Safety
		Good Manufacturing Practice
	In-process control:	
		Computer
		Technical skills
		Dealing with 'out of specification' situations
	Revalidation	
	Cleaning down in aseptic areas	
	Batch security:	
		During processing
		Changeover
		Storage
Manufacturing of batches	Receipt and issue of materials	
	Recording of delivery	
	Connecting of tanker to tanks	
	Quality assurance sampling of tanker	
	Checking of sieves	
	Check batch numbers and issue of materials	
	Batch changes	
	Operation of dispensing system including balance checks	
	Dispense materials	
	Mix materials	
	Connect manufacturing vessel	
	Clean area and equipment	
	Maintenance of laminar flow cabinets	
	Changing of sieves on manufacturing vessels	
	Repairs to pumps and refrigeration equipment on the manufacturing vessels	
	Testing of in-line propellant filters	
	Changing of temperature humidity records	
Filling lines	Starting-up of filling lines	
	Setting-up of ink jet printers	
	Cleaning of ink jet printers	

Table 5.7 (*cont.*):

Setting-up and challenging of checkweights
Weight control during filling, recording
Monitoring filling operations, i.e. checking of crimp dimensions and other parameters
Checking of line at end of batch
Bulk reconciliation
Operations of tray loader
Routine maintenance of can cleaners
Routine maintenance of Pamasol filling machine
Maintenance of Anritsu checkweighers
Adjustment of valve feed machanism
Clearing jammed cans from Rondo
Clearing jammed cans from can-cleaning machine
Clearing jammed cans from Pamasol, including resetting star wheels
Adjustment and repairs to pneumatic control system on Pamasol
Checking outers to Pamasol machine
Changing of gassing head 'O'-rings
Changing of gassing head seals
Adjustment to crimp heads
Routine maintenance of crimp heads
Routine maintenance of filling heads
Routine maintenance of gassing heads
Repair and adjustments to fluidic controls to filling line

Data and information collection 143

                Repair of electrical
                  equipment on filling line
                Routine maintenance of
                  Morgan Forest/Mills
                Cleaning and checking of
                  filling nozzles
                Repairs to structure and
                  doors of Pamasol flow
                  cabinet
                Checking of filters and flow
                  rates
                Packing of cans into trays
                Line-cleaning procedure
                Quality assurance sampling
                  procedures
                Analysis of filled cans

                                      Analysis of can contents
                                      Analysis of drug/can
                                      Analysis of shot weight
                                      Analysis of shot dose
                                      Analysis of relative dose
                                      Analysis of twin impinger,
                                          deposition
                                      Analysis of non-volatile
                                          matter
                                      Analysis of correct materials
                                      Analysis of component
                                          reconciliation
                                      Analysis of overprint
                                      Analysis of checkweigher
                                      Analysis of leakage rate
                                      Analysis of water content
                                      Analysis of valve recovery
                                      Analysis of pressure test
                                      Analysis of particle counting
                                      Analysis of silica gel dry
                                      Analysis of can
                                          reconciliation

                Manufacture document
                  checks
Actuator testing Issue of actuators
                Inspection of actuator test
                  machines
                Testing of actuators
                Challenge tests
                Procedures for product/batch
                  change

Table 5.7 (*cont.*):

Packaging lines	Cleaning procedure Repair and maintenance of mechanical parts of actuator test machines Switching on/off of department air compressors Cleaning and checking of line clearance Setting-up of packaging line:	
		Setting-up of checkweigher Challenging checkweigher Challenging spray test unit Checking components onto line Setting-up of overprint units Setting-up of code readers Challenging scan pack unit Documentation of line monitoring
	Packaging line clearance Packaging line reconciliation Operation of turntable (feeding cans) Operation of sessions machine:	
		Feeding of labels to label head Alignment of print Checking of print
	Feeding tested actuators to cam-cartoning machine Feeding cartons/leaflets onto cam-cartoning machine Hand cartoning Hand packaging into cases Operation of case-packing machine Clearing of carton/leaflet jamming in cartoning machine Clearing cases jammed in case packer Resetting case packer Adjustments and repairs to weight cells	

Data and information collection

Adjustments and repairs to spray test units
Cleaning of spray test units
Adjustments and repairs to cartoning machine
Adjustments and repairs to case packers
Adjustments and repairs to Scanpack machine
Labelling of outers
Removal of labels
Palletization of outers
Trucking of pallets to stores
General area cleaning:

    Wiping
    Scrubbing
    Sealing

Watch over machine(s) and its (their) functions
Keep tablet hopper supplied with correct batch
Clean machine at batch and product changeovers
Clean air lock (if appropriate) when necessary
Provide assistance to other operators
Conduct production monitoring tests
Ensure free flow of tablets down shuttle channels
Watch for and remove any tablet faults in open blister packs
Operate stop/start function in conjunction with other operators
Recover tablets from rejected, faulty and damaged strips
Relieve other operators
Keep carton and leaflet stack filled as necessary
Identify and remedy jams and stoppages in cartonner
Periodically remove and examine strips from cartonner

Table 5.7 (*cont.*):

    Feed accumulated and sorted strips into feed stack when appropriate
    Identify faults on strips as and when they arise
    Make up fibreboard outers
    Apply stencil to fibreboard outers
    Check stencil to campaign/product demand information
    Check overwrapped bundles against correct weights
    Check overwrapped packs
        Alignment
        Damaged cartons
        Overprint legibility
        Carton print copy
    Ensure sufficient fibreboard outers are made up and stencilled
    Check on quality and supply of overwrap film reels
    Check on quality and supply of PVC film reels
    Strip down, clean and search equipment
    Reconcile materials used with materials supplied
    Call in both components and tablets
    Changeover procedures for both batch and product changes

Packaging labeller
    Understand programmable logic controller, mechanics of machine and parts in system
    Diagnosis of faults – logics of system
    Service of machine
    Control of spares
    Print blocks:
        Setting
        Security
    Training specific to planned preventive maintenance

Data and information collection 147

PERFORMANCE MONITORING	Setting and improvement of standards:	
		Outputs
		Downtime
		Material loss
		Rejects
		Customer service
		Training
		Quality
		Safety
		Plant performance
	Measuring against standards	
	Taking corrective action	
	Communicating performance:	
		Teams
		Individuals
	Ownership of problems	
	Support for action and agreement	
	Budget	
	Collection and production of accounts information	
	Reports:	
		Monthly reports
	Equipment group recording:	
		Line logs
	Audit other teams:	
		Regulatory compliance
		Quality improvement
		Safety
SAFETY	Environmental monitoring	
	Occupational hygiene	
	Auditing of facility – hazard operations	
	Equipment – design:	
		Environment
		Equipment
	Accident investigation	
	Safety improvement groups	
MATERIALS MANAGEMENT	Inventory control	
	Forward planning	
	Machine loading	
	Capacity planning	
	Materials movement	

Table 5.7 (*cont.*):

		Warehouse
		Collection
		Driving
		Receipt
		Despatch to warehouse
	Packaging technology	
	Packaging development:	
		New packs
		New artwork
	Customer orders and needs	
	Purchasing:	
		Orders
	Non-stock items	
	Scheduling:	
		Timescales – hours
	Materials usage	
	Write-offs	
	Returns	
	Reworks	
	Rejects	
	Expiry dating	
	Use of computers	
	Understand specifications for raw materials and packaging components	
	Job pack	
	Ordering of components and raw materials	
		Information provided on material availability
		Awareness of staffing levels and skills
		Schedule in overprint areas
		Stock control of materials
		Collation of components and materials
		Location of material in stores
USE OF COMPUTERS	Keyboard skills	
	Data processing	
	Operate a computer	

Collection of task-related data

The rough task list that has been developed forms the basis for the next series of steps.

1 Sort the initial task list in terms of occurrence in the production process or other process area and at the same time allocate to one or more existing performers. This will result in a series of lists for each existing job-holder.
2 This initially sorted task list should then be printed out in data collection sheet format (see Figures 5.3–5.5).
3 The initial task data collection sheets should then be shared with existing job-holders whose tasks are listed and/or with 'experts' among the supervisors and managers. With how many and with which people the task lists are shared depends upon the openness with which the study is being conducted. By sharing the task lists it should be possible to fill in gaps and correct wording and task descriptions. The output of this stage is a final task listing which can then be used as the basis of a data collection sheet.

   An alternative method to these three steps is described under 'Establishing the level of task definition'.
4 Data collection should be designed to include spaces for task number and task description and as many other variables as are relevant to the study. For example, the more strategic and the wider the scope of the study, the less the detail required. However, in even the most general of studies it is necessary to collect task frequency, task duration and task complexity variables. If the study is going to derive new job roles and build up the organization from the bottom, qualifying task variables will be required. Before collecting any additional variable it is important to be clear why it is needed and how it will be used in the final analysis.
5 It is now possible to collect task data and to rate each task. This can be done in a number of ways.
   (a) Interviews can be conducted with individual job-holders who are asked to go through the list of tasks and rate each one against the chosen variables. It is useful if a series of prompts is used to help in the interviewing individuals, e.g. explaining the various task rating scales etc.
   (b) A mix of job-holders, their supervisors and managers can go through the task lists, either as a group or as individuals, and fill in all of the task ratings.
   (c) Reliance upon a single expert, who might be a manager or a supervisor, to rate the tasks.

Confidential **TASK ANALYSIS**

Process: ____________________

____

Discipline

P	Production	PD	Pack development
E	Engineering	AC	Accounts
QA	Quality assurance		
MM	Mat. management		

Degree of difficulty

1	> 6 months	4	< 1 month
2	> 3 < 6 months	5	< 1 week
3	> 1 < 3 months	6	< 1 day

Equip./Stage	Task	Discipline	Performed by	Degree of diff.	Duration (mins)	Frequency/ day	External contact

Sheet ____ of ____ Date: ____

Completed by:

Figure 5.3 *Data collection sheet – example*

ENGINEERING SKILLS PROFILE

Task no.	Description	Current performer	Duration (hrs)	Frequency (per year)	Complexity (1–8)	External support	Category

Complexity scale
1. < 1 day. 2. 1 day – 1 week. 3. 1 week – 2 weeks. 4. 2 weeks – 1 month. 5. 1 month – 3 months. 6. 3 months – 6 months. 7. 6 months – 1 year. 8. > 1 year.
External support scale
1. Stores. 2. Security. 3. Contractors. 4. Purchasing. 5. Safety. 6. Projects. 7. Validation. 8. Prod. support. 9. Material services.
Category scale
1. Maintenance. 2. Repair. 3. Replacement. 4. Diagnosis. 5. Change over. 6. Construction. 7. Install. 8. Commissioning. 9. Calibration. 10.   11.   12. Miscellaneous.

Figure 5.4 *Data collection sheet – example*

Task no.	Task description	Batch type	Location	Performer		Involvement of other people '0' or '1'									Support '0' or '1'		Frequency (no. of times/ day)	Duration		Difficulty/ complexity	Impact/ significance '0' or '1'				
				Ind.	Team '0' or '1'	O	F	S	D	Q	C	P	M	E	Info.	Equip.		Mins	Secs	1–8	S	P	Q	PF	CS

Area .... Study group member .... Date ....

Figure 5.5 *Data collection sheet – example*

While the last method may be the quickest, it can suffer from the bias of depending upon a single source. This is not always the case: in one study where task data was collected via routes (a) and (c) the results were almost identical. The first route allows for maximum participation, for all extremes to be averaged out, and generates a widely owned database.

6 As soon as all of the tasks have been rated, by whatever route, the data should be loaded into a computer (most micros can cope with quite large task data sets of 1500 or more tasks with 15–20 entries per task and up to 25 sets for each task rating). The actual cleaning, validation and analysis of the data are described in the next chapter.

Irrespective of the detail collected or the individuals interviewed, it is important to be able to explain the purpose of the task data collection and how the task data will be analysed, and also to answer such questions as: 'This is only work study, isn't it?' Throughout the data collection stage everyone making an input must be at ease with the process.

Summary

Work can be described in a number of ways, ranging from the collation of time and motion data to wide-ranging descriptions of production processes at task level. This chapter has described how task data and its associated variables differ from work study and work measurement. Taking the task as the basic unit of work, it has been shown how a comprehensive profile of a production process and the work involved can be generated by two routes. The various steps involved and the data which needs to be collected have been described. It should now be possible for the reader to generate reliable task data. The development and use of the resulting task database are outlined in the next chapter.

6
Data analysis

Introduction

The purpose of this chapter is to explain how to use the task data collected by means of the steps in Chaper 5. This chapter is divided into eleven steps:

1 Task data cleaning and verification.
2 Task data validation.
3 Task data – first plots.
4 Task data reduction.
5 Task data – second plots.
6 Design principles and evaluation criteria.
7 Task data – rules for analysis.
8 Task data – third plots.
9 Possible new combinations/configurations of roles and organization.
10 Task data reduction.
11 Task data – fourth plots.

These steps are now described and illustrated by examples.

Step 1. Task data cleaning and verification

1 Run off printout of the task data for each of the current jobs, task-by-task.
2 Examine each task entry for consistency across each of the interview returns. Pay particular attention to the following variables:
   Task frequency.
   Task duration.
   Task complexity.
   Also ensure consistency for other variables:
   Batch type.

Location.
Performer.
Impact/significance.
Involvement of other people.
Support.
3 Check for double entries.
4 Where inconsistencies and differences occur, go through the following procedure:
   (a) Is the inconsistency due to a coding error?
       Check entry against original task data sheet.
   (b) Are there differences as regards frequency?
       Is this task determined by production rate/volume?
       If 'yes' check frequency against existing throughput levels.
       Sources: Agreed standards in terms of units filled/packed, trays, outers, etc.
       Production logs.
       Production schedules.
       Work study reports.
       Planned preventative maintenance records.
       If 'no', keep a note of the task and refer it back to the study group.
   (c) Are there differences as regards duration?
       After excluding mis-entries and errors, average out the entries.
   (d) Are there differences as regards complexity?
       Again, average out all entries.
       Note: On the printout, complexity scores are usually averaged out and will probably need rounding to the nearest whole number. If complexity is 1.5 or 2.5 etc., then round up or down depending upon the number of entries greater or less than the averaged score. For example, if the averaged score is 1.5, there are 23 entries in total, 10 scores are greater than 1.5 and 13 are less than 1.5, then round down. If the number of entries had been the reverse, the 1.5 average would have been rounded up to 2.0.
5 There will remain some problem task entries.
   (a) Overlapping tasks, neither of which satisfies the definition of a task, i.e. that a task is a unit of work, is performed by an individual of a group, has a definite beginning and end and results in a product or a service: here, combine the tasks, rewriting the entry to delete at least one of the tasks.
   (b) Continuous tasks are usually part and parcel of another task and should be as regarded as sub-tasks. These tasks can either be treated as overlapping tasks, or re-entered with a new, more appropriate task description.
   (c) Loss of cover/cover provided elsewhere needs to be considered in two ways:

156   *Changing Job Structures*

     (i) As a specific task in its own right with its own frequency, duration, complexity scores etc.
    (ii) In terms of a knock-on to the loss of service within the department. For example, if cover is being provided to another department, this must adversely affect the quality of response to the tasks arising in the employing department – it will increase the duration of some tasks, and also affect related tasks of other people, e.g. ordering of spares might be delayed, fitter's time might be wasted waiting for advice etc. This adverse effect must therefore be reflected in the task database.
  (d) Training received by the task performer needs to be recorded in terms of the amount of time spent on training, the complexity score not being relevant. This relates to consideration of the total volume of work performed by an individual.
  (e) Training provided by the task performer also needs to be recorded in terms of frequency, duration, complexity etc.
  (f) A duplicate task undertaken by a different performer needs to be treated initially as a completely separate task. Check that the complexity ratings are broadly similar (fall within adjacent scores – ideally they should be the same). These tasks will need to be challenged as regards their real need during Step 4, 'Task data reduction'.
6 Some gaps in the task data may still exist, e.g. level of contractors' work, communication meetings (departmental, site etc.). It is important to record the work contractors undertake in task terms, and it is necessary to establish how much time is taken up by the receiving of communications etc. Time devoted to quality circles, corrective action teams, safety circles etc. also needs to be established. Again, these figures are necessary to validate the task volume recorded in the task database.
7 There may remain a number of tasks (usually a few per cent of the total) which need further discussion within the study group, and possibly with the current performer, in order to clarify them. Keep a note of the task numbers so that ready reference to the master task sheets can be made.

Step 2. Task data validation

Before it is possible to run off the first plots of the task data it is necessary to enter into the cleaned and verified task data the number of current performers. It is then possible to equate the task data volume (frequency × duration = volume) with the actual existing manning levels. If these figures match (after having allowed for policy times: breaks, meals, washing-up, communication meetings, training etc.) then the first plots can be run off.

If the task data volume does not agree with the current manning levels it means that there are gaps in the task data which still need to be filled. Go back to either the study group or the task performer to establish what gaps exist, and fill them in.

Step 3. Task data – first plots

1 Once the full task data set has been established, the following plots can be run off:
 (a) Summary of all of the task data by complexity (in percentage and absolute terms) by main areas, e.g. manufacturing/filling, packaging, other, total – or any other major grouping of tasks identified from the mapping of the process.
 (b) Manufacturing/filling by current performer by complexity (in percentage and absolute terms).
 (c) Packaging by current performer by complexity (in percentage and absolute terms).
 (d) 'Other' by current performer by complexity (in percentage and absolute terms).
 Complexity has been scored on a scale of eight:

Hours	1
One day	2
Greater than 1 day, less than 1 week	3
Greater than 1 week, less than 1 month	4
Greater than 1 month, less than 3 months	5
Greater than 3 months, less than 6 months	6
Greater than 6 months, less than 1 year	7
Greater than 1 year	8

For ease of presentation it is advisable to reduce this range to three or four categories, e.g.

Scale of 4	Scale of 8	Scale of 3
1	$\{1, 2\}$	
2	$\{3, 4\}$	1
3	$\{5, 6\}$	2
4	$\{7, 8\}$	3

158 *Changing Job Structures*

2 These plots provide a broad description of the existing content of the work in a department and related areas.
3 These plots are worth considering initially and briefly summarizing in a few words. They also represent the base position which we will be seeking to improve upon.

Step 4. Task data reduction

1 The purpose of this step is to challenge the existing task database. From the improvement projects for manufacturing/filling and packaging, from SWOT/5P work and from the independent changes arising from a new project or from on-going engineering improvement work, changes will be introduced which will add new tasks, delete tasks and modify tasks. We need to identify which tasks are likely to be affected and then plot the resulting task data again.
2 It is also useful at this stage to challenge existing procedures, especially where standard operating procedures do not exist and/or are being updated, and where they have become outdated.
3 At this stage it is also useful to build into the task database other relevant tasks. For example, for engineering this would mean including commissioning/validation of plant and equipment, the assembly of equipment and improvement projects. This can mean adding into the task database many high skill/complexity tasks.

Step 5. Task data – second plots

1 Once the full task data set has been challenged, the following plots can be run off:
   (a) Summary of all of the task data by complexity (in percentage and absolute terms) by main areas, e.g. manufacturing/filling, packaging, other, total – or any other major grouping of tasks identified from the mapping of the process.
   (b) Manufacturing/filling by current performer by complexity (in percentage and absolute terms).
   (c) Packaging by current performer by complexity (in percentage and absolute terms).
   (d) 'Other' by current performer by complexity (in percentage and absolute terms).
   Again, use the modified complexity score range.

Step 6. Design principles and evaluation criteria

1 Before the task data can be further analysed it is necessary to consider what type and form of organization and jobs we are trying to develop. Here, for example, we can refer to the SWOT/5P work which resulted in the following for the 'People' category (see Chapter 4, page 91):
  Strengths
    Committed/cooperative/loyal
    Willing to learn
    Skilled
    Openminded
    Objective
    Hard-working
    Confident
    Open to change
  Weaknesses
    Two populations
    Insufficient training
    Communication
    Career development
    Promotion within/over-related to qualifications
    Too many channels
    No incentives
    High absence levels/counselling system
    Boredom
    Friction
    Organization
  Opportunities
    Promotion/development
    Recognition
    Company commitment and cash rewards
    Greater role/part in the operation
    Meet people
    Greater job satisfaction
    Better working environment
  Threats
    Reluctant to change
    Might not get the rewards
    Down-grading
    Job losses
    Lack of interest
    Pressured in too short a time to change

Too much responsibility in the wrong places
Trained people leave

From these four lists we can identify the characteristics of the organisation we want to develop.

2 It is useful also to include here any job design survey data from which it is possible to list a number of features of the organization and jobs that are needed. Such a survey will identify the strengths and weaknesses of existing jobs across a series of core dimensions.
3 Personal views, preferences and experiences are also important. For example, the following describes the features of a nearly autonomous work group. Is this what we are looking for? And, can the task data support it?

Characteristics of a semi-autonomous work group

Essential characteristics

The work which the group carries out is a 'whole' job and produces a meaningful output or end product.

The tasks performed within the group are interdependent, so that the performance of a task affects or is affected by another task.

The group's work is relatively independent of the work of other people or groups.

The group is of optimal size i.e. between 5 and 20 members.

The group members can communicate with each other and with other key groups in the environment, and it is physically possible for them to speak to each other and be heard.

The group has some degree of autonomy in the areas listed below.

Other possible characteristics

Group goals

The group negotiates with management what it is expected to do and how much freedom it has in doing it.

The output targets for the group are agreed with management.

The quality standards of the work are agreed with management.

Acceptable levels of wastage of materials are agreed with management.

Group membership

The number of group members needed is agreed with management.
The group is allowed to choose its own members.

The group can choose new members.
The group can discipline members.
The group can expel a member under defined circumstances, agreed with management and unions.
The group can choose which members are 'loaned' when the workload decreases.
The group can negotiate which people it 'borrows' when the workload increases.

Rewards

Differences between the wages/salaries of group members have been agreed with management.
Ways of sharing productivity increases have been agreed with management.

Resources

The group has the information it wants about contribution to the total enterprise.
The group can requisition information it needs to do the job.
The group gets the factual information it needs to do the job.
The group can requisition supplies of materials and equipment.
Supplies of materials and equipment are available when the groups needs them.
The group gets the advice and help it needs to do its job, when it requests them.
The group gets feedback of the information it needs to assess how well it is doing its job.

Control over workplace

The group can decide where it works.
The group decides what machines and equipment it will want and negotiates these with management.
The group decides where the machines and equipment are positioned.
The group can requisition needed maintenance or repair services.
The group can carry out maintenance of the machines and equipment it uses, subject to negotiated agreement with any unions involved.
The group can repair the machines and equipment it uses, subject to negotiated agreement with any unions involved.

External relationship

The group is involved in the selection of its external supervisor or coordinator.

The group gets the cooperation it needs from other work groups.

Managers and supervisors refrain from interfering with the group's decisions and activities while they are taking place within the guidelines negotiated by the group.

Internal organization

The group can decide its own hours of work and those of individual members, including leave of absence, within the constraints established by union agreements.

The group can decide when rest-breaks are taken and how long they last.

The group can decide its own work methods.

The group decides the order in which it does the work.

The group can decide which member does which task at any particular time.

Each member of the group can choose to be trained to carry out any task.

The group decides what formal and on-the-job training each member will receive.

The group assesses and decides whether or not a member has acquired a particular skill.

Staff appraisal of group members is carried out by the group.

Record-keeping and other paperwork is carried out by the group.

The group carries out quality control and checks its own work.

The group can set its own safety targets.

The group can choose its own internal leader.

The group decides how and when the internal leader is selected.

4 Also the terms of reference provide a series of 'musts' for the evaluation criteria.

5 At the end of this step we should have a list of statements which help to direct our initial analyses of the task data.

The key to this step of the process is to consider the design criteria under three headings: input criteria, output criteria and content criteria. Input criteria refer to actions and resources required to develop the new organization and jobs. Output criteria refer to the expected achievements of the new organization and jobs. Content criteria can be split into one of two groupings: (a) criteria which cover the internal workings and behaviour of the new organization; (b) those which refer to the physical characteristics of an organization and its constituent jobs. It is this last set of criteria which are of importance here in deriving the rules and guidelines for analysing the task data, e.g.

(a) Build up from a line/manufacturing base using the point at which the task is generated as a key anchor for the task, i.e. build up jobs and the organization from the 'core' of the process.

Data analysis

(b) Design/develop jobs by means of a bottom-up rather than a top-down approach in order that the individual makes the best use of his/her skills and abilities, i.e. the job is designed to demand up to and including the maximum competences/skills/knowledge that the individual can attain. The reverse of this process is to design a job upon one of two principles: (i) all high-skill work is hived off to an individual job or jobs; (ii) the highest skill requirement of a job is identified and the job is filled by someone who can achieve this skill with minimal effort – it is assumed that he/she can also perform down the skill range, and is willing to do so.

(c) The work profile of the product-based departmental team includes all day-to-day tasks and the responsibility and authority to act on them. This by implication means that most longer-term development work and capital investment activity are not the direct responsibility of this team but are performed by another team.

(d) The purpose, objectives and strategies of all functions should be common, as far as possible, and mutually reinforcing, so there should be at least some shared measure(s) of successful performance that reconciles cost, quality and customer service etc.

(e) Assuming that all jobs and teams should engage in some form of improvement work, it is necessary to create the headroom for this in all new jobs, especially engineering jobs.

(f) 'Career and development opportunities for all' implies that the existing restricted single career ladders need to be developed to cover all new roles.

6 Also to be produced during this stage is a series of evaluation criteria by which the options can be evaluated/tested (see Chapter 7). These criteria should be divided into 'musts' and 'wants' and, again, should be grouped as 'input', 'output' and 'content' criteria. Examples of team/job/organization 'musts' include:

Department team/production team.
Authority to act/react to day-to-day situations.
Holds and develops own budget.
Ability to handle most day-to-day decisions and actions.
Resources available for training.
Consistent with company and national safety standards.
Common targets for all groups.
Equal opportunities for career progression and rewards.
Time for improvement work.
Retention and transfer of learning between teams to maintain standards and specialist skills, within existing numbers.
Fair and consistent reward structure.

Clear goals and objectives that are known.
Improves efficiency by x per cent.
Improves effectiveness by x per cent.
Copes with existing and foreseen changes in product and process technology.
Maintains and improves upon existing safety standards.
Complies with good manufacturing practice.
Provides meaningful jobs.
Realizable with existing staff.
Endorses manufacturing centre/focused factory concept.
Training material readily available.
Minimizes existing demarcations and does not generate any new ones.
Provides the basis upon which to build in the future.
Acceptable to staff and trade unions.
Achievable with no threat to continuity of production and customer service levels.
Principles can be applied across a whole site.
Makes better use of the existing talents of people on site.
Improves line utilization by x per cent.
Reduces changeover times.
Reduces the number of unpredictable stoppages.
Provides means to release people for training.
Rewards sufficient for staff.
Rewards sufficient for company.
Resulting jobs recognizable outside the company.
Training used is nationally recognized.

These are adequate as general statements but they must now be expressed in terms of organizational structure and individual jobs/roles.. The general statements act as a series of prompts to help to generate the organization and the jobs.

As a first step it is useful to think of the organization structure as a series of possible groupings, e.g. of processes, of like products/outputs, of like technologies or of like specialisms. Similarly it is possible to group individual roles, e.g. single role/skill, then (with minor enhancement) dual skill/process/function etc. Both the organization structure and role options can then be combined in one matrix (page 165).

This matrix can be completed by going through the 'content' design criteria list of 'musts' and 'wants'. Which of the above structure and role options satisfies the criteria? It is found in completing the matrix that it is not possible to combine all of the role options with all of the structure options, i.e. some are mutually exclusive. This procedure does, however, generate those role and structure options that are compatible.

Table 6.1 shows how one list of 'content' design criteria was used to

	Role				
Structure	Process/function focus		Overlap with unrelated roles		
	Single	Dual	Minor	Major	Full

Process
  (Part)
  (Full)
Product
Technology
Function/Specialism					

Table 6.1 *'Content' design criteria used to complete a structure/role matrix*

	Roles			
Structure	Single process/ function	Dual process/ function	Overlap with other areas	All tasks (multiple tasks)
2 packaging teams + 1 filling team	Yes	–	Yes	–
1 filling team + 2 packaging teams	Yes	Yes	Yes	Yes
Current structure	Yes	–	Yes	–
Product-based teams	Yes	Yes	Yes	Yes

1 filling team
  + 2 packaging teams
  (3 sub-teams)
	Yes	–	Yes	–

Packaging = 1 team, filling = 1 team	Yes	–	Yes	–
All department as one team	Yes	Yes	Yes	Yes
Narrow, functional teams	Yes	–	–	–
Machine-based teams/ specialists	Yes	–	Yes	–

complete the matrix which was then used to guide use of the task data. In order to fill in this matrix one study group took their own 'content' criteria and applied them. It became clear to them that it would be worth analysing their task database according to three possible structures: one filling team and two packing teams; product-based teams; the whole department as one team.

Step 7. Task data–rules for analysis

1 On the basis of the design principles it is necessary to devise a set of rules which can then be applied to the task data set. These rules usually involve three variables:

   Task location.
   Task frequency.
   Task complexity.

   For example, on the basis of location the task data can be allocated to the three groups:

   Direct manufacturing tasks.
   Direct support manufacturing tasks.
   Indirect support manufacturing tasks.

   The data can be divided, according to task frequency, into:

   Tasks occurring at least 12 a year ('direct/core tasks').
   Tasks occurring less than 12 times a year ('indirect/support tasks').

   The complexity scores can be reduced, as for the earlier plots to three categories, 1 (1–4), 2 (5–6), and 3 (7–8).
2 It is important to devise several sets or variations of the rules based on the design principles.
3 These rules should then be applied to the cleaned, validated and reduced task data set.
4 For the example described in Step 6 the task data would be sorted by the whole manufacturing process, and then by splitting the manufacturing process into two parts which would include their direct and indirect tasks. This means that all relevant testing, inspection and quality tasks get built into the 'core' organization.

This step is now beginning to provide a series of smaller databases which can be reshaped. First it is useful to consider an example of the types of output which this step can produce.

Data analysis

1 Taking the complete task database for an engineering department, we obtain the following profile:

Complexity of task	Hours of work	
1–2	3784	9%
3–4	11924	30%
5–6	10691	27%
7–8	13458	34%
Total	39857	

2 This can be divided into tasks directly supporting the manufacturing process and tasks supporting the site:

Core manufacturing tasks

Complexity of tasks	Hours of work	
1–2	3217	11%
3–4	9412	32%
5–6	8206	28%
7–8	8943	30%
Total	29778	

Site/support tasks

Complexity of tasks	Hours of work	
1–2	567	6%
3–4	2512	25%
5–6	2485	25%
7–8	4515	45%
Total	10079	

3 These sets of task data can be further subdivided according to both the discipline of the performer and whether the task is equipment-specific or not:

Equipment-specific tasks

Complexity of tasks	Hours of work	
1–2	2787	11%
3–4	7700	32%
5–6	7655	32%
7–8	6135	25%
Total	24277	

These task data can then be classified according to the discipline of the performer:

Discipline of performer (hours)

Complexity of tasks	Instrument		Electrical		Mechanical	
1–2	322	9%	515	14%	1950	12%
3–4	1310	36%	990	27%	5400	32%
5–6	1080	29%	725	20%	5850	35%
7–8	961	26%	1474	40%	3700	22%
Total	3673		3704		16900	

And classified by process:

Process (hours)

Complexity of tasks	Filling		Packaging		Other	
1–2	1708	11%	815	12%	264	11%
3–4	5618	38%	1232	18%	850	34%
5–6	3823	26%	2990	43%	842	34%
7–8	3760	25%	1849	27%	526	21%
Total	14909		6886		2482	

4 Then there are those equipment-non-specific tasks which have the following profile:

Complexity of tasks	Hours of work	
1–2	430	8%
3–4	1712	31%
5–6	551	10%
7–8	2808	51%
Total	5501	

These tables together begin to suggest that there is a wide range of work that can be undertaken by a wide range of people (see Figure 6.1).

Another way of dividing task data is to consider the task frequency profile. Again taking the data for the whole department from an engineering aspect, the profile shown in Table 6.2 is generated.

	Task complexity level			
	1-2	3-4	5-6	7-8
Whole Department	9%	30%	27%	34%
Core/direct tasks	11%	32%	28%	30%
Support/indirect tasks	6%	25%	25%	45%
Equipment-specific tasks	11%	32%	32%	25%
Instrument equipment-specific tasks	9%	36%	29%	26%
Electrical equipment-specific tasks	14%	27%	20%	40%
Mechanical equipment-specific tasks	12%	32%	35%	22%
Filling-specific tasks	11%	38%	26%	25%
Packaging-specific tasks	12%	18%	43%	27%
Other process-specific tasks	11%	34%	34%	21%
Equipment-non-specific tasks	8%	31%	10%	51%

Key: Complexity level 1–2 = 1 week or less
3–4 = 1 month or less
5–6 = 6 months or less
7–8 = greater than 6 months

Figure 6.1 *Task complexity profile*

Table 6.2 *Task frequency profile*

Task frequency/year	Number of tasks	Total number of tasks	
0.5	2	1	
1	117	117	
2	66	132	
3	9	27	
4	64	256	889 tasks (7%)
5	6	30	(less than once per month)
6	8	48	
8	4	32	
10	15	150	
12	8	96	
13	49	637	
15	7	105	
17	1	17	1326 tasks (11%)
18	1	18	(approx. once per month)
20	25	500	
24	1	24	
25	1	25	
26	31	806	
30	10	300	2146 tasks (18%)
40	11	440	(approx. fortnightly)
50	12	600	
52	31	1612	
60	2	120	
72	1	72	
78	4	312	
100	5	500	5840 tasks (48%)
104	5	520	(approx. weekly)
130	2	260	
156	6	936	
208	1	208	
240	2	480	
260	2	520	
300	1	300	
364	1	364	1979 tasks (16%)
365	3	1095	(approx. daily)
520	1	520	
Total	515	12198	

All of these manipulations and plots of the task data provide profiles of the work required to ensure the successful completion of a stage, or stages, in the production process or system. In each case the purpose of the task profile is to generate smaller sets of task data which contain within them all of the necessary tasks, irrespective of their current performer or complexity. It is these smaller sets of task data which can be used to develop teams and individual job roles.

Step 8. Task data – third plots

1 Apply the rules developed in Step 7 to the cleaned, validated and reduced task data set.
2 First do a plot showing the divisions made across the task data set. Divide the task database by location and frequency, each split being expressed in terms of complexity. Do plots for all the task data, and plot separately manufacturing/filling tasks and packaging tasks by the current performer of the task.. These plots will describe the current work profile.

Step 9. Possible new combinations/configurations of roles and structure of the organization

1 The analysis of the task data set has now reached the position when a series of overall job roles and the organization structure can be spelt out in detail.
2 Here we apply the rules developed in Steps 6 and 7, but relate them more specifically to:

   (a) The elements of an 'ideal job':
       Gives the holder satisfaction from the exercise, develops his/her abilities and results in the achievement of worthwhile personal goals.
       Allows the job-holder to participate in setting personal and team objectives.
       Motivates the job-holder to achieve these objectives.
       Encourages the job-holder to identify with the team, manufacturing centre and site, with fellow employees, with the process and their own personal aims.

Requires a healthy level of physical and mental activity with an allowance for personal adjustments.
Provides fair pay, status and security.
Is conducted in an environment without extremes of noise, temperature, humidity, etc.

(b) The following features of the tasks:
Commonality of tasks.
Relatability of tasks.
Nature/scope of tasks.
Distribution/location of tasks.
Self-containment of tasks/families of related tasks.
Volume of tasks.

Taking these two sets of factors together with the rules developed earlier, we can begin to speculate about possible 'new' roles for existing job-holders. For example, in considering the membership of a line/manufacturing team in a food factory, could such rules contain, or totally consist of, the following 'components'?
Technical operator.
Machine-biased/relative specialist technical operator.
Machine-biased operator.
Operator.
Mechanical craftsman.
Mechanical craftsman in support team.
Electrical craftsman.
Electrical craftsman in support team.
Mechanical craftsman as operator.
Electrical craftsman as operator.
Mech-electrical craftsman.
Mech-electrical craftsman in support team.
Electro-mechanical craftsman.
Electro-mechanical craftsman in support team.
Working team leader.
Non-working team leader.
(Semi-)autonomous team with no designated team leader.
Team leader, job biased to:
  Operating.
  Planning/scheduling.
  Quality.
  Technical.
Quality control in all jobs.
Separate quality control job in team.
Quality control in support team.

Data analysis

Mechanical craftsman as deputy team leader.
Mechanical craftsman also as team leader.
Electrical craftsman as deputy team leader.
Electrical craftsman also as team leader.
Mech-electrical craftsman also deputy team leader.
Mech-electrical craftsman also as team leader.
Electro-mechanical craftsman as deputy team leader.
Electro-mechanical craftsman also as team leader.
Mechanical craftsman as a separate job in team as technician.
Electrical craftsman as a separate job in team as a technician.
Mech-electrical craftsman as a separate job in team as a technician.
Electro-mechanical craftsman as a separate job in team as a technician.
Team training role is shared among all team members.
Team training role is the responsibility of the team leader.
Craftsman/technician (irrespective of discipline) is the main technical trainer for the team
Training is a support service.
Support teams provide service to several teams.
Support teams provide service to only one team.
Support team is multi-functional.
Support teams are uni-functional.
All team administration requirements are undertaken by a single job-holder.
All team administration requirements are shared among all team members.
Administration is provided by support team.
Planning/scheduling as a separate job in the team.
Planning/scheduling is shared among all team members.
Planning/scheduling is provided by support team.
Mech-electrical craftsman as operator.
Electro-mechanical craftsman as operator.
Machine-biased operators who rotate.
Technical operators who rotate.
Operators who rotate
   etc.

3 After running through this type of list it should be possible to build up a series of pictures of the manufacturing and related jobs and organization structures for the department. These form the basis for further development.

The key to this step to the selecting of the possible job configurations is as follows. First, the subdivided task database has to be profiled to cover the particular stage of the process. These task data profiles will have a specific volume (task frequency, multiplied by task duration) which will be one, two, three etc. people-equivalent in size. We now know approximately how many jobs are involved. Second, the overall task profile for this subset of the task data can be one of four main types: biased to low-complexity tasks; biased to high-complexity tasks; peaks at medium complexity tasks; peaks at both low- and high-complexity tasks. Now taking each of these profile types in turn we can identify which job configurations they indicate:

(a) If the bulk of the work is of low complexity there should be no problem in all the job-holders performing all of the work in this part of the process. It may also be necessary to reconsider the tasks allocated to this stage-specific task data set and to add additional ones.
(b) If the reverse task complexity profile is found, it may be pointing towards the creation of jobs which many current job-holders could not, or would not want to, aspire to. Again, the make-up of the task database may require some modification.
(c) If the tasks are predominantly of medium complexity, it may be possible to combine them to create jobs which span both low- and high-complexity work. In this case it could also mean that all of the job-holders can undertake the full range of tasks at their stage of the process.
(d) Finally, if the task profile is bimodal with groupings of low- and high complexity tasks, then the jobs might best be held by two different types of job-holder. The volume of work involved is the key here in determining whether whole jobs can be justified.

Task profile	Example roles
Low-complexity bias	General operators
High-complexity bias	Technicians
Medium-complexity bias	Technical operators
High and low complexity	General operators and technicians

Once these general directions for job configurations have been established, it is necessary to examine the detail of the tasks covered in terms of electrical, mechanical, operational, quality etc. tasks; this then indicates the possible 'biases' of the new roles.

4 Another way of tackling this issue is to plot the task data by performer, by task complexity and by a general heading. The following listings provide one example of this approach, which can be used to consider task similarities and possible areas of task overlap.

First, allocate each of the jobs included in the task analysis to one of the five main areas. In this example there are forty-two jobs to be allocated.

Data analysis

General area	Job
1 People	Personnel officer
	Personnel assistant
2 Engineering	Engineering section head/Plant engineer
	Electrician
	Instrument mechanic
	Fitter
3 Operations	Filling section head
	Packaging section head
	Operations manager
	Packaging supervisor
	Filling supervisor
	Overprint operator
	Filling operator
	Packaging operator
	Cleaner
4 Science	Quality control manager
	Quality compliance
	In-process control inspector
	In-process control technical assistant
	Quality control admin. section
	Packaging material quality control section head
	Packaging material quality control supervisor
	Hygiene services
	Lab. section manager
	Lab. supervisor
	Lab. steward
	Lab. technician
	Quality review
	Raw material testing
	Packaging material quality control technical assistant
	Product quality manager
5 Commercial	Materials stock controller
	Supplier auditor
	Packaging admin. section
	Audit and validation coordinator
	Main stores – receipt and dispatch
	Planner
	Collation supervisor
	Accounts dept.
	Collator
	Warehouse/line serviceman
	Office services

176   *Changing Job Structures*

Next, analyse the five main areas according to task complexity: here, Level 1 represents task complexity ratings 1–2; Level 2, ratings 3–4; Level 3, ratings 5–6; Level 4, ratings 7–8.

1(a) People – Level 4
   Report writing.
   Coaching one-to-one.
   Training (imparting).
   Running team meeting, e.g. for safety.
   Disciplining others.
   Team-building.
   Developing of subordinates.
   Maximize staff utilization.
   Absence counselling.
   Make presentations.
   Review training records, programme development, delivery etc.
   Conduct interviews.
   Conduct appraisals.
   Implement site charter.
   Run working parties.
   Allocate work.
   Manpower planning.
   Handle personnel matters.

1(b) People – Level 3
   Encourage staff to work within charter.
   Make training presentations.
   Conduct monthly briefings.
   Absence counselling.
   Show visitors around.
   Absence monitoring.

1(c) People – Level 2
   Conduct weekly briefing.
   Chair site committees.
   Organize social events.
   Explain pay system principles and operation.
   Conduct occupational testing.

1(d) People – Level 1
   Organizing and handling visitors.
   Allocating telephone calls.

2(a) Engineering – Level 4
   Planning and scheduling of engineering work.

Standard operating procedure initiation, training and monitoring.
Equipment modification, development and design.
Keeping up to date with latest technology.
Liaison with suppliers to site and inter-site.
Handling shutdowns and start-ups.
Safety certificates and inspections.
Projects from authorization to handover.
Planned preventative maintenance initiation through to recording.
Build up maintenance budget.
Service conditioning.
Contract management.
Check, clean and renew plant and equipment parts.
Repair, replace and renew plant and equipment parts.
Attend to machine breakdowns.
Check, calibrate and overhaul instruments.
Diagnose, fabricate and fit parts, check, fault-find on plant and equipment.

2(b) Engineering – Level 3
Reset earth leakage.
Simple plant and equipment fault diagnosis.
Remove strainer and clean mesh filter.

2(c) Engineering – Level 2
Replace lamps.
Renew clock batteries.
Reset overloads.
Check equipment action.
Isolate equipment.
Greasing and lubrication.
Strip, clean and replace conveyors.
Replace filters.
Open valves.

2(d) Engineering – Level 1
Record equipment conditions.
Clean equipment.
Replace ink jet filters.
Check connections.
Check seals.

3(a) Operations – Level 4
Ensure standard operating procedures are up to date.
Conduct safety inspections and initiatives.

Maximize equipment utilization.
Prepare budget.
Stock-taking.
Maintain quality.
Handle customer complaints.
Investigate customer quality queries and reply to them.
Investigate and report on serious incidents.
Planning (general).
Packaging problem solving.
Identify and purchase equipment,
Prepare monthly report.
Permits to work.
Organize safety projects.
Visit suppliers.
Control and monitor expenditure.
Monitor performance.
Handle major projects.
Conduct validation work.
Handle complaints.
Pre-registration pharmacy projects.
Authorize purchases.
Maintain quality standards.
Achieve production performance standards in service, cost and quality.
Make up rubber stereos.

3(b) Operations – Level 3
Organization work schedule.
Monitor condition of systems and production.
Write new documents.
Check documentation.
Write standard operating procedures.
Handle new technology and development.
Handle suggestions.
Check job packs.
Investigate accidents.
Conduct safety inspections and act on them.
Conduct safety meetings and audits.
Reduce material losses.
Hazard-spotting.
Handling projects.
Conduct quality audits.
Conduct packaging material quality control investigations.
Stock-taking.
Ensure capacity utilization.

Data analysis 179

Check equipment condition.
Book off raw materials and components.
Book off filled cans.
Check documentation.
Manage project workload.
Ensure high staff utilization.
Ensure line clearance.
Split bulk as needed.
Reconciliation of job pack.
Use planning and scheduling programme.

3(c) Operations – Level 2.
Check preparation room.
Prepare batch.
Set up equipment.
Check weighing of product.
Check suspensions.
Do in-process checks.
Clean equipment/vessels.
Charge lines with raw materials.
Remove waste.
Change filters.
Ensure availability of cans and valves.
Order raw materials and consumables.
Maintain dispensing systems.
Stock control of materials.
Produce monthly reports.
Fill in line documentation.
Organize labour.
Investigate incident reports.
Hazard-spotting.
Handling flexitime and holidays.
Conduct safety meetings.
Authorize purchases.
Schedule production batches.
Order and issue documents, trays, and labels.
Allocate staff.
Collate batch information and other forms.
Customer quality queries investigations.
Allocate jobs to lines.
Check job packs, components, and overprint.
Organize changeovers.
Check and challenge plant and equipment.
Adjust equipment and remove jams.

Do in-process control checks.
Order extra components.
Clean equipment.
Collect components.
Complete customer quality queries forms.
Investigate component shortages.
Set up overprint machine.
Check and count batches and components.
Match overprint labels to job pack.

3(d) Operations – Level 1
Pull job on to line.
Charge line and keep replenished.
Count rejects.
Deal with jams.
Clean area.
Run line.
Liaise with outside support.
Do hand packing.
Wrap pallets.
Clean preparation room and line.
Reconcile line output and materials used.
Log output and materials used.
Dispose of waste.
Cleaning duties – (brushing, mopping, polishing, waste removal, scrubbing, scrapping, buffing, spraying and washing.
Check components and match them to job pack.
Check overprint sheets and stereos with manual.
Print and return printed tags and labels.

4(a) Science – Level 4
Final product release.
Validation work.
Procedure updating.
Intermediate release.
Reject reconciliation.
New product debriefing/product development.
Handle inter-site complaints.
Liaison with other sites – microbiological service.
Site standards.
Develop product guide.
Multiple batch checking.
Production standard operating procedures checking.
Reject/reprocess instructions purchase requisitions.

Reference samples.
Certificate of analysis.
Planned preventive maintenance routine approvals
Handling atypical results.
Update standard operating procedures.
Enviro/monitoring review and recommend.
Good manufacturing practices audit.
Validation assessment, coordinate and results coordination.
Organize and follow-up department audit.
Compilation of findings on complaints and customer quality queries.
Batch-checking.
Handling engineering requisitions.
Handling batch rejects.
Check manufacturing documents, components and overprint.
Sample multiple batches.
Enter and update product formulations into computer.
Raise quality assurance specifications.
Check, control and circulate PQs.
Handle registration and product-related queries.
Sentence or reject raw materials.
Final release of materials..
Quality compliance batch release.
Check certificates.
Develop in-process control.

4(b) Science – Level 3
Return suppliers' note.
Split samples for testing.
Check documents for multiple batch samples.
Check bulk batch against job pack.
Inform of specification changes.
Routine laboratory work.
Update methods.
Initiate reports on components.
Check finished work.
Check certificate of performance.
Create workbooks and check completed ones.
Check approval copies of new materials.
Complete reject forms.
Liaise with purchasing and suppliers.
Plan for stock replacement.
Check returned goods.
Act on incident and accident reports.
Audit and approve suppliers.

Agree content of specification with other sites.
Approve artwork.
Dispose of hazardous materials.
Empty waste skips.
Clear and clean blocked drains.
Arrange contract disposal of waste.
Clean up unforeseen spillages.
Erect scaffolding.
Move machinery.
Order laboratory stocks.
Planning of work.
Pass and check batches.
Handling complaints.

4(c) Science – Level 2
Quarantine label application.
Customer quality queries.
Review enviro/monitoring of trends.
Good manufacturing practice audit review.
Validation communication.
Check vessels, labels, documents and materials.
Set up HPLC system.
Do water KF, IR, odour, NVM tests.
Test can valves, weight and dimensions.
Do performance test.
Check delivery conditions.
Calibrate equipment.
Input quality data and compile report.
Create work schedule and update as necessary.
Coordinate quality control meeting.
Dispose of cans and waste arcton.
Clean upper void areas.
Clean glass.
Load laboratory results on to the computer.
Receive laboratory stocks.
Set up autoanalyser, operate and analyse the results.
Prime cans.
Conduct tests on product, e.g. d/short, weigh, deposition, pressure, water, leakage and absence.

4(d) Science – Level 1
Enviro/monitoring sampling, tabulation.
Process documentation systems audit.
Sort samples.

Weigh cans, prime cans, and leak-test.
Prepare, clean, set up test equipment.
Chloride test.
High boiling matter.
Read barometer.
Current temperature readings to standard.
Do dilution and neutralizing work.
Do testing calculations.
Titrate materials.
Clean and assemble test equipment.
Split sample.
Weigh cans.
Valve visual inspection.
Identify valve components.
Check actuator appearance.
Check actuate labels.
Inspect and microscopically examine actuators.
Test actuator performance, dust and fit and can fit test, dimensions and spray-hold diameter.
Check cartons and label.
Reconcile batch and delivery note information.
Calibrate micrometers, shadowgraph, mandos, HP85, danalec, balance, pamasol, screw, vernier.
Do rub and rewind test.
Investigate material complaints.
Liaise with supplier auditor.
Dispose of printed matter and cardboard.
Clean changerooms and toilets.
Calibrate balance, spectrophotometer.
Dispose of product samples.
Control laboratory stocks.

5(a) Commercial – Level 4
Work with strategic purchasing.
Sentence components with quality compliance.
Audit component suppliers.
Develop suppliers on quality matters.
Improve suppliers' quality ratings.
Scrutinize appropriate component specification.
Confirm new pack and delete old ones.
Order new print block.
Investigate packaging complaints.
Update packaging specification.
Develop test methods.

Develop cheaper packaging components.
Agree artwork.
Liaise with production, purchasing and planners on pack changes.
Progress-chase components.
Check overprinting.
Develop accounting system.
Handle capital proposals/projects.
Set standard product costs.

5(b) Commercial – Level 3
Chasing quality assurance.
Stock control of components and raw materials.
Downdating on computer.
Dealing with wrong overprint sheet.
Communication supplier
Liaise with suppliers on component compliance.
Respond to customer needs.
Typing.
Downdate date stock on computer.
Deliver goods to user department.
Act on audits.
Make old artwork redundant.
Handle site transfers.
Stock control of home warehouse.
Update head office computer on parameters.
De-suspend new export orders.
Organize eight week schedule (detailed and rough) and accurate two week schedule.
Stock control.
Computer system component ordering and downdating.
Control of complete pack.
Issue goods to finished goods.
Calculate elements of product/production.
Audit of work-in-progress.
Set departmental annual budgets.

5(c) Commercial – Level 2
Adding stock control parameters to new items.
Progress on suppliers – new/old orders.
Checking batch on box, cans, labels and cartons.
Pulling batch on to line.
Ordering, returning and dealing with components.
Dealing with re-sampling problems and wrong counts.
Order goods, check condition and offload.

Sort suppliers' batches.
Locate and deliver goods and assemble for delivery.
Delete redundant items and packs for MENTOR.
Negotiate amendments to export orders and contract order dates.
Adjust filling schedule.
Raise job pack.
Create weekly planning report.
Progress-chase late component delivery for orders.
Liaising with laboratory, stores and purchasing for collation.
Service lines with materials.
Draw batch from bond room.
Compile production report.

5(d) Commercial – Level 1
Splitting-up job pack.
Check codes on components.
Pulling components to lines.
Checking returned stock.
Ordering extra stock.
Handing out schedule to overprint.
Photocopying and laminating.
Circulate material to relevant parties, e.g. copy of new artwork.
Planning ticket entry for planning board.
Allocate and highlight priorities to packaging material quality control and quality assurance.
Issue components and materials to lines.
Store actuator in holding area.
Move pallets from lines to warehouse.
Inform despatch of recall batches.
Charge stacker truck.
Check components.

These task listings can be used by existing task performers to identify which kind of tasks could be shared. Thus rather than mechanically apply the 'rules of analysis' (Step 7), it is equally possible to re-allocate tasks by highlighting their similarities and overlaps among a group of performers (see Chapter 7, Step 6 'The Balance Sheet', where one approach to total productive maintenance is described).

Step 10. Task data reduction

1 The reallocation of tasks between performers will have a knock-on to the task data set, which needs to be recognised; an effort must be made to

modify the task data set accordingly. For example, if batch/order changes were undertaken by the operators, what would be the impact on the task data set? Also, if 'minor' stoppages on the cartonner/labeller were handled by the operators, what would be the impact on the task data set?

2 Continue with the above line of reasoning which will both reduce the number of tasks in absolute terms and also reduce the frequency and duration of the remaining tasks.

Step 11. Task data – fourth plots

1 Run off final plots using the further reduced data set, applying the rules developed in Step 9.
2 This will result in a final list of tasks which will form the work of a team and/or an individual. These lists can then be summarized to form the team and work profiles. The resulting task listings for the new roles and teams can be compared with the original task data listings to assess the potential benefits (see Chapter 7, Step 4).

Summary: Designing an efficient and effective organization

Going through each of the eleven steps involved in the analysis of the task data is intended to refine and focus the task base upon the primary objective of the organization. On a manufacturing site, the primary objective is to raise the efficiency and effectiveness of the conversion of raw materials into finished products. Therefore, in the designing of the appropriate manufacturing organization there are a number of basic requirements. First, there is a need to have an organization so structured as to allow the production system's availability to be maintained at an appropriate level. This might require the raising of the ability of operators to respond to a greater range of changes in operating conditions, e.g. adjustments, alignments, changeovers etc. Second, it might also pay to focus engineering and appropriate technical resources on the more longer-term work involved in raising the production system's reliability. The exact mix of skills and knowledge and the range of tasks to be undertaken by the 'operating' and the 'reliability' teams is never readily apparent.

The eleven steps involved in the analysis of the task database can be divided into two groups that cover:

1 The creation of valid and reliable task data base built up of a range of existing, amended and new tasks.

Data analysis

2 The allocation of the tasks based upon their contribution and role in ensuring the successful operation of the production system.

Two of the most important are Steps 7 and 8. It is in these steps that the whole task database is divided into smaller sets according to their contribution to the production process. In the description of Step 7 two key rules were introduced which classified tasks on the basis of their frequency and in a more general regrouping based on their complexity levels. Also introduced at the same step was the allocation of tasks based on the possible divisions of the production system. Most production systems can be divided into a series of highly interrelated but distinct 'cells'. One way of deciding on the divisions in the production system is to trace along the production chain and to identify those points where the raw material/product changes in some way. For example, a series of liquids might be mixed together and bottled: the bottle then becomes the raw material/product. The bottle might then be labelled, placed in a box, over-wrapped and packed in a case.

Other aspects of the production system to look for are storage points, which may represent buffers to ensure continuous production and/or may be important parts of the process itself. For example, in some industries (e.g. pharmaceuticals) the product may have to be stored for a fixed period to ensure no deterioration in its performance. In the case of a buffer it is important to establish its purpose, and also who 'owns' it.

Application of the rules of Step 7

1 Divide the task data base using task frequency. Here there are three main concepts:

   (a) *Core activities* are those necessary to carry out the physical transformation of product and allow the production process to flow.
   (b) *Direct support activities* are those necessary to allow the production process to continue over the short term. They include maintenance, quality control etc.
   (c) *Indirect support activities* are those necessary for longer-term development, e.g. project engineering, new product development etc.

(Note that these three types of activity correspond to the 'improving', and 'ongoing' levels in an organization, described in Chapter 2).

The rule of thumb used in Step 7 to identify a 'core' task was that the task must occur more than 12 times a year, i.e. once a month. This is not a rigid rule but a guide. Detailed scrutiny of subdivided task lists will identify any misplaced task. What is being achieved here is the establishment of the boundary between direct operational requirements, i.e. the adherence to set procedures (and the adjustment of the process to ensure that it does adhere to a set procedure), and the development of the process, i.e. the setting and improvement of operational procedures.

Also included in this step is the allocation of tasks to provide the basis for the design of individual jobs and teams with a high level of self-regulation. Thus a job or team would possibly cover a whole cycle of the production process, the individual job-holder or members of a team having the full range of skills required to operate a complete cycle.

2 Divide the task database using task complexity levels. Here there are four key concepts.

(a) *Top-down job design.* Many if not most existing jobs have been developed on the basis of filling them with somebody with the ability to do the most complex task of the job. It is assumed that a job-holder who can undertake the most complex task will be able to undertake all of the less complex ones as well. The net result of this way of developing and filling jobs is that many job-holders are wasting, or at least not using much of, their potential. For example, as a general rule manufacturing tasks have the following skill/complexity profile:

20–30 per cent	high/specialist skills
40–60 per cent	general skills
40–60 per cent	multi-semi-skills

High/specialist skills require three-four years of education and training, and an equivalent period of experience before they can be deployed. General skills require six months or so of education and training, and an equivalent period of experience before they can be deployed. Multi-semi-skills require little or no time to acquire and deploy. As soon as the skills have been acquired over a few days or weeks they can be deployed with little or no experience.

Accepting for the moment that this '20–40–40 skills profile' is a true representation of day-to-day manufacturing activities, it means that those people with the ability to perform high/specialist skilled work are using their full abilities only 20 per cent of the time. One conclusion to be drawn from this is that the range and depth of work they undertake could be expanded. The second conclusion is that, with some training, most people could competently undertake a large proportion of the work.

(b) *Task transferability.* Building upon the above concept, it is reasonable to assume that many if not most tasks can be transferred from an existing performer to a new performer. Thus, the use of task

Data analysis

complexity is one way of dividing the task database since it can be assumed that an existing performer who can complete a task at, say, Level 4 or 5, i.e. a training time of greater than one month and less than three months, could also undertake other tasks of a similar complexity currently being performed by someone else.

(c) *Bottom-up job design.* As a basis for designing a job it is suggested that this is better done by matching the capabilities of the job-holder with an appropriate range of interrelated tasks. It follows from this hypothesis that someone who has the ability to perform highly skilled work should be given every opportunity to use and develop those skills. This concept is the reverse of the 'top-down job design' approach.

(d) *Job quality.* At the same time as attempting to raise the efficiency and effectiveness of an organization, it is also possible to strive to achieve the development of high-quality jobs. The criteria an ideal job should satisfy are:

> Gives the job-holder satisfaction from the exercise and development of his/her abilities and the achievement of worthwhile personal goals.
> Allows the job-holder to participate in setting individual and team objectives.
> Motivates the job-holder to achieve these objectives.
> Encourages the job-holder to identify with the company and site, fellow employees, the process, and his/her own personal aims.
> Requires a healthy level of physical and mental activity with an allowance for personal adjustments.
> Provides a natural environment without extremes of noise, temperature and humidity.
> Provides fair pay, status and security (see Toon, 1979).

Here we are trying to ensure that the groupings of tasks allocated to an individual job-holder meets these criteria and so provides the necessary core job dimensions (Hackman and Oldham, 1975: 161) for satisfying, motivating and productive jobs. The meeting of these criteria is also made all the more likely because of the guidelines implicit in the socio-technical systems approach, i.e. compatibility, minimal critical specification, variance control, boundary location, information flow, power and authority, multi-functional workers, support congruence, transitional organization and incompletion (Cherns, 1987). These last three concepts are explained as follows:

(i) 'Support congruence' suggests that systems supporting work designs, such as information and reward systems, should reinforce the nature of those designs. Most people using the socio-technical systems approach are geared to high levels of employee involvement and self-control, and the organization's support systems should promote those characteristics. This generally means making significant alterations in marketing, sales, financial controls, and reward and information systems. In most cases of socio-technical systems design, employees are afforded some control over those systems, although this varies according to company policy, national laws and government regulations.

(ii) 'Transitional organization' suggests that changing from a traditional work design or organization to one based on socio-technical systems principles requires a transitional structure for managing the change process. This transitional organization helps employees to gain new skills and knowledge and facilitates the learning necessary to make the new design work. The transition period involves considerable innovation, learning and change, and usually differs from and is more complex than either the old or the new design.

(iii) 'Incompletion' points to the reality that socio-technical systems designing is never really complete but continues as new things are learned and new conditions are encountered. Thus, the ability continually to design and redesign work needs to be built into existing work teams. Members must have the skills and knowledge to assess their work unit continually and to make necessary changes and improvements. From this view, socio-technical systems designing rarely results in a stable work design but provides a process for continually modifying work to fit changing conditions.

3 Split the production process/system at key transformation points. Outlined in Chapter 4 was a mapping of a manufacturing process and this 'map' was further extended by considering both the support activities required to allow the process to proceed and also those factors preventing progress. The purpose of this rule is to think through the possible configuration of the production process both with and without divisions. For example, in the description of the 'role-structure matrix' earlier in this chapter the production process was treated in three main ways: split according to production technology, split according to the product manufactured and, finally, as a single unit. These three broad structure options provide the first possible divisions of the task database. Application of these rules generates a series of task databases, reduced in size and specific to one part of the production process. Each of these process task bases is then subdivided by task frequency and then, within task frequency bandings, tasks are further subdivided by their complexity.

Data analysis

It is at this point that the analysis begins to focus on individual roles and groups of roles.

At this stage there are two main guidelines to follow:

(a) *Task distribution*. Within each of the specific task databases the tasks can be plotted in histogram form according to level of complexity. This plot could reveal an even distribution of the tasks, i.e. there are equal numbers of low- and high-complexity tasks. This can now be pursued via two routes:
  (i) Task location: rather than use the general task-locating code to sort the tasks, it is useful to use more specific task codes, e.g. to sort by line, by machine etc. and then plot task complexity histograms. Again, is it an even or a peaked distribution?
  (ii) Task type: rather than mix all of the tasks together, they can be sorted by their type, e.g. operating, maintaining, changeovers etc. Do both high- and low-complexity tasks fall into one of the task type categories?
(b) *Task volume*. This is determined by the multiplication of task frequency by task duration. Here the key questions revolve around the volume of tasks required in a specific area and the volume for a particular type of task, or complexity of task.

The main features that are being looked for here are:

1 Do the task profiles suggest that one person could master and undertake all of the tasks? Is the range of tasks too great for one person in terms of locations, times of occurrence and complexity? (This second question is posed only after the first one has been answered.)
2 Do the task profiles reveal a volume of tasks which could justify the inclusion of functional specialists? For example, is there sufficient electrical or mechanical engineering work to justify a full-time electrician and/or fitter?

It is not expected to have final answers to these questions at this stage, but it does mark the focusing of the task database at the individual role level.

The next step is to generate listings of tasks for each of the production process areas, which will form the input to the design of individual roles. It is at this stage that all of the additional variables collected on each task are used. As before, there is a series of guidelines:

(a) *Core activities*. One of the main principles of the approach is the creation of self-contained teams and individual roles focused on the core purpose of the organization. This therefore means integrating

all of the tasks relevant to progressing the production purpose of the organization.
  (b) *Task transferability.* Here there are five factors to consider:
    (i) Task volume: if the volume of tasks is insufficient to justify a single specialist performer, the tasks should be built into the roles of the most appropriate team/job. Reliance upon specialist and other infrequent inputs should be minimized.
    (ii) Task geographic distribution: the very location of a task can preclude its completion by an individual because of its inaccessibility, its dependence on support equipment etc.
    (iii) Task temporal distribution: if two tasks require to be undertaken at the same time and they are geographically separated, it means that one person cannot complete them. Thus it is important to identify the bunching of tasks in time, otherwise impossible roles may be devised for job-holders.
    (iv) Task safety: before any tasks are shared between performers, and/or transferred between performers, it is vital that all of the necessary safety considerations are taken into account.
    (v) Support resources: many tasks require equipment, tools etc. It is important to determine the viability of the adequate provision of support resources; in many cases they should probably be shared.
  (c) *Bottom-up job design.* The application of the principle of matching the capabilities of the job-holder with a range of tasks that makes use of, and offers the opportunity for the development of, those capabilities.

The actual application of these three guidelines is not a straightforward mechanical procedure, and it is often best to identify the purpose and the general profile allowing the actual job-holders to provide the detail. What has been established at this point is the number of people required to carry out a range of tasks on a given process or part of a process, and the make-up of those jobs. For example, in a manufacturing operation this might require the pulling together of the direct production tasks of operators, the supervision, and the relevant support tasks undertaken by engineering, quality control, scheduling etc.

In summary, there are four key steps in the analysis of the task data each one being the application of a finer sieve:

  (a) The creation of a valid and reliable task database.
  (b) Sorting of the tasks by complexity, frequency and location to create the initial organization options.
  (c) Sorting of the reduced task lists by volume and distribution to create the initial team composition options.

Data analysis

(d) Sorting of the still further reduced task lists by core activities, task transferability and bottom-up job design principles to create individual roles.

In terms of producing a reliable and robust result from the application of this method, it is important that the first sort is successful in dividing the task database into core and support activities.

7
Selecting the 'best option'

Introduction

The products of the eleven-step process described in Chapter 6 are usually a series of organization options. Each option represents a possible combination of task data into specific structures, team and individual roles. The purpose of this chapter is to describe a two-stage evaluation process which allows 'the best option', or perhaps more correctly 'the most appropriate option', to be selected.

The evaluation procedure divides into two parts:

(a) The evaluation of the options against the evaluation criteria (Steps 1 to 3).
(b) The evaluation of the option selected based on Steps 1 to 3 in terms of the costs and benefits of the chosen option (Steps 4 to 6).

This chapter is divided into six sections, each of which describes one of the above steps.

Step 1. Developing evaluation criteria

The evaluation criteria are not generated at this stage of the process of changing job and organization structures. Most of the design criteria have emerged during the initial stages of the process (see Chapter 4, Stages 1 to 3). From these early stages of the process came a 'vision' of the new organization based on the personal views of individual employees and also on the analysis of the strengths, weaknesses, opportunities and threats facing the existing operation. At this stage it is more a matter of collecting together the previously generated evaluation criteria and reducing them to a manageable list. It is important to remember throughout this step that the design criteria are being developed in response to the question: what must (and should) the organization and jobs achieve? For example, if the overriding conclusion of a study group is that the new organization should be highly participative, it will need to have most of the features listed in Table 7.1.

Table 7.1 *Design features for a participative system (Lawler, 1982: 298–99)*

Organizational structure	Flat
	Lean
	Mini-enterprise orientated
	Team based
	Participative council or structure
Job design	Individually enriched
	Self-managing teams
Information system	Open
	Inclusive
	Tied to jobs
	Decentralized – team based
	Participatively set goals and standards
Career system	Tracks and counselling available
	Open job-posting
Selection	Realistic job preview
	Team based
	Potential and process-skill orientated
Training	Heavy commitment
	Peer training
	Economic education
	Interpersonal skills
Reward system	Open
	Skill based
	Gain-sharing and/or employee share ownership
	Flexible benefits
	All salary
	Egalitarian
Personnel policies	Stability of employment
	Participatively established through representative group
Physical layout	Around organizational structure
	Egalitarian
	Safe and pleasant

This example developed by Lawler goes beyond the structure and content of the organization and individual jobs, describing the systems that allow the structure and jobs to work. It serves to illustrate also that it is necessary to design the other key elements of an organization at the same time, and they must support the structure. In fact it is through the training, reward system, career system etc. that the new organization and jobs will be brought into being.

Four examples are provided here to illustrate other, similar design criteria which can form evaluation criteria lists.

Example 1. Being in front – developing the most competitive means of manufacturing

Continuing on from an example used earlier, one study group developed three lists of possible criteria which were then combined into a single list of seventeen criteria. These four lists are presented below. The first three lists were developed by sub-groups made up of members of the study group.

Evaluation criteria from Group 1

1 No job losses.
2 No downgrading.
3 Sufficient rewards.
4 Job satisfaction.
5 Cater for people who don't want to change.
6 Better career development.
7 Better training.
8 Better recognition.
9 Good safety standards.
10 Opportunities for everyone (career development).
11 More involvement (e.g. selecting own teams).
12 Better communication.
13 Team to have more information on workload.

Evaluation criteria from Group 2

1 No job losses.
2 More safety awareness.
3 Set training programme/enough slack to allow full training.
4 Better communication/less complex channels.
5 Clear picture of the whole operation.
6 Better working environment.
7 Career development/let experience and performance count.

Selecting the 'best option'

8 Open to change/willing to learn.
9 More responsibility/accountability shared/more variety of tasks.
10 Financial recognition.
11 Better grading system/fewer grades/easier vertical movement.

Evaluation criteria from Group 3
(All items in the terms of reference of the study, see pages 87–8)

1 Ensure no job losses.
2 Provide sufficient incentives/financial rewards in line with job development.
3 Acceptable to all levels of trade unions.
4 Ensure the continuity of supply of the right people, i.e. apprentices/SPTs – college/day release.
5 More formal training on (new) equipment previously put out to contract.
6 More say in planning/scheduling consultation at all levels involved, i.e. local control to maximize availability of equipment.
7 Improve quality of planning (i.e. pack spec./changeovers).
8 Must cope with two populations.

These three lists were then brought together to form a single list of criteria for the evaluation of the options.

1 Must be a team-based organization within a manufacturing centre structure.
2 Must demonstrate cost benefits to the business.
3 Must cater for all existing staff, including those who do not feel able to take on new skills, and remove the need for downgrading.
4 Must be built upon the principles within the Site Charter.
5 High standards of customer service, quality and safety must be maintained and should be even further improved.
6 Should encourage individuals to increase the variety of their skills to the limit of their ability.
7 Must create a clear view of team objectives.
8 Teams should have responsibility and the skills and facilities to respond to at least day-to-day situations.
9 Teams must have the information they need, e.g. performance against schedule, quality, safety etc.
10 Structure must help communication between team members, support groups and management.
11 Should be compatible with a training/payment system that encourages individuals to develop through the business by learning new skills.

12 Teams should be responsible for, or at least have influence in, scheduling their own work.
13 Structure should encourage staff involvement.
14 Team should have all the relevant skills and resources it needs to achieve its objectives.
15 Team must have enough resource to allow training to be an integral part of team activity.
16 Teams should be responsible for their own output in terms of quality, customer service and cost and should apply appropriate controls to ensure this.
17 Activities inconsistent with or not directly related to a particular team objective should not be based in that team.

Eleven of these criteria (Nos 1, 3, 4, 6, 8, 10, 12, 14, 15, 16 and 17) have a direct input into the design of the physical structure of the new jobs and organization.

Example 2. Creating a future for engineering on site

Again this example was used earlier and produced the following evaluation criteria as a part of the effort to develop an improved engineering department on the site.

1 Flat structure

1 Department team, product-based.
2 Team has authority to act/react to the day-to-day situation.
3 Holds and develops own budget.
4 Information available directly at individual/team level.

2 Multi-skilled individuals/teams

5 Team has the ability to handle most day-to-day decisions/actions.
6 Acquisition of skills and knowledge through evolutionary means.
7 Resources within the team to allow training to proceed successfully.
8 Competence of existing people/achievable with existing people.
9 Individuals are accountable for their actions.
10 Consistent with company and national safety standards.
11 Training to national standards where possible and appropriate.

3 Production – maintenance partnership

12 Integrated/joint management structure.

Selecting the 'best option'

13 Common targets/purposes.
14 Equal opportunities for career progression and rewards.

4 Focus on improvement

15 Skills and knowledge in team relevant to improving day-to-day activities at least to specification level, and a budget to support them.
16 Provides time for increased resources to be devoted to improvement work.

5/6 Workable demarcations/jobs and teams operate to TAS principles

17 Individuals work to TAS principles irrespective of current job or role (TAS = time, ability and safety).

7 Production/manufacturing centre orientation

18 Project skills and knowledge integrated into manufacturing centre teams.
19 Mobility between teams (between manufacturing centres) for cover within a manufacturing centre and on a planned basis (collective learning).

8 Minimal direct supervision

20 Ownership of clear goals and objectives.
21 Clearly defined and understood team and individual roles.

9 Maintains high level of skills, standards and motivation

22 Retention of specialisms.
23 Retention and transfer of learning between teams to maintain engineering standards.

10 Precludes waste of time and talent

24 Mechanism/structure to avoid duplication of work.
25 All changes in role and structure can be achieved broadly within existing numbers.

11 Supportive reward structure

26 Fair and consistent application of any rewards system across and within teams.

Example 3. Organizing for manufacturing excellence

In this case the evaluation criteria developed reflect the nature of the study in that the study was concerned with establishing a broad indication of the appropriate team and job structures across three manufacturing sites. The criteria which were developed are mainly concerned with outputs rather than with content or input.

1. Raise plant productivity/availability/utilization.
2. Maintain and improve on quality.
3. Improve customer service levels.
4. Cope with unforeseen changes.
5. Provide meaningful jobs.
6. Achievable with existing people.
7. Achievable within a reasonable time period.
8. Minimize safety risk.
9. Implications for industrial relations.
10. Revenue cost implications.

These are far more remote criteria in organization terms than the previous two examples because of the terms of reference of the respective studies.

Example 4. 'Towards 2000 – An Engineering Challenge'

This example is based on a study to generate proposals to change the roles of engineering and operator jobs. For one of these roles, engineering, the following terms of reference were adopted:

1. To examine the existing practices within the works, highlighting where inefficiencies are created due to the lack of flexibility. This can be within the craft and process areas or between the two.
2. To propose how improvements can be made, specifying the effect on numbers and defining the potential savings.
3. Based on 2, to propose outline training programmes and indicate the order of cost.
4. To propose a programme of consultation, training and implementation.
5. To indicate how further steps towards the ultimate goal should be managed.

In fulfilling these terms of reference the management study team developed the following criteria for evaluation of the three options and the current situation.

Selecting the 'best option'

1. Minimize trade demarcations.
2. Merge electrical/instrument operation (technology driven).
3. Reduce the engineering hours budget.
4. Be acceptable to the statutory bodies.
5. Develop joint commitment at local level.
6. Maximize existing engineering abilities.
7. Able to react to change.
8. Provide a meaningful job.
9. Retention of trainees (likely to be achieved with proposed rewards package).
10. Training (ease and cost).
11. National recognition for training.
12. Supportive of area team development.
13. Permits inter-company transferability of labour.
14. Training materials readily available.

Step 2. Sorting and weighting of the evaluation criteria

Having established the evaluation criteria it is then necessary to sort them in terms of 'musts' and 'wants': what must the new organization and jobs achieve, and what would it be 'nice' for the new organization and jobs to achieve?

Here there are no specific rules other than to say that the evaluation criteria must reflect the terms of reference, the purpose of the new organization and jobs, remove the weaknesses, minimize the threats, and build upon the strengths and opportunities. The four examples used in the previous step serve to illustrate how this step can be tackled.

Example 1. Being in front – developing the most competitive means of manufacturing

From the initial list of seventeen evaluation criteria, nine were agreed within the group as being the most important, which any new organization must satisfy:

1. Must be a team-based organization within a manufacturing centre structure.
2. Must demonstrate cost benefits to the business.
3. Must cater for all existing staff, including those who do not feel able to take on new skills, and so remove the need for downgrading.
4. Must be built upon the principles within the Site Charter.

5 High standards of customer service, quality and safety must be maintained and should be even further improved.
6 Must create a clear view of team objectives.
7 Teams must have the information they need, e.g. performance against budget, quality, safety etc.
8 Structure must help communication between team members, support groups and management.
9 Teams must have enough resource to allow training to be an integral part of the team's activity.

It was felt by the group that these nine criteria, if satisfied, would yield the organization that they required and that it would be more efficient than their existing structure.

In this case, weighting was done on a personal basis, i.e. each member of the study group ranked the evaluation criteria in terms of importance; this ranking was later used in scoring the various options.

Example 2. Creating a future for engineering on site

In this the whole group discussed the initial 26 evaluation criteria and derived the following list of 'musts':

1 Department team, product-based.
2 Team has authority to act/react to day-to-day situations.
3 Team has ability to handle most day-to-day decisions/actions.
4 Resources available within team to allow training to proceed successfully.
5 Consistent with company and national safety standards.
6 Common purpose/targets.
7 Equal opportunities for career progression and awards.
8 Provides time for increased resources to be devoted to improvement work.
9 Ownership of clear goals and objectives.
10 All changes can be achieved broadly with existing numbers.
11 Fair and consistent rewards system.
12 Retention and transfer of learning between teams to maintain engineering standards.

It was these twelve evaluation criteria which would lead to an appropriate new engineering organization. Note here that evaluation criteria were generated in most of the key areas required for the design of an organization, e.g. structure, jobs, interdepartmental relationships, orientation, rewards etc. (see Table 7.1).

Selecting the 'best option'

Example 3. Organizing for manufacturing excellence

In this company-wide project the evaluation criteria were split into two parts – objectives of the new organization and constraints to the implementation of the new organization – and ranked as follows.

1 *Evaluation criteria – objectives*	*Weight*
(a) Line productivity/availability/utilization	10
(b) Quality	10
(c) Customer service	10
(d) Provide meaningful jobs	8
(e) Cope with unforeseen changes	6

2 *Evaluation criteria – constraints*	*Weight*
(a) Industrial relations implications	9
(b) Achievable with existing people	7
(c) Safety risk	4
(d) Revenue cost implication	3
(e) Time period	1

This example explicitly introduces the idea of implementation at this stage of the work. It is necessary to adopt a 'step forward–step back' approach, i.e. an iterative approach where each step forward has a retrospective effect on the previous step. The introduction of implementation into the evaluation criteria also raises the possibility that selection of the ideal option might not be based on the cost, time-scale, risks etc. of its introduction.

Example 4. 'Towards 2000 – An Engineering Challenge'

In this case only four 'musts' were established and these were seen of equal importance:

1 Minimize trade demarcation.
2 Merge electrical/instrument operation.
3 Reduce engineering hours.
4 Acceptance by the statutory bodies.

A further fourteen evaluation criteria were then put into a 'wants' list and weighted as follows:

Evaluation criteria   *Weight*
1. Reduce engineering hours to 500,000 by 1990 — 10
2. Develop joint commitment at local level — 9
3. Training (ease and cost) — 9
4. Maximum trade union acceptability at national level — 8
5. Reward criteria to the company — 8
6. Area team development — 7
7. Ability to react to change — 6
8. Meaningful job — 6
9. Maximize existing engineering abilities — 5
10. Reward criteria to the staff/retain trainees — 5
11. Training availability — 3
12. Single site negotiation — 2
13. National recognition of training (ability to obtain) — 2
14. Inter-company transferability — 1

These criteria were then applied to the four options under consideration.

Step 3. Applying the evaluation criteria

Having generated the evaluation criteria and weighted them, they can be applied to the various options being evaluated.

Example 1. Being in front – developing the most competitive means of manufacturing

First it is necessary to identify the current situation and alternative options, and their potential advantages and disadvantages. Each option must be fully understood before they can be evaluated. In this example, in addition to the current situation, three alternatives were developed. Each of these four possible options is now briefly described.

The current situation (see Figure 7.1)

In the early stages of this study the issues raised by the existing structure were assessed as strengths, weaknesses, opportunities and threats.

Strengths of people
    Committed/cooperative/loyal.
    Willing to learn.
    Skilled.

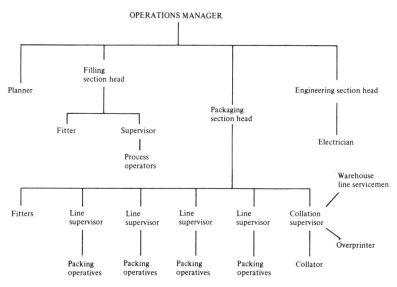

Figure 7.1 *The current situation*

Openminded.
Hard-working.
Confident.
Open to change.

Weaknesses of existing organization
Two populations, i.e. those looking for change and those reluctant to change.
Insufficient training.
Communication poor – too many channels.
Career development limited.
High absence level.
No incentives.
Promotion within/over-related to qualifications.
Boredom.
Friction.

Opportunities
Promotion/development.
Recognition.
Company commitment and cash.
Rewards.
Greater role/part in the operation.
Meet people.

Greater job satisfaction.
Better working environment.

Threats
Reluctant to change.
Might not get the rewards.
Down-grading.
Job losses.
Lack of interest.
Pressured in too short a time to change.
Too much responsibility in the wrong place.
Trained people leave.

Option 1. Product-based teams (see Figure 7.2)

Basis of design: each team comprises the staff and skills needed to take total responsibility for a single product range. This divides all work between two teams, with additional input from a technical support team. The tasks of the following performers are carried out by these teams:

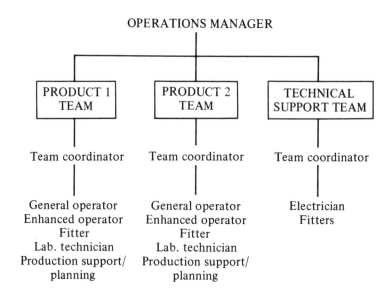

Figure 7.2 *Product-based teams*

Filling operator.
Packaging operator.
Collation.
Line supervisor.
Section head.
Collation supervisor.
Fitter.
Lab. technician.
IPC assistant.
Filling supervisor.
Planner.
Warehouse/stores.
Line serviceman.
Overprinter.
Cleaner.

A degree of overlap between roles is assumed in these teams.

Advantages
1 Total variety of tasks covered.
2 Would cater for all existing staff (including those not looking for future development).
3 Teams would have good identity with product/market.
4 Would promote a good understanding of the whole process.
5 Teams self-contained with a long-term view of the business.
6 Would allow development of individuals.
7 Specialized one-product groups.
8 Less downtime for product changeovers.
9 Would reduce risk of cross-contamination or rogues.
10 Teams would have a greater control of resources for improvement work.
11 Greater pay progression opportunities.
12 Lab. would become part of operation – improved communications.

Disadvantages
1 Teams could not cope with volume fluctuations on one product.
2 Teams would have no knowledge of other products.
3 Existing health problems could make this option unacceptable.
4 Possibly too many roles within team.
5 Would be a reluctance of staff to move to other areas.

Option 2. Fill/pack teams (see Figure 7.3)

Basis of design: each team has one filling line and two packaging lines. The teams comprise the skills necessary to run the lines and supply the lines with materials. Some degree of overlap is assumed between roles within the teams.

Team responsibility A
Improvement work.
Project work.

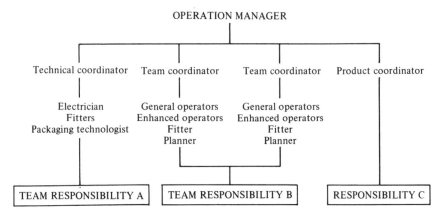

Figure 7.3 *Fill/pack teams*

Technical assistance to team.
Problem solving.
Back-up resource.
Development of new equipment/packs.
Validation work.
Plant maintenance.
Safety monitoring.

Team responsibility B
Line maintenance and repair.
Manufacturing.
Planning/scheduling own work.
Liaison with product coordinator.
Ordering/collating own materials.
Overprinting off-line.
In-process control.
Sampling.
Housekeeping.
Quality.
Output.
Financial performance.
Safety monitoring.

Responsibility C
Customer liaison.
Long-term planning.
Allocation of orders to teams.
Stock control of home packs.
Inventory policy.

Advantages
1. Would enable teams to cover wide variety of tasks.
2. Greater knowledge of product.
3. Would allow personal development within the teams.
4. Would cater for all existing staff, including those not looking for future development.
5. Would encourage flexibility.
6. Self-contained teams with medium-term view of business (long-term view held by product coordinator).
7. Teams would have full picture of the process.
8. Should increase line efficiency.
9. Would create considerable development opportunity for staff.
10. Teams would retain knowledge of whole product range.

Disadvantages
1. Possibly too many individual roles within each team.
2. Team objective could become clouded by the number of individual roles.
3. Team structure would be biased towards packaging possibly at expense of filling.
4. Possibly not enough staff to release for the training that would be necessary.
5. Development opportunities not equally shared.
6. Lab. would remain isolated.
7. Reluctance of staff to move to other areas.

Option 3. Lab./fill – Pack/plan teams (see Figure 7.4)

Basis of design:

1. The aims of the filling section are different from those of the packaging section.
2. Product filling/packaging should not be viewed as one operation.
   (a) There is an imposed 1 month delay between fill and pack.
   (b) Cans are not filled to a packing order but to a weekly demand against stock level.
3. The aims of the filling section are closely related to those of the product lab., i.e. supply of filled cans for subsequent packaging (very little lab. work on packed material).
4. Filling section is just another supplier to packaging.
5. The new facility offers opportunity to bring lab. role nearer to production.

A degree of overlap is assumed within the teams.

210 Changing Job Structures

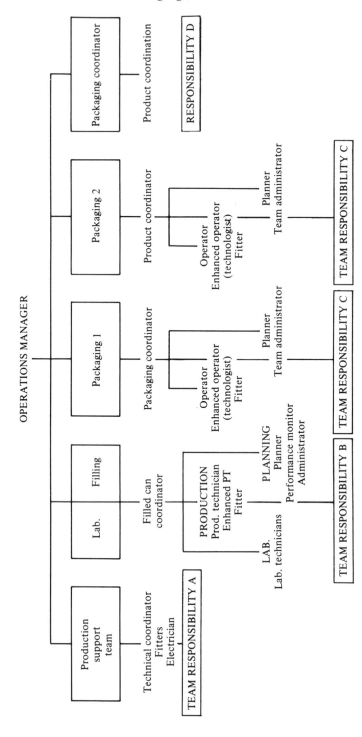

Figure 7.4 *Lab./fill and pack/plan teams*

Team responsibility A
  Improvement work.
  Project work.
  Technical assistance to team.
  Problem solving.
  Back-up resource.
  Development of new equipment/packs.
  Validation.
  Plant maintenance.
  Safety monitoring.

Team responsibility B
  Running filling line.
  Manufacturing batch.
  Line maintenance and repair.
  Scheduling.
  Liaison with pack coordinators.
  Ordering materials.
  In-process control.
  Sampling.
  Housekeeping.
  Quality.
  Matching output to schedule.
  Financial performance.
  Safety.
  Testing of filled cans.

Team responsibility C
  Running packaging.
  Line maintenance and repair.
  Planning and scheduling own work.
  Liaison with product coordinator.
  Ordering and collating own material.
  In-process control.
  Sampling.
  Housekeeping.
  Quality.
  Matching output to schedule.
  Financial performance.
  Safety.
  Handling of packaging.
  Materials problems including liaison with supplies.
  Department/component suppliers.
  Overprinting.

Responsibility D
    Customer liaison.
    Long-term plan.
    Allocation of orders to packaging teams.
    Stock control of home stocks.
    Inventory policy.
    Packaging administration.

Note. Responsibility of main stores could be extended to cover actuator dispensing. Housekeeping responsibility stays with team but other cleaning tasks migh be better covered by staff in a hygiene team, e.g. polishing floors, cleaning offices, walls and partitions etc.

Advantages
1. Clear view of team objectives.
2. Would allow team to concentrate on their objectives.
3. Wide variety of tasks covered by each team.
4. Will create opportunity for individual development within the teams.
5. Would cater for all existing staff, including those not looking for future development.
6. Creates specialism in packaging area and therefore new development opportunities for packaging operators.
7. Opportunity for filling/lab. development moves.
8. Would raise responsibility of filling technician role – would create opportunity for lab. staff to gain production experience.
9. Self-contained teams with a medium-term view of business (long-term view held by product coordinator).
10. Better control of process.

Disadvantages
1. Part of the lab. testing happens several weeks after testing.
2. Would reduce opportunity for packaging operators moving into filling and the laboratory unless moves out of team can be arranged.
3. Would reduce team view of entire operation.

Evaluation of the options

The options were evaluated by individual study group members, and the resulting scores were collated. Table 7.2 gives an example of such an exercise. The result of the exercise undertaken by the study group was the selection of Option 3.

Table 7.2 *Evaluation of options against design criteria*

Criterion	Ranking	Option 1	Option 2	Option 3
Team-based organization	5	689	753	847
Cater for all existing staff	1	1176	1140	1270
Cost benefits to business	2	–	–	–
Built within Site Charter	4	652	613	750
Service/quality/safety maintained	8	428	514	703
Allow individuals to increase skill variety	9	587	416	601
Clear team objective	3	742	710	867
Give team responsibility for day-to-day situations	14	305	252	357
Supply teams with information	11	660	543	607
Improve communications	6	723	567	750
Training/payment to encourage individual development	10	506	502	652
Team schedules own work	15	295	305	384
Encourage staff involvement	12	409	401	478
Teams have skills and resource needed	13	336	388	498
Training integral part of team	7	492	412	663
Team responsible for own output	16	186	171	233
Total		8816	7687	9677
		2nd	3rd	1st

Example 2. 'Towards 2000 – An Engineering Challenge'

A number of possible alternative methods were available to increase the efficiency of the site's engineering workforce.

1 *Retain the present situation.* Maintain the present single-skill status operating within the craft workforce.
2 *Introduce dual skills.* Combine those craft groups which have core skills of a similar nature, e.g. electrical and instrument, pipefitter and welder, fitter and machinist.

3 *Introduce a flexible craft system*. Combine all current craft groups ensuring that, in addition to the core skills of their own craft, employees obtain the basic skills applicable to other crafts.
4 *Introduce multi-skilling*. In addition to obtaining the basic skills in the craft range, the employee is trained in process technology in order that he may be utilized in the process sphere.

Between the introduction of dual skilling and that of the flexible craftsman lie other alternatives, e.g. craft groupings – fitter group (comprising fitters, pipefitters, riggers etc.); power and control group (comprising electricians and instrument mechanics); fabricator group (comprising sheet metal worker, welder and leadburner). Combinations such as these, intermediates between dual skilling and a flexible craft system, were not considered in any detail.

Which of these alternatives is selected depends, primarily, upon the cost and efficiency benefits to the company and, secondly, on the ability of the alternative to allow further steps to be taken towards the establishment of a fully multi-skilled workforce.

In order to evaluate each of the above alternatives, the Kepner Tregoe Decisions Analysis technique was utilized (Kepner Tregoe Ltd, Windsor, Berkshire, UK). This process, by defining the required objective, allows a clear focus on the results to be achieved and the resources to be used to achieve them, while providing a criterion for evaluation of the alternatives.

The boundaries of the exercise, defined in the brief, were to highlight inefficiencies in, and to propose improvements to, the method of operation of the site engineering workforce. The following decision statement was, therefore, used to define the objective: 'To select the most effective means for improving the utilization of the site engineering workforce'. Details of the resulting decisions analysis are shown in Table 7.3.

When considering the alternatives against objectives mandatory for the success of the decision it will be seen that 'Stay as you are' is rejected. Each of the remaining alternatives was then examined against objectives considered desirable for the success of the decision, these objectives being weighted according to importance.

As a result of this further analysis it is apparent that the introduction of a flexible craft system most closely meets the requirements of the decision statement.

The possible adverse consequences of implementing each alternative were then examined (Table 7.4). It can be seen that while the introduction of flexible craft status and of multi-skilling have similar consequences, the latter is considered to present additional difficulties in respect of both recruitment and the on-going training cost.

Step 4. Estimating the benefits

First it is necessary to identify where benefits might be gained and how they can be assessed. As regards manufacturing, increased line output and productivity would accrue from any of the following results:

1 Reduced task duplication.
2 Reduced changeover times.
3 Reduced breakdown waiting times.
4 Shorter communication lines.
5 Improved job performance.
6 Raised familiarity with the equipment.
7 Greater motivation for improvements.
8 Reduced wasted/dead time.
9 Reduced product wastage.
10 Increased awareness of performance.
11 Sustaining the benefits.
12 Getting the best from new equipment.
13 Reduced validation and commissioning costs.
14 Increased running times.
15 Increased machine capacity.
16 Reduced capital expenditure.

The following seven changes would reduce lead times:

1 Shorter time to process orders.
2 Faster throughput times.
3 Eliminate quality control/inspection delays.
4 Eliminate off-line production activities.
5 Reduce work-in-progress levels.
6 Increase capacities/scheduling buffers.
7 Increase available machine capacities.

Let us now apply these ideas by means of an example.

Example 1. Organizing for manufacturing excellence

The benefits from the new organization were categorized as direct and indirect, as outlined below.

The direct benefits were those which resulted from the creation of the new roles of team leader, technical and general operators with broader

Table 7.3 Decision statement: selection of the most effective means for improving the utilization of the engineering workforce

Objectives	Alternative choices				
	Stay as you are	Dual skill	Flexible craft		Multi-skill
MUSTS					
1 Minimize trade demarcation	No go This is not possible with current pay and attitude	Go Very limited impact	Go Considerable impact		Go Most impact on site overall operation
2 Merge E/I operation (technology driven)	No go	Go EETPU driven	Go EETPU driven plus additional skills		Go EETPU driven plus additional skills impacting on process operation
3 Reduce engineering hours	Go Reduce O/T as current	Go Useful contribution	Go Very considerable impact. Reduce waiting time		Go Most effective means by using spare production hours
4 Acceptance by statutory bodies	Go Current practice	Go Current practice in some companies	Go Current practice in some companies. May require further capital investment		Go Limited external experience. No more than five UK sites in the processing industry
WANTS	Weight	Score Weight Total score	Score Weight Total score		Score Weight Total Score
1 Reduce engineering hours to 500,000 by 1990 (direct contribution employees only)	10	3 30 90 Limited effect 12 to 15% of target	10 100 1000 Training need obtainable within time constraints		7 70 490 Additional advantages Further training need × factor of 4
2 Maximum trade union acceptability at national level	8	7 56 392 Union driven at national level	6 48 258 Some movement by AEU greater EETPU		3 24 72 Green field site. No problem. Established sites under extreme threat only
3 Develop joint commitment at local level	9	4 36 144 This is seen as similar to national level	8 72 576 Maintains engineering cohesion		6 54 324 Seen as a dilution of engineering skill

#	Criterion	N	Proposed practice			Added (Single group)			Added (Single group larger number)		
5	Single site negotiation	2	1	2	Little movement	7	14	Single group	7	14	Single group larger number
6	Ability to react to change	6	2	12	Effect mainly in the E/I area	6	36	Greater perception of engineering objectives	8	48	Greater perception of overall objectives
7	Meaningful job	6	2	12	Little change	9	54	Challenging job	8	48	May be viewed as a skills dilution
8	Reward criteria – staff (retain trainees)	5	2	10	Minimal benefit	7	35	Additional responsibility. Need for retention	9	45	Full flexibility. Very marketable.
9	Reward criteria – company	8	2	16	Minimal benefit	9	72	Greatest use of engineering workforce. Short timescale	9	72	Benefits as flexible craft but timescale much longer
10	Training (ease and cost)	9	9	81	Easiest	4	36	Train all engineering craft (250)	2	18	Train all engineering and prod.
11	National recognition of training (ability to obtain)	2	9	18	Existing	6	12	Require negotiation with City & Guilds	6	12	Require negotiation with City & Guilds
12	Area team development	7	2	14	Relates to E/I and fabrication	9	63	Engineering related	10	70	Complete team situation
13	Inter-company transferability	1	10	10	Common practice	7	7	Similar engineering basis	6	6	Fine tuning of process needs
14	Training availability	3	10	30	All in-house	5	15	External requirement built on technical base	2	6	External requirement. Previous experience extremely limited
	Total	337		2057			614	4964		532	4066

Table 7.4 Adverse consequences of implementation

Dual skill	P	S	Flexible craft	P	S	Multi-skill	P	S
Demarcation between groups could increase	H	H	Dilution of core skill	L	M	Dilution of core skill	M	M
Low reward structure for participants	H	M	Marketable operative	M	M	Marketable operative	L	M
Pairing of non-craft group leading to increased industrial muscle	H	M	Inability to recruit locally	H	L	Inability to recruit locally	H	M
Sustains general worker concept	M	L	On-going training cost	H	L	High on-going training cost	H	M
Overtime not reduced	M	M	Off-the-job training block release	H	L	Off-the-job training block release	H	L
Revert to original skill base	L	M	Revert to original skill base	L	M	Revert to original skill base	L	H
			Increased use of specialist labour	H	L	Increased use of specialist labour	H	L

P = probability.
S = seriousness (impact).
L, M, H = low, medium, high.

Selecting the 'best option' 219

skill levels, greater expertise, effectiveness and flexibility. These benefits accrued primarily in the areas of productivity and reduced factory lead times.

In addition to the direct financial benefits, significant indirect financial benefits arose from increased capacity, reduced factory lead times and the enhanced computer systems required to support the new structure (these benefits, once identified, can be 'costed'). Although the indirect gains were considerable, no financial claims were included as part of this study.

Direct benefits from the new organization

1 Productivity – more effective and efficient production

  (a) Increased line output
      Improved machine performance.
      Reduced changeover time.
      Reduced breakdown waiting time.
      Improved material conversion/reduced wastage.

  (b) Reduced supervisor/management structure
      Reduction in levels of hierarchy.
      Shorter communication channels.
      Elimination of duplicate checks.
      Greater responsibility/job satisfaction/commitment at operating level.

  (c) Integration of engineering into operating role
      Elimination of general fitter role – staff reduction.
      Elimination of organization/supervision of general fitters.
      Greater familiarity/more rapid fault recognition on equipment.
      More rapid fault diagnosis.

  (d) Integration of in-process QA into operating role
      Elimination of in-process QA inspectors – staff reduction.
      Elimination of organizational supervisors of QA inspectors.
      Greater operator responsibility for QA – improved QA standards.

  (e) Greater operating performance awareness
      Greater motivation for performance improvement.
      More rapid identification of performance inhibitors.
      Maximize and sustain benefits of productivity improvement.
      Maximize and sustain benefits of capital investment.

2 Improved customer service and competitiveness resulting from reduced factory lead times through:

(a) Increased line output
   Increased machine running times.
(b) Shorter planning/material processing times
   Integration of these functions into the manufacturing centres.
(c) Faster production throughput times
   Faster changeovers and elimination of engineering waiting time.
(d) Elimination of delays from in-process QA testing
   Having a larger pool of more technically competent operators.
(e) Increase in available machine capacity
   More efficient equipment utilization.

3 Reductions in raw material, work-in-progress and finished goods inventories.
   Reduced factory throughput times.

Indirect benefits from the new organization

1 Reduced capital expenditure
   The resultant increase in capacity will delay or, in some cases, remove the need for capital expenditure to meet potential volume changes.

2 Increased workload
   Reduced product costs and factory lead times could attract additional workload to existing factories.

3 Inventory
   In addition to the direct inventory reduction, there will be further inventory savings as a consequence of improved material conversion and reduced wastage.

4 Enhanced support system
   Maximizing productive output from operators, while removing supervisory levels, requires the provision of accurate, 'real-time', user-friendly systems, particularly at the operating level.

5 Simplification and computerization of process documentation
   Reduced operator time in documentation/recording.
   Better understanding of process requirements and instructions.
   Reduced time in preparation for batch processing.
   Greater flexibility and simplicity in updating/modifying procedures.
   Greater accuracy in data recorded.

6 Improved planning and scheduling system
   More efficient use of labour and production resources.

Greater ability to smooth production loads.
Earlier recognition of labour over- or underloads.
Reduction in line changeovers.
Greater accuracy in measurement of capacity utilization.
Greater accuracy in assessing new capacity requirements.

7 Improved material usage information for operators and managers
Greater awareness and motivation for improvement.
More rapid attention to performance problems.
Reduction in material wastage.
Better data to assess capital expenditure requirements.
More accurate batch/product costing.

8 Improved labour recording
Greater accuracy in labour usage analysis.
More rapid identification of areas for improvement.
Better identification of batch and support labour requirements.
More accurate linking of staff to specific operations.
More accurate batch/product costing.
Automatic absence and holiday monitoring.

9 Improved equipment performance monitoring
More accurate machine downtime analysis.
More rapid identification of recurring problems.
More rapid identification of specific machine bottlenecks.
Better justification for machinery replacements.
Assistance in future machine selection.
Automatic monitoring of maintenance schedules.

Direct financial gains from reorganization

As productivity gains relate to savings in direct labour requirements, it is necessary to define the labour pool affected. The 'production associated labour' was defined as the staff affected by the proposed reorganization, i.e. current production staff and production-associated engineering and QA staff:

Site A	840
Site B	510
Site C	190
	1540 staff in total

1 Productivity – more effective and efficient production

(a) Increased line output
  (i) Improved machine performance
    The improved performance on this parameter was quantified by a survey of 13 external production sites, which had previously implemented a similar reorganization of operating roles. The main benefits noted on these sites were as follows:
      Resolution of frequent stoppages.
      Long-term rectification of packaging material faults.
      Running equipment consistently at design speeds.
      Improved production start time adherence.
      Improved production finish time adherence.

    The performance improvement found across the thirteen sites was as follows:

    Range   5–65%
    Mean   18.5% (see Table 7.5)

    However, for costing purposes only a 10 per cent performance improvement was assumed.

10% reduction in production-associated staff (1540)	154 staff
154 staff at a total remuneration cost of £16,000 each	£2.5m
Therefore 10% performance improvement	**£2.5m**

  (ii) Reduced changeover time.
  (iii) Reduced breakdown waiting time (see Table 7.6).
    The task analysis data generated on all three sites showed that the performance improvements achievable on these parameters together accounted for a further 1.5 per cent.

1.5% reduction in production-associated staff (1540)	23 staff
23 staff at a total remuneration cost of £16,000 each	£0.4m
Therefore 1.5% performance improvement	**£0.4m**

Table 7.5 *Improved machine performance – external evidence of 'held' gains*

Site[1]	No. of employees	Gains	Time period of measurement
1	1700	20%	3 years
2	2200	14%	4 years
3	340	10%	3½ days
4	1750	44%	6 years
5	345	18%	3 years
6	750	10%[2]	3½ years
7	2000	15%[3]	4½ years
8	475	32.5%[4]	4 years
9	625	12%	2½ years
10	700	19%	5 years
11	495	28%	2½ years
12	500	15%	3 years
13	295	15%	3 years

[1] All sites operate a minimum of ten filling/packaging lines.
[2] Range 5–15%.
[3] Range 10–30%.
[4] Range 20–65%.

Sources of main gains
 Adherence to start times.
 Adherence to finish times.
 Reduced number of frequent stoppages.
 Long-term rectification of packaging material faults.
 Reduced changeover times, but increased frequency of changeovers.
 Increased predictability of both plant/line availability and consistent achievement of design run speeds.
 Range of improvements   5–65%.
 Average improvements made   18.50%.

(iv) Improved material conversion/reduced wastage.
 Current wastage costs across three sites were £11m per annum. Recent work study exercises at one site had reduced wastage by 37 per cent.
 Improved responsibility, accountability and machinery and pro-

Table 7.6 Impact of the preferred model on line downtime – examples of events quantified by work study exercises at two of the study sites

Fault	Percentage time lost (work study data)	How resolved – Existing organization and job roles	How resolved – New organization and job roles	Estimated effects
SITE 1				
Batch/order changes	3.1	Undertaken by QA/Production/ Engineering/Supervision	Undertaken by technical and general operators	Reduced by 75%: whole team utilized, without need for outside support. Waiting time eliminated
Cartonner/labeller minor stoppages	10.6	Resolved by Production and/or Engineering. Root cause often remains	Undertaken by technical and general operators	Reduced by 50%: better trained, multi-skilled operators with enhanced equipment understanding and commitment to performance improvement
Major breakdown Infrequent but can cause long delays		Fault cause often unknown. Production/Engineering Supervision identify craft required prior to resolution	Problem identified by technical operators. Assistance sought of the specialist engineer from Technical Support	Reduced lines of communication leading to quicker response to and rectification of problems by more specialized technicians

SITE 2				
Start-up/clean-down	7.6	Undertaken by IPC/QA/Engineering (electrical/mechanical)/Production/Supervisors	Undertaken by technical and general operators	Reduced by 50%+ by utilizing whole team without the need for outside support
Await engineer	3.7	Line stopped awaiting engineer – whole team idle	Eliminated except for D of D6 work[1]	Faults up to D of D5 (approx. 90%) rectified by technical or general operator. No waiting time
Vials fall over	3.0	Often tolerated. Engineering involvement requested when incidence becomes excessive	Adjustment by technical or general operator	Reduced by 50%. Better trained, multi-skilled operators with enhanced equipment understanding and commitment to performance improvement

[1] D of D indicates 'Degree of difficulty' rating

cess skills were expected to reduce material losses by at least 15 per cent across all sites.

Therefore 15% saving on £11m	**£1.6m**
Total savings from increased line output	**£4.5m**

(b) Reduced supervisory/management structure
Task analysis data was examined to determine the labour savings from within the current production departments achievable by raising the responsibility level of operators and eliminating superfluous levels of hierarchy and cross-checking. The data from the three sites confirmed a labour saving of 2 per cent in production-associated staff.

2% reduction in production-associated staff (1540)	31 staff
31 staff at a total remuneration cost of £16,000 each	£0.5m
Therefore 2% staff reduction	**£0.5m**

(c) Integration of engineering into operating role
Task analysis data was examined to determine the savings from reduction in minor stoppages, more rapid fault diagnosis and elimination of the current independent role of a fitter/engineer with supervisory support. The data from the three sites confirmed a productivity improvement of 3.5 per cent.

3.5% reduction in production-associated staff (1540)	54 staff
54 staff at a total remuneration cost of £16,000 each	£0.9m
Therefore 3.5% productivity improvement	**£0.9m**

(d) Integration of QA into operating role
Task analysis data was examined to determine the savings from eliminating the existing duplication of in-process control checks by, in future, having operators conduct all required IPC checks themselves during processing. Also there would be a significant saving from eliminating separate IPC personnel and their supervisory hierarchy. The task analysis data from the three sites confirmed a productivity improvement of 3 per cent.

Selecting the 'best option'

3% reduction in production-associated staff (1540)	46 staff
46 staff at a total remuneration cost of £16,000 each	£0.8m
Therefore 3% productivity improvement	**£0.8m**

(e) Greater operating performance awareness

Greater responsibility, accountability and skills at operator level would enhance performance, particularly in sustaining the benefits of improved performance from new equipment. Previous work study data indicated that after initial new equipment installation, performance generally reduced with normal running. However, with a dedicated team approach, enhanced performance was maintained at a much higher level. Available data indicated that the productivity improvement equated to 3 per cent overall.

3% reduction in production-associated staff (1540)	46 staff
46 staff at a total remuneration of £16,000 each	£0.8m
3% productivity improvement	**£0.8m**

2 Improved customer service and competitiveness through reduced factory lead times

The overall gains can be summarized and costed through reductions in raw material, work-in-progress and finished goods inventory because of shorter factory lead times.

The reduction in inventory levels which would accrue from the operational reorganization was quantified by a study of thirteen other production sites that had already implemented a similar reorganization of operating roles. Inventory reductions found were as follows:

Range	1–18%
Mean	10.9% (see Table 7.7)

For this study a more cautious inventory reduction of 7.5 per cent was assumed.

Total inventory level across all three sites	£37m
7.5% reduction of £37m	£2.8m
Therefore 7.5% inventory saving	**£2.8m**

Table 7.7 *Improved customer service and competitiveness through reduced factory lead times*

External evidence of 'held' gains

Site	No. of employees	Gains	Time period of measurement
1[1]	4500	1%	3½ years
2	675	4%	2 years
3	535	6%	3 years
4	900	10%	4 years
5	500	15%	4 years
6	1050	14%	4 years
7	250	15%	3 years
8	1450	15%	6 years
9	375	12%	3 years
10	1200	11%	4 years
11	1100	12%	3 years
12	850	8%	3½ years
13	500	18%	3 years

[1] Covers 5 sites in all.

Sources of main gains
   Reduced buffer required because of consistently running to design speed and predictable availability.
   Reduced waste of product and packaging raw materials in the ratio of 60:40.
   Long-term improvement in packaging design.
   Reduced warehouse space.
   Reduced work-in-progress/intermediate store levels.

Range of improvements made   1–18%.
Average improvement made   10.85%.

Overall benefits achieved

Site	Work reduction (%)	Source of Savings (%) Direct	Indirect
A	21.5	56	44
B	30.1	46	54
C	26.5	46	54

Sources of main direct benefits
   Reduced breakdown waiting time.
   Reduced fault diagnosis time.

Selecting the 'best option'

Reduced organization levels.
Reduced changeover times.
Sustained performance improvement.
Absorption of minor adjustments.
Removal of duplicate checking.

Sources of main indirect benefits
Improvements in systems.
Set aids/tools for changeovers.
Capital improvement projects raising performance.

No matter what the situation, it is worth listing all of the items that might be improved and then deriving some measure of the magnitude of the improvement. In many cases the task data will provide a major source of information, e.g. tasks transferred between performers, tasks shared between performers, the elimination of some tasks etc. This type of task information can be directly translated into a measure of the potential saving. In the same way a benefits picture can be pieced together for other areas.

Step 5 Estimating the costs

As in estimating the benefits, first it is necessary to list the items which might result in expenditure with the implementation of the new organization and jobs. Such a list might be as follows:

1 Rewards
   Increase in pay.
   Pension/NI increases.
   One-off payments.
   Recurrent payments.
   Overtime cover for trainees.
2 Displacement
   Redundancy.
   Early retirement.
   Community support.
   Training for new career/job.
   Pension enhancement.
   Counselling.
3 Training
   Trainers.
   Materials.

Time of trainees.
Travel and subsistence.
Assessment/monitoring procedures.
4 Communication
Materials (launch).
Materials (on-going).
Time for attending meetings/briefings.
External public relations.
5 Assistance
EEC Social Fund grants.
Training Agency grants.
TEC grants.
6 Process
Change project team
Support infrastructure and services.
External assistance/support.
7 Negotiation
Negotiating team.
Support infrastructure and services.
8 Revenue
Contractors.
Recruitment/screening.
Induction training.
On-going training.
9 Failure/risk
Disruption to production.
Quality of customer service.
Inventory levels.
Alternative production sources.
Loss of potential/momentum due to poor management of changes.
10 Procedures/systems
Appraisal.
Production control and monitoring.
Planning and scheduling.
Quality control.
Standard operating procedures.
Good manufacturing practice.
Display and accessibility of information.
Pay structure development and maintenance.
Career development.
11 Capital
Changed line/plant layout.
Equipment modification.
Physical environment.

Selecting the 'best option'

Tools/equipment for line teams.
Facilities for line teams.

Costs can then be ascribed to each of these items on the basis of experience elsewhere, depending on the time scale and approach adopted.

1 Rewards
   Increase in pay   8–12 per cent
   One-off payments   £100–£150 per head minimum up to £2000–£4000 maximum
   Secondary base rate increases   1½–3 per cent on top of annual pay award
   Overtime for trainee cover   2–3 per cent increase on annual budget

2 Displacement
   Redundancy   £10,000–£12,000 (with enhancement)
   Community support   £1000 per head of those leaving (also related to dominance of local labour market)
   Pension enhancement   £1800 per head of those leaving
   Counselling   £150 per head of those leaving (also provided for those not leaving)

3 Training
   Trainers   About 1 trainer per 15–20 trainees initially dropping to about one trainer per 60–70 trainees after first phase of training
   Training material   £125 per head (population in excess of 750)
   Training (technical)   £3000–£4000 per head (on new, technically advanced plant – all costs)
   Training (organizational)   £1500–£1800 per head (all costs)
   Training budget   2 per cent of CRV of plant and equipment
   Training budget   15–20 per cent project costs (projects worth £20m+ and technically advanced – all costs)
   Training budget   8–10 per cent of labour budget, possibly reducing to about 6 per cent
   Assessment/monitoring system   £50,000 for a full software system

4 Communications
   Materials (launch)   £75,000–£80,000 for sites in excess of 1000 (includes video, booklets etc.)

5 Assistance
   EEC Social Fund grants — Possibly a third of all costs for training see *Paying for Training* (The Planning Exchange, Glasgow, annual publication)
   Training Agency, Training and Enterprise Councils, grants etc.
6 Process
   Change project team (2–4 people per site for about two years from announcement of major changes) — £400,000 (all costs) per year
7 Negotiating
   Negotiating team — Probably full-time for about a year (at least two per bargaining group)
   Support offices — £150–£400 per square foot
8 Revenue
   Contractors — Possibly increase to about 20 per cent of those leaving
   On-going training — About 6 per cent of labour budget

Example 1. Organizing for manufacturing excellence

This is a continuation of the example used to describe the benefits of intoducing a new organization and jobs. Here the costs were divided into three parts: first, a summary of the overall costs; second, the likely training and development costs; and third, the likely management implementation costs.

Costs of the new organization structure

The costs of operational re-organization were split into two main categories, initial implementation costs and annual recurring costs.

1 Initial non-recurring implementation costs
   This covered the main initial investment required to achieve the change, although the expenditure would not all occur in one year, but would be spread across the length of the implementation period.

   (a) *Training*
       The training and development requirements are outlined in detail after this summary of the costs. The costs specified include the full cost of trainers, development of training programmes, materials

and the cost of employing temporary staff to continue operation while permanent staff were released for training programmes.

Total cost of training programme *over 5 years*	£11.5m
Deduct normal training costs over 5 years on three sites	−£3.5m
Net cost of additional training for operational reorganization	**£8.0m**

(b) Communication
This related primarily to initial communication with staff on the background and reasons for the reorganization, both initially and throughout the process of restructuring. It also included external public relations.

   (i) *Materials*
   Preparation of videos, brochures, handouts for initial launch of reorganization programme, also on-going support during implementation

   £1m

   (ii) *Labour*
   Staff and management attendance at initial briefings, working parties, individual counselling etc., also cost of external communication/public relations

   £1.5m

   Total communication cost **£2.5m**

(c) *Management*
Implementation of such a major site-wide reorganization would require considerable input from management at a senior level. It was therefore costed on the basis of a number of full-time management equivalents dedicated to the implementation of this project.

   (i) *Company and site change groups*
   In order to ensure correct implementation on each site, it was envisaged that there will be a requirement for company-wide change groups. This was costed at the equivalent of managers full time for a period of 3 years, with senior manager total remuneration at £50,000 per year.

   Eight managers for 3 years **£1.2m**

(ii) *Union negotiation*
Due to the multiplicity of unions involved, this was assumed to require the equivalent of three senior/middle managers for a period of 1 year full time.

Three senior managers total remuneration cost at £50,000 per year	**£0.2m**

(iii) *Materials*
Support function for managers including material   £0.3m

Total management costs	**£1.7m**

(d) *Labour reduction*
The reorganization would allow a net reduction of 354 staff (23%). However, taking into account the volume-related forecast staff levels on each site over a three-year period, this number would be reduced to 210. Since the existing employee age and service profile would not allow this to be achieved by natural wastage, it would be necessary to develop an early retirement/voluntary redundancy package.

The costs of early retirements and voluntary redundancies were considered to be equivalent for the purposes of this calculation and were based on the terms used previously, inflated to reflect current costs.

Early retirement or voluntary redundancy costed at £21,500 each:

210 staff at £21,500 each	**£4.5m**

2 Annual recurring costs

These are the long-term increased costs resulting from reorganization which would recur annually post-implementation.

(a) Salaries
As a result of reorganization, production-associated staff would be reduced to 1186. However, the remaining staff would have undergone considerable training to become multi-skilled and to operate at a higher level of responsibility and accountability.

It was therefore estimated that the remaining staff would on average receive 10% salary increase for greater flexibility and increased skill levels, in addition to any normal increases.

Average operator total remuneration cost	£16,000

10% increase for 1186 staff costing £16,000 each   £1.9m

(b) Training
Apart from the initial major training exercise to achieve implementation, it was recognized that there would subsequently be a requirement for a much higher level of training to support flexible, more highly-skilled operators. This might well involve technical operator apprenticeship.

Additional training to maintain higher skills   £0.3m

Total annual recurring costs   **£2.2m**

3 *Systems costs*
A number of computer-based systems had been quoted as requirements to support the reorganization. However, the requirement for many of these systems had already been recognized to support current operations, regardless of reorganization.

Several of the systems, computerized process instructors and computer scheduling were already under development. The requirements for improved material and labour usage and machine performance monitoring had already been recognized and would also be required, regardless of the reorganization, e.g. production accounting recording system.

Thus no costs were included in this exercise for development of these systems, nor were benefits from the system included.

Implementation costs: training and development

1 Aims
   (a) To develop individual competencies.
   (b) To develop team working.
   (c) To generate commitment to and understanding of the proposed changes.

2 Key elements
   (a) Thorough analysis of the training needs of all key positions, e.g.:
       Operator.
       Line managers.
       Support technicians.
       Support managers.
   (b) Specification of appropriate training programmes.

(c) Identification of resources required to conduct the training programmes, e.g.:

> Development resources.
> Cover for trainees.
> Training staff (internal).
> Training centre or centres.
> External training consultancy.
> Advice and support.
> Time (anything up to five years) to complete the training programmes, and the commitment of all concerned.

3 Main new roles to be developed
   (a) *Team leader*

   The role of team leader is so different from any technical role that it was considered advisable to train the successful applicant before appointment rather than after. Compared with, say, the training of existing supervisors or section heads there would have to be a quadrupling of management-orientated training for the team leader. The entire recruitment, selection and training period would probably be of the order of one year.

   Initially, most of the team leaders would be drawn from the ranks of supervisors or section heads, which would contain the level of expenditure on training, i.e. mainly conversion training would be required.

   (b) *Technical operator*

   Consideration of the training of the technical operator raised the concept of a 'production apprenticeship' which was likely to last about 2 years. The technical operator would be required to acquire a significant number of complex skills in machine maintenance and repair, quality assurance, problem solving and information processing. The team coordination role would require leadership training over and above the teamwork training given to the general operator.

   Like the general operator, the trainee technical operator would require to be covered during parts of the apprenticeship, but the exact extent and content of the training would depend on the trainee's background. An engineering craftsman, for example, might well take less time to become effective in the new role.

   (c) *General operator*

   General operators would make up the majority of the manufacturing team membership. Compared to existing jobs, the jobholders would need to acquire additional skills, particularly those of minor

machine maintenance or adjustment and product quality checking or sampling. There would be greater emphasis on process and product knowledge, backed up by diagnostic and problem-solving skills. Training in team working also feature strongly in the training programme.

Although none of the learning times for skills acquisition exceeded one month, and many were much less, it remained likely that the total training period for the general operator would be of the order of six months. Not all of this period would be unproductive time; possibly as little as eight weeks would be non-productive time. A considerable trained temporary staffing resource would therefore be required to cover the trainee general operators. Considerable resources would also be required to develop training programmes suited to the new style of operation and organization.

(d) *Costs (over 5-year period)*
   (i) Team leader
       Assumptions:
         145 team leaders.
         50 days training at £60 per day (£3000).
         3 months non-productive time to include on-job training secondment.
         £25,000 p.a. wages costs.

Development costs	£100,000 (non-recurring)
Training per team leader = 145 × £3000	£435,000 (non-recurring)
Team leaders' pay during training, 60 person years × £25,000	£1.5m (non-recurring)
On-going training, probably about 10 days per year	£87,000 p.a. (recurring)

   (ii) Technical operator
       Assumptions:
         450 technical operators (from analysis of task data).
         6 months of the 2-year training period non-productive.

Some of the costs would be contained in the general operator programmer particularly development costs and temporary cover costs. Even so, the running costs could be, say,

450 staff × 6 months non-productive work
 (in training) = 225 person years
225 × £16,000   £3.6m (non-recurring)

(iii) General operator
Assumptions:
880 general operators to be trained, plus, within the 5-year period, 220 other general operator trainees to cover natural wastage; in total, 1100 trainees.
£10,000 p.a. for a temporary member of staff (50 weeks).
8 weeks training to be covered by temporary staff.
One full-time trainer per 50 staff (22 required).
£20,000 wages costs for the full-time trainer.
Temporary cover costs: 1100 staff x 8 weeks = 8800 weeks of training cover = 176 person years.

176 person years × £10,000 p.a.	£1.76m (non-recurring)
Development costs (including material): probably of the order of 50 new programmes at £12,000	£600,000 (non-recurring)

Running costs: full-time operator trainers

22 at £20,000 p.a. = £440,000 p.a.	£2.2m over 5 years (non-recurring)

On-going training for general and technical operators was estimated to cost £400,000 p.a. This would provide one week's refresher training for each employee. The cost included temporary cover and instructor time (recurring).

(iv) Other staff/managers

Assumed 875 staff/managers at £1500 each	£1.3m (non-recurring)
On-going training, probably 10 days p.a.	£525,000 (recurring)
Grand total non-recurring costs (5 years)	£11.5m
Less current training budget (3% of total costs 5 years)	−£3.5m
Net non-recurring cost	**£8.0m**
Total additional recurring costs (p.a.)	£1.102m
Less current training budget	−£700,000
Net recurring cost	**£300,000** (rounded down)

Implementation costs: Management

1 Purpose
   (a) To develop the necessary individual and collective managerial competencies to implement the change programme.
   (b) To generate management commitment to, and understanding of, the proposed changes.
   (c) To identify and redeploy uncommitted/unwilling managers to positions where they could not influence behaviour through the promotion of different standards and practices.

2 Key elements
   (a) Identification and redeployment of managers likely to block rather than facilitate the change programme. Such managers were to be identified by the board and moved to non-sensitive roles or out of the company. The uncommitted/unwilling managerial population might be as large as 25 per cent of the existing managerial stock at each of the sites.
   (b) Exposure of the board and site management teams to 'change management processes and experiences': the purpose was to make progress on the whole change programme and to learn concepts and methods which would aid organizational and individual change.
   (c) Development of the change management competencies of individual managers on site/manufacturing/support centre teams: an in-depth exercise run with mixed company participation over at least a two-week period, with follow-up at each of the sites by a site change agent/ organizational development consultant. As the level of managerial competence developed it would be possible to begin to build individual and collective commitment to the change programme philosophy (not the detail) and to make the commitment to change evident through a consistency of managerial style, e.g. setting the example, providing 'space' for subordinates, putting down key markers on managerial inconsistencies, and raising managerial visibility.
   (d) Upon this base the formal communications programme could be launched.

These four steps represented part of the enabling/transition programme which helped to prepare management for the development and implementation of long-term change away from traditional jobs and roles.

During this same enabling period of about 18 months, supportive changes were introduced into 'systems' and 'training and development policies'.

3 Resources
In order to support the management part of the implementation strategy it would be necessary to acquire the following resources:
   (a) New recruits to the company on a full-time basis to fill any of the gaps left by redeploying management.
   Preferably rely upon internal candidates where possible.
   Conduct major trawl for management talent across the company.
   (b) Site/company support by internal/external change agent/organizational development consultant.
   Consider appointing one consultancy for whole company, though preferred route is to let sites acquire their own support in most appropriate form.
   External support at about one person one day per week per site for 2–3 years.
   (c) 'Change programme' courses to develop individual and team competencies for coping with and managing change programme.
   Worth considering establishing a company organization development programme.
   (d) Cross-functional/cross-level 'change workshop' programme of 4–5 days duration.

4 Timetable
   (a) Acceptance of study recommendations.
   (b) Identify potential 'promoters' and 'blockers' of proposed change among management on each of the sites.
   (c) Board and site management teams' conference to begin to open up the debate on the implementation process.
   (d) Translate study recommendations into specific actions.
   (e) Site management teams work up site implementation plans.
   (f) Identify and establish release dates for implementation task force members.
   (g) Begin to develop 'new' management through promotion, redeployment (internal and external) and recruitment.
   (h) Run initial 'managing change' workshops with the board and each of the site management teams.
   (i) Intensive on-site support for key managers as they begin to introduce changes in their individual and collective styles.
   (j) Launch of first visible changes in systems and personnel/training through high involvement/participation process.
   (k) Implementation of changes in systems (probably performance measurement and local budget/cost control) and in personnel/training (level of resource available, quality of on-site facilities, and training appraisal/development review system introduced).

(l) Formal launch of the move to multi-role/multi-skill operators, team leaders etc.

5 Costs

(a) Recruitment of new managers.
(b) Replacement of promoted managers.
(c) Redundancy/early retirement of redeployed managers.
(d) Change programme:

	Team events for board and site management teams (24 in all, at £350 per participant)	Estimated cost £8,000
	Team events for manufacturing and support centre management teams (72 in all, at £200 per participant)	Estimated cost £14,400
	'Change workshops' programme for all employees (3000 in all, at £90 per participant)	Estimated cost £270,000
(e)	External organizational development support (between £25,000 and £30,000 per site)	Estimated cost: £150,000–£180,000 (over 2 years) £225,000–£270,000 (over 3 years)
	Total (excluding VAT and expenses)	**£517,000–£562,800**
	Grand total (with VAT and expenses)	**£720,000–£775,000**

These costs, which were not included in the costs detailed for the implementation of the recommended new organization and job roles, were to be taken into account in the cost analysis of the manufacturing centre implementation. Some of them would replace existing expenditure and would be off-set accordingly.

Step 6 The balance sheet

Having generated estimates, based on the best available information, of the costs and benefits, it is necessary to bring them together in a single balance sheet. The costs and benefits of the example used in Steps 4 and 5 are brought together in Table 7.8. In this case a very simple payback calculation has been undertaken.

Another approach to the same issue is to view the costs and benefits over a seven-year period: Table 7.9 covers the benefits to be derived from the introduction of 'flexible craft status' on a site. While the figures are adverse in the formative years of the scheme, the saving at current costs (1986 prices) would amount to over £900,000 five years later. It is important to note that this saving should be compared to the annual maintenance budget of the site, which was £11 millions in 1986.

All of the items included in Table 7.9 are based on actual costs derived from the implementation. No account has been taken of the additional benefits associated with reductions in plant downtime due to individual efficiency gains and the additional hours available to engineers allowing

Table 7.8 *Benefits and costs – payback calculation*

Benefits (Step 4)	£ million	Costs (Step 5)	£ million
Recurring benefits		*Recurring costs*	
Increased line output/material conversion	4.5	Salary increases	1.9
		Additional recruitment/ training	0.3
Reduced supervisory/ management structure	0.5	Total recurring costs	2.2
Integration of engineering work into operating role	0.9	*Non-recurring costs*	
		Training	8.0
Integration of in-process QA work into operating role	0.8	Communication	2.5
		Management	1.7
Greater operating performance awareness	0.8	Labour displacement	4.5
		Total non-recurring costs	16.7
Reduced inventory	0.2		
Total recurring benefits	7.7		
Non-recurring benefits			
Reduced inventory	2.0		
Nett recurring benefits		*Nett non-recurring costs*	
Recurring benefits minus recurring costs		Non-recurring costs minus non-recurring benefits	
= £7.7m − £2.2m	= £5.5m	= 16.7m − 2.0m	= £14.7m
Benefits/costs analysis			
$\dfrac{\text{Nett non-recurring costs}}{\text{Nett recurring benefits}} = \dfrac{14.7m}{5.5m} = 2.7$			
Return on investment (payback) = 2.7 years			

Table 7.9 Costs and benefits over a 7-year period (based on 1986 costs)

Cost factors	1986	1987	1988	1989	1990	1991	1992
Implementation costs							
Redundancy 100 Eng. workers	–	136	227	273	273	–	–
Redundancy 6 Eng. supervisors and 7 Eng. foremen	–	65	65	65	86	–	–
Min. 10% increase in rate for 250 Eng. workers		32	67	135	281	281	281
20 additional contractors	–	–	139	208	276	276	276
Training to implement	–	70	105	105	105	–	–
Training to maintain	–	–	–	10	20	30	30
Training for future needs	–	–	10	15	15	20	20
Publicity	5	20	–	–	–	–	–
Ave. 5% increase in rate for Eng. staff	–	20	30	45	59	59	59
Consultancy fees	–	10	10	10	–	–	–
Total	5	353	653	866	1115	666	666
Implementation gains							
Reduction of 100 Eng. employees	–	204	544	952	1360	1360	1360
Reduction of 6 Eng. supervisors	–	36	72	90	108	108	108
Reduction of 7 Eng. foremen	–	15	30	61	107	107	107
Total	–	255	646	1103	1575	1575	1575
Nett benefit	(5)	(98)	37	237	460	909	909

them to take on more planning, engineering and systems work, as a consequence of the reduced administrative load as individual employees take on more responsibility.

Both Tables 7.8 and 7.9 represent balance sheets for the introduction of new organization and job structures on a project basis. It is also possible to introduce changes in job content and organizational structures in an incremental fashion and to monitor the progress made in benefit terms. This approach was adopted on one chemicals site employing 12,000 people as the basis of its total productive maintenance (TPM) programme which sought to create a partnership between operations and maintenance to improve product quality, reduce waste and improve the state of maintenance.

At this chemicals site TPM was made up of a series of concepts which were based on operators and craftsmen working together to understand how their roles interact and what they must do to support one another. The main concepts were:

1. Utilization of operators to perform certain routine maintenance tasks on their equipment. Operators assuming responsibility for their equipment will help to eliminate potential causes of failure. By dealing with dust, rattles, loosened bolts, scratches, deformation and wear, all of which combine to cause failures, the operators can do their part to prevent failures.

   The operators will be properly trained and certified to perform the specifically identified tasks. Also, the proper tools and supplies required to perform the tasks will be provided.

   Safety will be given utmost consideration in training individuals to perform tasks identified by the teams.

2. Utilization of operators to assist craftsmen in the repair of their equipment when it is down. Frequently, several pieces of equipment fail at the same time, and maintenance does not have enough trained people to respond to all of the failures. Under this concept, operators would be properly trained to assist maintenance personnel in the repair of the equipment. In return, maintenance would be 'enlarged', and ultimately the failed equipment would be returned to service much quicker.

3. Utilization of craftsmen to assist operators in the shut down and start-up of the equipment. There are times when operators need assistance in shutting down and/or starting up the equipment but do not have the help. This prolongs the shutdown, causing maintenance to wait on the job. By utilizing properly trained craftsmen to help operators get the equipment shut down, the outage time of the equipment will be reduced. Also, once the craftsmen finish the repairs, they assist the operators in returning the equipment to service by correcting leaks and other mechanical and electrical problems as it is being brought up. By staying at the job site and assisting until the operators have the equipment running, many repeat calls will be eliminated, and overall downtime will be reduced.

4. Utilization of trained operators to perform routine jobs not requiring skilled craftsmen. There are many routine tasks that could be done by just about anyone, with very little training. Under the TPM or multi-skilling programme these tasks will be identified; if it is not feasible for operators or craftsmen to do them in their spare time, other people will be used to do them. The people doing the tasks could report to either operations or maintenance.

5 Utilization of computerized instrumentation to do calibrations using operators. Quality management requires that instruments be properly calibrated. Use of SPC charts to control operations is based on using data that is as accurate as possible. As part of the TPM or multi-skilling programme, maintenance should purchase a computer and calibration test unit. This system will enable the site to be more effective by routinely checking and monitoring the calibration of critical instruments.
6 Interface between operating groups. Through natural evolution, operating job structures frequently develop which are not as practical as desired. In many cases, unnecessary wait times and equipment downtime are the attendant results. Identifying these unproductive interfaces and restructuring job responsibilities can remove such inefficiencies. This is a major extension of the craft–operator partnership into other support areas.

These six concepts centre around the 'zone concept of TPM' which seeks to achieve maximum flexibility of both operating and maintenance forces. This requires the identification of those tasks which, in belonging exclusively to one group or the other, cause unnecessary delays, loss of productivity, generation of waste or lost product, and ultimately increase manufacturing costs. Training both groups to perform those tasks which originally belonged to one group or the other improves flexibility of people and alleviates many of the problems arising from 'one-group' ownership.

The actual identification, transfer and training of tasks in this example was managed by a series of interlinked teams covering the site, the plant and specific areas or shifts. To start with, a series of three pilot projects were undertaken to prove that the value of TPM and the transferring of tasks between various groups had real benefits to the site. The three pilot areas had the following major characteristics: one was a continuous process, one was a batch process and one was a service group.

Gains were monitored at the local level, recording in detail every task transferred; e.g. in one film plant 4200 transferred tasks were performed saving 2200 hours per year; in one organics plant 1300 transferred tasks were performed yielding a saving of 3200 hours per year and giving an increased equipment uptime of 1800 hours per year. In all, three task transfer sheets were used: one detailed the nature of the task to be transferred, and then two detailed the benefits depending on whether the task has been transferred from maintenance to operations or vice versa. These three forms are reproduced in Figures 7.5, 7.6 and 7.7. By completing one of the Time Savings Worksheets (Figures 7.6 and 7.7) it was possible to piece together the savings which were made between 1985 and 1988.

SITE: _____ DEPARTMENT: _____

FUNCTIONAL AREA: _____ DATE: _____

TASK: _____

CURRENT WORK ORDER PRIORITY: A ☐   B ☐

1. In Local Process   Yes ☐   No ☐

2. Task time (in minutes): _____

3. Task frequency:

   Daily ☐   Weekly ☐   Monthly ☐

   Other (please indicate)

4. Complexity:
   0 — 5 — 10
   Low   Moderate   High

5. Skill requirements:
   0 — 5 — 10
   Low   Moderate   High

6. Task criticality (What happens if task is done improperly?)
   – Impact is: Immediate   Delayed

   Consequence:
   0 — 5 — 10
   Low   Moderate   High

7. Safety considerations:
   – Likelihood of accident is
   0 — 5 — 10
   Low   Moderate   High

   – Particular safety concern(s): _____
   _____

8. Tool requirements: _____
   _____

9. Supplies needed: _____
   _____

10. Operator/craftsman is willing: Yes ☐   No ☐

APPROVALS: _____   _____   _____

Figure 7.5 *Task evaluation sheet*

Date _____ Operations/building _____
Task _____
Work order priority _____ Frequency _____
Currently done by _____ Persons assigned _____
Will be done by _____ Persons assigned _____

Process before multi-skilling/TPM

Action/conditions	Time (in minutes)
1. Problem identified and work order prepared	_____
2. Work order in system until assigned	_____
3. Craftsman travels to job site	_____
4. Job being done	_____
5. Craftsman travels to next job or shop	_____
A. Total equipment downtime (from Items 1, 2, 3, 4)	_____
B. Time involved for craftsman (Items 3, 4, 5 × assigned)	_____

Process after multi-skilling/TPM

Action/Conditions	Time (in minutes)
1. Problem identified/operator gets tools and supplies	_____
2. Job being done	_____
3. Tools and extra supplies replaced	_____
C. Total equipment downtime (from 1, 2, 3)	_____

Downtime savings (Item A minus Item C) _____
Craftsman time saved (see Item B) _____

Figure 7.6 *Time savings worksheet (maintenance-to-operations tasks)*

Changing Job Structures

Date _____ Operations/Building _____

Task _____

Work order priority _____ Frequency _____

Currently done by _____ Persons assigned _____

Will be done by _____ Persons assigned _____

Process before multi-skilling/TPM

Action/Conditions	Time (in minutes)
1. Craftsman locates operator (beginning and end of task)	
2. Operator and craftsman travel to job site (beginning and end)	_____
3. Operator does support task (beginning and end)	_____
4. Operator returns to assigned area (beginning and end) ****Craftsman performs repair task****	_____
5. Craftsman checks out repair – operator waiting (if applicable)	_____
A. Total operator time required (Items 2, 3, 4, 5)	_____
B. Total craftsman time required, excluding repair/checkout (Items 1, 2, 3)	_____
C. Downtime due to interface (Items 1 and 2)	_____

Process after multi-skilling/TPM
(Craftsman does entire task)

D. Operator time required	0.0
E. Craftsman time required excluding repair/checkout (Item 3)	_____

Downtime savings (Item A minus Item C)	_____
Craftsman time saved (B minus E)	_____
Operator time saved (A minus D)	_____

Figure 7.7 *Time savings worksheet (operations-to-maintenance tasks)*

The savings

18,600 hours reduction in operations and maintenance time.
Task duration reduced by a ratio of 4:1 once transferred.
Shutdown duration reduced by 40–60 per cent.
Training headroom in maintenance increased by 25 per cent.
Maintenance work undertaken by operators 15 per cent of the 1985 total.
Engineering time devoted to high priority/schedule 'A' work reduced from 50 to 2 per cent.
Machine reliability increased by 1–2 per cent (worth about $40m a year).
Product quality improved by 1–2 per cent.
Maintenance budget reduced by 12 per cent (worth about $12 millions).

The main inputs/costs

TPM facilitator – one per group, and requires to be 3 months full-time.
TPM meeting – initially four or five 2-hour meetings.
Training material development – 3–4 weeks per area or major grouping of tasks.
Training in tasks: about 1 hour per task per employee.
Steering committee meetings: four of 2 hours over 6 months.

The most significant cost was the release of front-line supervisors to be trained in TPM methods (task analysis as described in Chapter 5) and the time for them to function as full-time TPM facilitators.

This second approach to the pulling together of the costs and benefits is very pragmatic and builds up a picture of the benefits on an on-going basis. It works, and means that the changes proposed will all definitely yield benefits.

Summary

The selection of the most appropriate or 'best' option takes place in two stages. First, the options are evaluated by means of a series of evaluation criteria (many of which will be described in the terms of reference). The evaluation criteria can also be regarded as 'success criteria', i.e. the project must satisfy these criteria if it is to be a success. In this chapter the development, sorting, weighting and application of the evaluation criteria have been described with reference to series of examples.

The second part of the evaluation process is the placing of monetary or other values on the costs and benefits associated with the new job and organization structures. Again it has been shown with reference to examples how this can be undertaken, and the likely size of the costs and benefits to be expected. In bringing together the costs and benefits into a consolidated balance sheet, the payback period was estimated. Also at this stage one detailed, task-level monitoring method was described which can give rise to information that can be used to construct a bottom-up task-based balance sheet.

The material in this chapter has also shown that it is possible and worthwhile to investigate the likely costs and benefits of proposed new job structures, and so identify the necessary resources required for their successful implementation.

8
Implementation

Introduction

Implementation of the seven stages of the method described in Chapters 4 to 7 divides into two parts. First there is the implementation of the method itself, and second there is the implementation of the outcome of the methods application. The eight stages of the method have been developed and structured in such a way as to raise the likelihood of a successful outcome (see Chapters 2 and 3).

The first part of this chapter outlines in detail the content of the sessions a group would go through in applying the method. These outlines would form the agenda of any application of the method. The second part considers three main aspects of the implementation of the method: training, pay and rewards, and monitoring and evaluation of the changes.

Implementation of the method (Stages 1 to 7)

In all, 27 one-day sessions are described, which would also involve activities between sessions. The content of the 27 sessions described here is based on one group's experience of using the method.

Session 1. Team training

Having established the membership of a study group (preferably on a voluntary basis) and its initial terms of reference, it is worth spending one or two days on some form of team training. This will raise the effectiveness of the team. Any readily available programme can be used to ensure that individuals are aware of and able to play a team role, and that they know the importance of reviewing their progress as a team.

Session 2. Raising of awareness and problem definition

1 Introduction

Shift of emphasis from the team training.
Introduce facilitator (if applicable) – Why? What role?
Purpose of the day.

   (a) To clarify the remit and the boundaries of the project.
   (b) To raise the awareness of external experiences and to raise the understanding of what is possible.
   (c) To begin the process of problem definition and focusing of the effort of the working party.
   (d) To map out the interrelationships of the problems in terms of their priority, significance and ownership.
   (e) To consider what methods are available and which ones are most relevant to this working party.
   (f) To produce an initial timetable and plan for the whole project.

2 External experience

What is happening elsewhere?
What are the options?
How have other companies gone about changing/developing their (new jobs/organizations?
Are there any companies we should consider visiting?

3 Problem definition and mapping (SWOT/5P analysis)

What is the focus of our study?
What are the strengths, weaknesses, opportunities and threats to the department?
Can we refine the problem?
Can it be subdivided?
How do the problems identified/barriers to progress interrelate?
What is their significance/impact?

4 Methodology

How do we tackle these problems?
What methods are available?
Are any of them appropriate to our problems?
How will we operate the relevant methods?

5 Timetable/plan

Given the issues to be tackled, what are the steps we need to go through?
Can we put a timing on these steps?
How long will each step take?
How much effort needs to go into each step?
How often, and what, will we need to communicate?

Session 3. Identifying the key issues

1 Review/recap

Review work (SWOT/5P analysis).
Where does this output take us?
How will the SWOT/5P analysis help us?
How will we develop and focus the remit?

2 Key issues

What are the key issues to be tackled?
Which ones can the study group tackle?

3 Study approach

What approaches are available to us as a study group to tackle the key issues?

4 Action plan and timetable

Can we begin to put some initial plan of action and timetable together?

5 Communication

What can be communicated to everyone in the department?

6 Meeting process review

How has the meeting gone?

7 Next meeting

Date and time of the next meeting.

Session 4. The study approach

1 Review/recap

Briefly review revised SWOT/5P analysis of Sessions 2 and 3.
Summarize the development of the remit and revised remit.
Check that the focus of the study covers systems and plant (in terms of inputs to the specification of user requirements – the SOURS process – and the commissioning of new plant and equipment) and in particular the core of the project, the jobs and organization structure in the department.
Map out how the various components of the study fit together.

2 Study approach

What approaches are available to the study group to tackle the design of a new way of manufacturing?
How will we select the best approach and methods? What are the selection criteria?
How will the whole study fit together?
What is the sequence of events the study needs to go through?
What are the key actions we must complete?
What is the detail of the preferred approach we can use?
How will we apply the preferred approach?

3 Action plan and timetable

Can we begin to put some initial plan of action and timetable together?
How will we use our time and divide the work?

4 Communication

What can be communicated to everyone in the department, and what to the rest of the site?
How will we communicate it? Who will do it? When? Where?

5 Meeting process review

How has the meeting gone?

6 Next meeting

Date and time of next meeting.

Session 5. Applying study method and data collection

1 Review/recap

Review revised remit.
Review communications – content and method.
Review progress made to date.

2 Study structure and method

Detail the key actions of the study method.
Detail data requirements.
Where does the listing of data sources fit in?
How does the mapping of the whole production process move us forward?

3 Data collection

Consider possible methods available.
Select method(s) to be used.
Design/develop the method(s) to be used.
Draw up a timetable and action list for data collection in terms of communications, administration, preparation of materials, allocation of tasks etc.

Communications

How is our market structured?
What are the possible routes/methods for reaching each market?
What support do we need?

5 External experience

Visits to other companies – first thoughts.
Develop a databank of other companies' experiences.

6 Meeting review

How has the meeting gone?

7 Next meeting

Date and time of next meeting.
Dates and times of future meetings.

Session 6. Process mapping and data collection

1 Review/recap

Review communications – progress on briefings.
Progress made on:

- (a) states of operations?
- (b) 'good' run charts?
- (c) 'bad' run charts?
- (d) task data collection sheet?
- (e) Visit to appropriate conferences/exhibitions?

2 Production process charts

Check for completeness.
Identification of key groupings of tasks.
Work through the data collection relevant to completing both 'good' and 'bad' run charts.
Combination of 'good' and 'bad' run charts to describe typical production runs.
Breaking down of the production process charts into individual tasks.
Identification of the main opportunities for improvement: are any evident by this stage with regard to plant and/or systems and procedures? How can these be examined further?

3 Data collection

Itemize the data still to be collected in order to complete the 'good' and 'bad' run charts.
Test out the data collection sheet individually and through interviews.
Timetable for data collection: communication, interview, location, printing of data collection sheets, setting-up of database on the computer, release of staff etc.

4 Communications

What has been done with regard to:

- (a) Site newspaper?
- (b) Noticeboard/diary?
- (c) Stationery?
- (d) Slogan/Theme?
- (e) Video disc?

Derive allocation of responsibilities and timetable to ensure a constant flow of information.

5 External experience

Progress on the discussion of Session 5.
Open files on specific companies.

6 Meeting review

How has the meeting gone?

7 Next meeting

Date and time of next meeting.

Session 7. Process mapping and improvement projects

1 Review/recap

Refinement of the 'good' and 'bad' run charts in terms of:

  (a) States of running.
  (b) Possible improvement projects arising for manufacturing/filling and packaging.

  Updating of study group members.
  Briefing of department (especially in manufacturing/filling).
  Reworked task data collection sheet.
  Contacts with/visits to third-party sites.

2 Production process charts/task data collection

Do we have complete plots now for each of the main states of running with all key steps identified?
Identification of all sources of task inputs into the department – including manufacturing centre, site, other company sites and elsewhere (e.g. raw materials suppliers, component suppliers etc.).
Trial of the task data collection sheet within study group and modification if necessary.
Design of the task data collection process.
Design of prompt cards giving examples, explanations, range of possible answers to select.

258   *Changing Job Structures*

Support actions required for data collection process – e.g. communications, release of people, location of interviews etc.
Timetable for task data collection.
Allocation of responsibilities for task data collection.

3 Production process improvement projects

How many emerged for manufacturing/filling and packaging?
How were the barriers to production process improvement interrelated?
How were the various 'barriers to improvement' evaluated?
Do we have sufficient information at this stage to 'scope' each of these projects?
Sources of information/actions required to take these projects forward.
Allocation of responsibilities to progress these projects.
Timetable for this exercise.

4 Data analysis

Setting-up of computer software to accept data for ease of entry, use and presentation.
Examples of the output of the process.

5 Communication

Notes for briefing in department and rest of the site.
Diary for the noticeboard in study room.
Stationery? Slogan/theme?

6 Summary

Actions arising from meeting.

6 Review of meeting

How has the meeting gone?

8 Next meeting

Date and time of next meeting.

Session 8. Data collection and analysis

1 Review/recap

Have the following been completed?

> Communication brief.
> Location coding system.
> Work study data located.
> Full set of standard operating procedures (SOPs) collected.
> Technical guide available.
> Video show training.
> Planned preventative maintenance (PPMs) schedules listed.
> Training modules/programmes collected.
> Task sheet modified.
> Interview explanatory and prompt cards drawn up.
> Draft timetable for task data collection drawn up.
> Release of people for interviewing agreed in principle (in this case at least 134 of the total of 198 involved in manufacture).
> Location of interviews established.
> Site tour conducted.
> Task data collection brief drafted.
> Possible visit to overseas sites.
> Union meeting set up.
> Visits to third-party sites.

2 Task data collection

Using existing sources of information, devise task listings for all of the key areas of production, engineering and quality using SOPs, work study data, PPMs etc. Also use the production flow charts for manufacturing/ filling and packaging as a prompt in this exercise.

Go through the full set of cards explaining the prompt study, the method and the purpose of the data collection exercise. These should cover study remit, study structure, where the task data fits into the study, development of options etc.

Using the modified task data collection sheet and the prompt cards, complete one sheet:

(a) Individually.
(b) Through one-to-one interviews.

Modify task data collection sheet if necessary to remove any problems encountered.

Review the timetable for the task data collection in the light of the above exercises.
Review the mechanics/logistics of the task data collection exercise.
Allocate responsibilities for task data collection briefing and task data collection interviews.
Agree task data collection interview review sessions.

3 Data analysis

Set computer software to accept the task data for ease of entry, use and presentation.
Go through examples of the output of the task data collection process from other sites.

4 Production process improvement projects

How many improvement projects have emerged for manufacturing/filling and packaging?
How were the reduced lists of projects developed?
Identify sources of information/expertise/advice and actions required to take these improvement projects forward.
Identify possible impacts of outputs of these improvement projects.
Allocate responsibilities to progress these projects.
Timetable for the progressing of the improvement projects.
Consider the possible secondary improvement projects in areas supporting the department.

5 Meeting with the unions

Put together a presentation/information pack for the unions for their next meeting.

6 Visits to company and third-party sites

Any additions/deletions to the list?

7 Communications

In addition to the task data collection brief for the department (the group of 134), what about the rest of the site, and those at head office?
Video show – progress beyond training?
Study room noticeboard – erected? Contents?
On-going briefs?

8 Summary

Actions arising from the meeting?

9 Review of the meeting

How has the meeting gone?

10 Next meeting

Date and time of the next meeting.

Session 9. Data collection

1 Review/recap

Have the following tasks been completed?
  Communication brief (pre-data collection).
  Communication brief for data collection.
  Prompt cards for interviewing prepared.
  Task inventory generated for all of the main roles involved in manufacture.
  Work study data located and copies obtained.
  Timetable for data collection agreed with key parties – is three days a week possible?
  Union agenda agreed.
  Task data collection sheet modified.
  Computer inputting of task data agreed.
  Stationery and other support materials obtained.
  Manufacturing/filling improvement project evaluation converted from number of occurrences to hours of production time lost.
  Survey within packaging completed and analysed.

2 Task data collection

  Check through the completed task inventory for each of the main roles involved in manufacturing.
  Are there any key roles not yet covered?
  Are the task lists consistent in terms of language used, level of detail worked to etc?
  Go through the task inventories for own role, and then other roles, in order to identify missing entries. Are the entries correct? Do they follow the flow of the product/process? Are the task descriptions

understandable to everyone? Have all tasks been qualified where necessary? Are the tasks described in a consistent way?

Task inventories must be completed for all of the key roles before beginning the interviews; if they have not all been completed, draft a timetable to ensure that they all prepared for Session 10.

Go through the prompt cards. Are they easy to read? Are they understandable to everyone? Mount them in A4 flip-chart holders.

Have the task inventories been printed out into the task data collection sheets, and are there enough copies for each of the job-holders? It is important to avoid mixing the task data collection sheets completed from different interviews.

Timetable for task data collection interviews – is it clear who will be interviewing who? Where? When? How long will interviews last? Do a trial run. What about the head office interviews?

3 Task data loading into the computer

For most of the roles involved in manufacturing, several people will be interviewed. We must therefore agree a way of entering the task data into the computer to allow everyone's task data sheets to be used. Thus, for most of the operating tasks in packaging there will be 30–40 sets of 'answers'. The data set in the computer must therefore be structured to allow all of this data to be entered, one task after another. Then the completed task data set for all operators can be sorted/listed by task so that the differences can be seen in terms of frequency, duration, complexity/difficulty, involvement etc. From this list of all individuals' assessments of a particular task we will need to obtain the average assessment. Probably the easiest way to do this part of the study is to enter all of the task data, sheet by sheet, and then have it printed out task by task and analyse it visually to select the average 'answer'. In most cases there will be a high level of agreement. Where agreement is not so evident it will be necessary to return to the task itself and possibly view it being done.

Task data should be entered as soon after the interview as possible so that we can keep to the timetable and can develop options of new organizations to be shared with everyone in the department and on the rest of the site.

4 Production process improvement projects

(a) Manufacturing/filling

Any changes to the list of main barriers to improvement when occurrences have been converted into hours of downtime/production lost?

Drafting of brief for the study of the key improvement projects.

Implementation

Who is best placed to take these projects forward?
Likely timetable for the completion of these projects?
Estimation of the impact of these projects on the task data set?
The overall benefits?

(b) Packaging
What is the outcome of the survey of packaging?
Drafting of brief for the study of the key improvement projects.
Who is best placed to take these projects forward?
Likely timetable for the completion of these projects?
Estimation of the impact of these projects on the task data set? The overall benefits?

5 Meeting with the unions

Agenda and style of union meeting.
Preparations for the union meeting.

6 Visits to company and third-party sites

Draft letter and decide enclosures to be sent to sites to be visited.
When is the best time to make the visits to various sites?
How many people per visit?
Who goes where?
What can we offer the sites visited?

7 Communications

Most recent pre-data collection brief.
Data collection brief and its delivery to site and head office.
Video-show: any progress beyond training?
Study room noticeboard – contents and upkeep?
Posters?

8 Summary

Actions arising from the meeting?

9 Review of the meeting

How has the meeting gone?

10 Next meeeting

Date and time of the next meeting.

Session 10. Data collection and improvement projects

1 Review/recap

Have the following tasks been completed?

    Task data collection brief.
    Follow-up session for task data collection brief.
    Work study report on department located.
    Prompt cards for interviewing prepared and mounted.
    Task inventory generated for:
      Packaging operators.
      Packaging supervisors.
      Manufacturing/filling operators.
      Manufacturing/filling supervisors.
      Laboratory/QC role.
      IPC role.
      Collation.
      Warehouse.
      Planning/scheduling.
      Engineering – mechanical.
      Engineering – electrical.
      Engineering – supervision.
      Others.
    Interview timetable generated and interviewee names agreed, and have they been informed?
    Task inventories loaded on to the computer and printed out into task data collection sheet forms.
    Head office interviews arranged.
    Computer data storage format and programs agreed.
    Stationery and other support materials agreed.
    Manufacturing/filling improvement project evaluations converted into hours of lost plant availability/output.
    Packaging improvement project survey progressed, with data sources identified and additions made for over-print.
    Video show up and running.
    Posters for noticeboard.
    Visits to company and third-party sites progressed, with letters ready in draft form.

2 Task data collection

Response to brief.
Any need for a follow-up session today?

Any missing task inventories for the roles to be covered in the interviews over the next three weeks?
Check through all support materials.
Do practice runs with the task data collection sheets and prompt cards.
Interview timetable agreed and known to all relevant parties.
Anyone unable to attend their interviews?

3 Task data loading into the computer

Has the data storage facility been designed and set up?
Has a trial run been done?
Have all of the task inventories been loaded?
Is a back-up resource(s) available to ensure that task data can be loaded into the computer as quickly as it is collected?

4 Manufacturing/filling production process improvement projects

What is the final list of possible projects?
Draft brief for the resolution of the improvement areas identified.
Who is best placed to take these projects forward?
Likely timetable for the completion of these projects?
Estimation of the impact of these projects on the total task data set. What tasks would be deleted, added or modified? What would be the overall benefits?

5 Packaging production process improvement projects

What is the final list of possible projects?
Draft brief for the resolution of the improvement areas identified.
Who is best placed to take these projects forward?
Likely timetable for the completion of these projects?
Estimation of the impact of these projects on the task data set. What tasks would be deleted, added or modified? What would be the overall benefits?

6 Meeting with the unions

Who will represent the study group?
What material do we have available?
Agree timetable for the preparation for this meeting (to be shared with the study group).

7 Visits to company and third-party sites

Draft letters all prepared?
Agree draft letters.
Send off letters this week with suitable support material.
Consider the possible data collection sheet/questions to be posed.

8 Communications

On-going information on study room noticeboard.
Video show display.
Piece for site newspaper.
Posters.
Follow-up brief from the task data collection exercise.

9 Review project timetable

On target?
What, and where, next?

10 Summary

List actions arising from the meeting.

11 Review of the meeting

How has the meeting gone?

12 Next meeting

Date and time of the next meeting.

Session 11. Data collection, cleaning and validation

1 Review/recap

Have the following tasks been completed/progressed?
    Task data collection brief for IPC, QA, labs/QC, warehouse, planning/scheduling.
    Any need for follow-up sessions?
    Work study report.

Timetable for remaining interviews.
Head office interviews arranged.
Task data loaded into the computer/keeping pace with the interviews.
Video show up and running.
Letters sent out for visits to third-party sites.

2 Task data collection

Response/cooperation with interviews.
Problems encountered?
Lessons learnt?
Any modifications necessary?
Which jobs/roles still remain to covered (especially for third-party inputs on site)?
Timetable for remaining interviews.

3 Task data loading into the computer

Have all of the remaining task inventories been loaded into the computer?
Have all of the results of the completed interviews been loaded into the computer?

4 Task data cleaning and validation

Identify multiple entries for a task and reduce to a single entry.
Identify remaining duplicates within individual roles, or where existing roles overlap.
Using existing production, quality etc. records (identified earlier in the project), check for task frequency, duration etc.
Review all other task entries for consistency and check that all tasks are fully completed in each category.

5 Manufacturing/filling production process flow improvement projects

What is the final list of possible projects?
Draft brief for the resolution of the improvement areas identified.
Who is best placed to take these projects forward?
Likely timetable for the completion of these projects?
Estimation of the impact of these projects on the total task data set. What tasks would be deleted, added or modified? What would be the overall benefits?

6 Packaging production process flow improvement projects

What is the final list of possible projects?
Draft brief for the resolution of the improvement areas identified.
Who is best placed to take these projects forward?
Likely timetable for the completion of these projects?
Estimation of the impact of these projects on the total task data set. What tasks would be deleted, added or modified? What would be the overall benefits?

7 Meeting with the unions

Who will represent the group?
What material is available?
Agree timetable for the preparation for this meeting (to be shared with the study group).

8 Visits to company and third-party sites

Have letters been sent out?
When will they be followed up?
Consider the possible data collection sheet/questions to be posed.

9 Communications

On-going information for video show display.
Piece for site newspaper.
Posters.
Follow-up sessions – small groups with the study group.
Who are we failing to get our message to?

10 Review project timetable

Are we on target?
What, and where, next?

11 Summary

List actions arising from the meeting.

12 Review of the meeting

How has the meeting gone?

13 Next meeting

Date and time of the next meeting.

Session 12. Data collection, cleaning and validation

1 Review/recap

Have the following tasks been completed/progressed?

> Task data collection briefs for IPC, QA, lab/QC, warehouse, planning/scheduling.
> Any need for follow-up sessions?
> Number of interviews completed.
> Head office interviews arranged.
> Number and timetable for remaining interviews.
> Task data loaded into the computer/keeping pace with the interviews.
> Letters sent out for visits to third-party sites.
> Manufacturing/filling production processes flow improvement projects progressing. (Ready by Session 13.)
> Packaging production process flow improvement projects progressing. (Ready by Session 13.)

2 Task data collection

How many interviews remaining? With whom?
Will they be completed by Session 13 (at the latest)?
Timetable for the remaining interviews?

3 Task data loading into the computer

Has all of the existing task data been loaded?
When will the final set of task data (without any cleaning) be available on computer?

4 Task data cleaning and validation

For each job/role, e.g. packaging operator, planner, etc., run off a printout task by task to begin the cleaning and data reduction process that will end up with a single entry for each task
Eliminate all duplicates, check for errors and inconsistencies.
Check against other sources of information for task frequency etc.

5 Meeting with the unions

What material has been prepared?
Feedback to the study group today?

6 Visits to sites

Have the letters been sent out?
Have they been followed up by telephone?
Questions to be used on visits – develop data collection sheet.
Get dates of visits cleared within the study group.

7 Communications

On-going information for video show display.
Piece for site newspaper.
More follow-up sessions – small groups with the whole of the study group.
How will we feed back the organization options to the site?

8 Job design criteria

Consider the possible process/methods available.
Do trial run within the study group.

9 Summary

List all actions arising from the meeting.

10 Review of the meeting

How has the meeting gone?

11 Next meeting

Date and time of next meeting.

Session 13. Data loading, cleaning and validation

1 Review/recap

Have the following tasks been completed/progressed?

Bring up to date the study group members who missed Session 12.
Task data collection interviews completed.
Interviews arranged/conducted with supplies.
Any need for follow-up communication sessions?
Any need for follow-up interview sessions?
Task data loaded into the computer.
Original task data printed out by current job-holder task by task, for initial cleaning and validation.
All letters sent out for the visits to third-party sites and follow-up telephone calls made.
Manufacturing/filling production process flow improvement projects ready to report back.
Packaging production process flow improvement projects ready to report back.
Meeting with senior management arranged.
Analysis of job design data trial run ready to report back.

2 Task data collection

How many interviews remaining? With whom?
When will they be completed? (By session 14.)
Timetable for remaining interviews?
Any need for follow-up sessions?
Is master set of original data collection sheets now in an identifiable set of folders?
Feedback to those interviewed?

3 Task data loading into the computer

Has all of the existing task data been loaded?
When will the final set of task data (without any cleaning) be available on computer? (By session 14.)

4 Task data cleaning and validation

Once all of the interviews have been conducted, run off a printout for each job task by task.
Examine each task entry for consistency across each of the entries.
Where differences exist and there are five or more respondents/entries, average the entry for a particular variable, e.g. complexity, frequency etc.
Where there are wide variations in the entries for a particular variable the entries can be checked against known sources of information, e.g. line

logs/diaries, job descriptions, SOPs, PPMs, work study line reports, GRNs, manufacturing documents etc. (see list generated in Session 4).
Reduce multiple entries for a single task to one entry.
Keep a check on the total number of people currently performing the single task.
Where inconsistencies for an individual task cannot be reconciled with reference either to other entries for a particular task (and an average taken) or to an existing source(s) of information, collect these entries together by keeping a record of the task sheet and task number; they can then be considered initially within the study group and possibly referred back to the interviewees themselves

5 Visits to company and third-party sites

Have all the letters been sent out?
Have all of them been followed up by telephone?
Do we need any replacements?
What dates have visits been arranged for?
Can the travel and accommodation arrangements be organized?
Any additional questions/points to be added to the data collection sheet?

6 Manufacturing/filling improvement projects

Feedback on work completed to date.
Can draft briefs for the resolution of each improvement area be drawn up?
Who is best placed to take these projects forward?
Likely timetable for the completion of these projects?
Estimation of the impact of these projects on the total task data set. Which tasks would be deleted, added or modified? What would be the overall benefits?

7 Packaging improvement projects

Feedback on work completed to date.
Can draft briefs for the resolution of each improvement area be drawn up?
Who is best placed to take these projects forward?
Likely timetable for the completion of these projects?
Estimation of the impact of these projects on the total task data set. Which tasks would he deleted, added to, or modified? What would be the overall benefits?

8 Communications

Review of methods, markets and timing (see Session 6 material).
Are we getting the (any) message across?

Piece for site newspaper? Copy date?
Weekly brief for department?
Monthly brief for site? Copy date?
Is the Session 19 date feasible for an interim report?

9 New facility and equipment

Begin developing a list of points to be progressed with the project manager.

10 Q & A session with senior management

Go through current round of concerns with senior management.

11 Feedback on job design survey

Explain to study group members not at Session 12.
Feedback results obtained from trial run.
Should we use this approach in the department?

12 Summary

List all actions arising from the meeting.

13 Review of the meeting

How has the meeting gone?

14 Next meeting

Date and time of next meeting.

Session 14. Data cleaning and validation

1 Review/recap

Have the following tasks been completed/progressed?
  Bring up to date the study group members who have missed previous sessions.
  Task data collection interviews completed.
  Any need for follow-up interview sessions?
  Task data loaded into the computer.
  Original task data printed out by current job-holder task by task, for

initial cleaning and validation. Are there enough copies (at least six)?

All letters for visits to third-party sites followed up.

Manufacturing/filling production process flow improvement projects ready to report back.

Packaging production process flow improvement projects ready to report back.

2 Task data collection

Any interviews remaining? How many? With whom?
When will they be completed?
Timetable for any remaining interviews?
Any need for follow-up sessions?
Master set of original data collection sheets now in an identifiable set of folders?
Feedback to those interviewed completed?
Have the head office interviews been written up?

3 Task data loading into the computer

Have all of the existing task data been loaded?
When will the final set of task data (without any cleaning) be available on computer?

4 Task data cleaning and validation

For how many jobs do we have a completed set of task data?

For those jobs where we have a completed set by task data, run off a printout task by task.

Examine each task entry for consistency across each of the interview returns.

Where differences exist and there are five or more respondents/entries, average the entry for a particular variable, e.g. complexity, frequency etc.

Also consider the overlapping of tasks where someone is performing two or more tasks on a continuous basis, which might change the duration of the task. This might lead to some tasks being re-written.

Where there are wide variations in the entries for a particular task, it can be checked against another source of information, e.g. line logs/diaries, job descriptions, SOPs, PPMs, work study line reports, GRNs, manufacturing documents etc.

Where possible, reduce multiple entries for a single task to one entry, using the above procedure.

Implementation

Keep a check on the total number of people currently performing the task.
Where inconsistencies for an individual task cannot be reconciled with reference either to other entries for a particular task (and an average taken) or to an existing source(s) of information, collect these entries together by keeping a note of the task sheet and task number; they can then be considered initially with the study group and possibly referred back to the interviewees themselves.
Repeat these steps for each of the completed task data sets.

5 Visits to third-party sites

Have all of the letters been followed up by telephone?
Do we need any replacements?
What dates have visits been arranged for?
Can the travel and accommodation arrangements be organized?
Any additional questions/points to be added to the data collection sheet?
Develop briefing notes for each visit to be made.

6 Manufacturing/filling improvement projects

Feedback on work completed to date.
Can draft briefs for the resolution of each improvement area be drawn up?
Who is best placed to take these projects forward?
Likely timetable for the completion of these projects?
Estimation of the impact of these projects on the total task data set. Which tasks would be deleted, added or modified? What would be the overall benefits?

7 Packaging improvement projects

Feedback on work completed to date.
Can draft briefs for the resolution of each improvement area be drawn up?
Who is best placed to take these projects forward?
Likely timetable for the completion of these projects?
Estimation of the impact of these projects on the total task data set. Which tasks would be deleted, added to, or modified? What would be the overall benefits?

8 Communications

Weekly brief for department?
Monthly brief for the site?

9 New facility and equipment

Begin developing a list of points to be progressed with the project manager at either Session 16 or Session 17. Derive points from the task data set and the improvement projects (see items 6 and 7 of this session).

10 Job design survey

Should we use this approach?
If yes, how should it be progressed?

11 Project timetable

Review progress against original timetable.

12 Summary

List all actions arising from the meeting.

13 Review of the meeting

How has the meeting gone?

14 Next meeting

Date and time of next meeting.

Session 15. Data analysis and external experience

1 Review/recap

Have the following tasks been completed?
  Task data collection interviews completed.
  Task data loaded into the computer.
  Original task data printed out by current job-holder task by task, for initial cleaning and validation.
  Remaining visits to third-party sites followed up.
  Manufacturing/filling production process flow improvement projects ready to report back.
  Packaging production flow improvement projects ready to report back.
  Task data set reduction achieved for packaging operator.
  Brief prepared and ready for site briefing timetable.

Implementation

Job design survey for study group members to complete.
Senior managers received copies of their 'answers'.

2 Task data collection

Any interviews remaining? How many? With whom?
When will they be completed?
Timetable for remaining interviews?
Master set of original data collection sheets now in an identifiable set of folders?
Brief gone out for feedback to thank those interviewed and to inform the site of progress made to date?
Head office interviews – have they been written up in any form?

3 Task data loading into the computer

Have all of the existing task data been loaded?
For which jobs do we have full task data set? (List them.)
Do any gaps exist?
Have the head office interview data been loaded in any way?

4 Task data cleaning and validation

For those jobs where we have a full task data set, do we have a printout by current performer task by task?
List the jobs for which we have a printout.
Use guidelines to go through task data for own jobs, taking a note of the 'problems', such as:

Overlapping tasks.
Continuous tasks.
Loss of cover.
Contractors.
Training.
Duplicate tasks undertaken by more than one performer. (See Chapter 6.)

All problem tasks to be considered by the whole group to establish an appropriate way of handling them.

5 Task data set analysis

Which plots should we have run off for the next meeting?
Begin the development of the design principles and evaluation criteria (see Chapter 6).

6 Visits to third-party sites

Status of visits to third-party sites:

Agreed.
Dates.
Numbers.
Form of visit.
Briefing notes for visit.

Companies to be visited – check against each of the above.
Do we need any other replacements?
Hotel/travel arrangements – who do we see about this?

7 Manufacturing improvement projects

Feedback on work completed to date.
Can draft briefs for the resolution of each improvement area be drawn up?
Who is best placed to take these projects forward?
Likely timetable for the completion of these projects?
Estimation of the impact of these projects on the total task data set. Which tasks would be deleted, added to, or modified? What would be the costs and the benefits?

8 Packaging improvement projects

Feedback on work completed to date.
Can draft briefs for the resolution of each improvement area be drawn up?
Who is best placed to take these projects forward?
Likely timetable for the completion of these projects?
Estimation of the impact of these projects on the total task data set. Which tasks would be deleted, added to, or modified? What would be the overall costs and the benefits?

9 Communications

Preparation for printer's session next week.
Do we need an interim brief before the interim report?

10 New facility room and equipment

Begin developing a list of points to be progressed with the project manager at Session 17.

Implementation 279

Derive points from the two sets of improvement projects, the SWOT/5P analysis, and the task data set itself.
Who will set up the session with the project manager?

11 Job design survey

Run within the study group for anyone who has not completed one yet.
Slot missing results into the study group's master score list.
Develop method to get cooperation in filling in the JDS questionnaire.
Printing of JDS questionnaire – how many? Who do we see about this?

12 Project timetable

Consider revised content of timetable for the remainder of the project.

13 Summary

List all actions arising from the meeting.

14 Review of the meeting

How has the meeting gone?

15 Next meeting

Date and time of the next meeting.

Session 16. Data analysis and communications

1 Review/recap

Have the following tasks been completed?
    Task data collection interviews.
    Task data loaded into the computer.
    Original task data printed out by current job-holder task by task, for initial cleaning and validation.
    First plots of the task data available.
    Task analysis handout – all got copies?
    Remaining visits to third-party sites followed up.
    Manufacturing/filling production process flow improvement projects ready to report back.
    Packaging production flow improvement projects ready to report back.

Job design survey – how do we implement it?
Preparation for printer's session this afternoon.

2 Task data collection

Any interviews remaining? How many? With whom?
When will they be completed?
Timetable for remaining interviews?
Head office interviews – have they been written up in any form?

3 Task data loading into the computer

Has all of the existing task data been loaded?
For which jobs do we have a full task data set? (List them.)
Do any gaps exist?
Have the head office interviews been loaded in any way?

4 Task data cleaning and validation (see Chapter 6, Steps 1 and 2)

For those jobs where we have a full task data set, do we have a printout by current performer task by task?
List the jobs for which we have a printout.
Use the guidelines to go through the task data set for your own job, taking a particular note of 'problems':
Differences of frequency, duration and complexity.
Overlapping tasks.
Continuous tasks.
Loss of cover.
Work done by contractors.
Training.
Duplicate tasks undertaken by more than one performer.
All 'problem tasks' to be considered by the whole group to establish an appropriate way of handling them.

5 Task data set analysis (see Chapter 6, Steps 3 to 11)

Consider plots already produced.
Which plots should we have run off for the next meeting?
Begin the development of the design principles.

6 Visits to third-party sites

Status of visits to third-party sites:

Date.
Numbers.
Confirmed.
Form of visit.
Briefing note for visit.
Travel arrangements.

Companies to be visited – check against each of the above.
Do we need any replacements?

7 Manufacturing improvement projects

Report back on progress.
Agree plan and timetable to complete.

8 Packing improvement projects

Report back on progress.
Agree plan and timetable to complete.

9 Communications

Preparation for printer's session this afternoon.
Objective of session.
Content and layout of site newspaper piece.
Structure, content and timing of interim report.

10 New facility and equipment

Develop a list of points to be progressed with the project manager at Session 17.
Set up session with project manager.

11 Job design survey

Develop method to get cooperation in filling in the JDS questionnaire.
Printing of JDS questionnaire.

12 Project timetable

Consider revised content of timetable for the remainder of the project.

13 Summary

List actions arising from the meeting.

14 Review of the meeting

How has the meeting gone?

15 Next meeting

Date and time of next meeting.

Session 17. Data analysis and communications

1 Review/recap

Have the following tasks been completed?

> Task data collection interviews.
> Task data loaded into the computer.
> Head office interviews entered into the computer.
> Original task data printed out by current job-holder task by task, for initial cleaning and validation.
> Task data cleaned and validated.
> First plots of the task data available.
> Task analysis hand-out – all got copies?
> All visits to company and third-party sites arranged.
> Manufacturing/filling production process flow production improvement projects ready to report back.
> Packaging production flow improvement projects ready to report back.
> Job design survey organized.
> Material for site newspaper organized.
> Actions, timing and dates agreed for interim report.
> Feedback on visits.
> Session fixed with the project manager.

2 Communication

Site newspaper article all finished?
Briefing for job design survey conducted/arranged?
Update on progress made for department/site?

3 Visits to third-party sites

Feedback on visits to date:
   Did the approach to the visit work?
   What were the experiences of the companies/sites visited?

4 Improvement projects

Report back on packaging and manufacturing/filling improvement projects.
Agree plans and timetable to complete/progress.

5 New facility and equipment

Cover points developed last time with project manager.
Consider impact on task data set.

6 Task data set analysis (see Chapter 6, Steps 3 to 11)

Consider plots already produced.
Which plots should we run off for the next meeting?
Can we generate our own plots?

7 Design principles and evaluation criteria (see Chapter 6, Steps 6 and 7)

Develop the design principles and evaluation criteria.

8 Project timetable

Consider revised content of the timetable for the remainder of the project.
Preparation for the next sessions.
  Session 18 – Options.
  Session 19 – Options and interim report.

9 Summary

List all actions arising from the meeting.

10 Review of the meeting

How has the meeting gone?

11 Next meeting

Date and time of the next meeting.

284   *Changing Job Structures*

Session 18. Communications, design principles and option development

1 Review/recap

Have the following tasks been completed?

>   Task data collection interviews.
>   Task data loaded into the computer.
>   Head office interviews entered into the computer.
>   Original task data printed out by current job-holder task by task, for initial cleaning and validation.
>   Task data cleaned and validated.
>   'Volume' measures put into the task data, i.e. number of performers of a particular task.
>   Plots of the task data available.
>   All visits to company and third-party sites arranged.
>   Arrangements made for convener to go with the study group.
>   Manufacturing/filling production flow improvement projects now ready to report back and hand on to department manager.
>   Packaging production flow improvement projects ready to report back and hand on to department manager.
>   Job design survey organized.
>   Site newspaper centre spread ready for printing – can we see it?
>   Actions, timings and dates agreed with printers for the interim report.
>   Visit notes typed for circulation/comment.
>   Project manager session typed for circulation/comment.

2 Communication

Site newspaper article finished? Can we see it?
Briefing for job design survey conducted/arranged?
When will we get the questionnaires back?
Update on progress made for department/site?
Feedback on visits? How? When? Who will write the notes?

3 Visits to third-party sites

All arranged now?

4 Improvement projects

Report back on packaging and manufacturing/filling improvement projects.
Consider impact of the improvement projects on the task data set.

5 Task data set analysis (see Chapter 6)

Consider the plots already run off.
Which possible regroupings of the task data set should be run off?
Which plots should be run off for Session 19?

6 Design principles and evaluation criteria (see Chapter 6, Steps 6 and 7)

Develop the design principles and evaluation criteria (build on those drawn up in Session 17).

7 Options development

List all possible options by which tasks, roles and structures could be organized in manufacturing (use this list to guide the selection of plots to run off from the task data set).

8 Project timetable

Consider revised content of the timetable for the remainder of the project – what else remains to be done?

9 Agenda for Session 19

Main objectives

(a) Analyse and evaluate options.
(b) Write the interim report.

Consider timings and process for the two days.
What preparation must be done for these two days?

10 Summary

List all actions arising from the meeting.

11 Review of the meeting

How has the meeting gone?

12 Next meeting

Date and time of next meeting.

Session 19. Option development and interim report

Objectives

1 To develop a series of role and organization structure options for the whole department.
2 To analyse and evaluate the series of options by means of an agreed set of design principles and evaluation criteria.
3 To write the interim report.

Part 1

08.30–12.30	Develop and agree on: (a) Design principles. (b) Evaluation criteria. (c) Role and organization structure options.
12.30–13.30	Lunch.
13.30–17.30	Evaluation and ranking of options.
17.30–18.00	Review of the day.

Part 2

08.00–12.30	Writing of the interim report: (a) Agree on structure and broad content. (b) Slot in existing material. (c) Write up individual options.
12.30–13.30	Lunch.
13.30–15.30	Pooling of inputs and comments and editing of text.
15.30–16.00	Review of the day.

Part 1 (detail)

08.30–09.30	Agree on objectives and structure of the two days. Share understanding of design principles and evaluation criteria. Circulation of role and organization structure material and support task data plots.
09.30–10.00	Coffee/tea.
10.00–11.30	Develop evaluation criteria in three cross-sectional groups.
11.30–12.30	Pooling of evaluation criteria and the formation of a common list in terms of 'musts' and 'wants'.

12.30–13.30	Lunch.
13.30–15.00	Application of evaluation criteria to role and organization structure options in three cross-sectional groups.
15.00–15.30	Coffee/tea.
15.30–17.30	Sharing of the evaluation of the options. Ranking of the options.
17.30–18.00	Review of the day.

Part 2

08.00–09.30	Recap on the output of the previous day – the list of ranked and evaluated options. Structure of the interim report. Any additions? Deletions? Modifications? What material do we currently have to hand?
09.30–10.00	Coffee/tea
10.00–12.30	Write up structure and content for the individual role and organization options – to be done in three small cross-sectional groups.
12.30–13.30	Lunch.
13.30–14.30	Circulate all written material and read it individually. Again, any additions? Deletions? Modifications? Any ideas on presentation format, diagrams etc?
14.30–15.15	Pooling of individual ideas and comments (continue over coffee and tea).
15.15–15.45	Coffee/tea.
15.45–16.15	Pooling of individual ideas and comments.
16.15–16.30	Review of the day. Summary of key actions on interim report.

Session 20. External experience, communications and option development

1 Visits

Feedback on visits.
What was learnt which would be useful for option development and evaluation?
How should the visit reports be fed back to the rest of the department and to the site?

2 Communication

Article for site newspaper.
Timing of the interim report.

3 Development and evaluation of organization structure and role options

Output of Session 19.
Development of options considered in Session 19.
Development and evaluation of other options.
Examination of options with task data.
What other information is required?

4 Summary

List all actions arising from the meeting.

5 Review of the meeting

How has the meeting gone?

6 Next meeting

Date and time of the next meeting.

Session 21. Communications, option development and evaluation

1 Recap/review

Any developments relevant to the study group?

2 Communications

Article for site newspaper.
Content of the interim report.
Timing of the interim report.
How will the interim report be given to people?
How will we get feedback?
How do we want to structure the feedback?
Should we pose a few specific questions?
On what should we pose specific questions?
How will we handle the feedback?

3 Development and evaluation of organization and role options

Examination of options with the task data – work through the three options to date.
What are the outstanding issues?
  Service structure.
  Leadership.
  Team membership.
  Movement between teams.
  Role content/overlap.
  Responsibility.

Consider sub-options within each of the main options.
Refine and develop options.
Test and examine options.
Take all options to the cost and benefits stage.
Can we go further than the current 'advantages' and 'disadvantages'?
What headings for costs and benefits could we use?
Benefits examples:

Reduced changeover time.
Reduced breakdown waiting time.
Improved material conversion/reduced wastage.
Shorter communication channels.
Elimination of duplicate tasks.
Greater responsibility/job satisfaction/commitment at all levels.
Greater familiarity/more rapid fault recognition on equipment.
More rapid fault diagnosis.
Greater operator responsibility for QA – improved QA standards.
Greater motivation for performance improvement.
More rapid identification of performance inhibitors.
Maximize and sustain benefits of productivity improvement.
Maximize and sustain benefits of capital investment.
Increased machine running time/increased line output.
Shorter planning/material processing times.
Faster production throughput-times/faster changeovers and elimination of waiting time.
Elimination of delays from in-process QA testing/having a larger pool of more technically competent people.
Increase in available machine capacity/more efficient utilisation.
Reductions in raw materials/work in progress/finished goods inventories.
Reduced capital expenditure.
Increased workload/win business.

Costs examples:

> Training.
> Communications.
> Pay.

4 Visits to third-party sites

How can the visit notes/reports be collated for feedback?
How should the visit reports be fed back to the rest of department and to the site?

5 Summary

List all actions arising from the meeting.

6 Review of the meeting

How has the meeting gone?

7 Next meeting

Date and time of the next meeting

Session 22. Communications, option development and evaluation

1 Recap review

Any developments relevant to the study group?

2 Communications

Article for site newspaper:

> Reactions of the study group?
> Reactions of others?
> Any questions raised?

Progress on the interim report:

> Site manager briefed – his reactions?
> Personnel manager briefed – his reactions?
> Dept managers briefed – their reactions?

Implementation

Availability of copies on site? Now? When?
Full timetable agreed with site management?
Briefing timetable before Session 23.
Support administration for briefing arranged?
Trial run with briefing materials.
Possible questions that might be raised.

3 Development and evaluation of organization and role options

Examination of options with the task data – work through the three options to date.
What are the outstanding issues?

>   Service structure.
>   Leadership.
>   Team membership.
>   Movement between teams.
>   Role content/overlap.
>   Responsibility.

Consider sub-options within each of the main options.
Refine and develop options.
Test and examine options.
Take all options to the cost and benefits stage.
Can we go further than the current 'advantages' and 'disadvantages'?
What headings for costs and benefits could we use?
Benefits examples:

>   Reduced changeover time.
>   Reduced breakdown waiting time.
>   Improved material conversion/reduced wastage.
>   Shorter communication channels.
>   Elimination of duplicate tasks.
>   Greater responsibility/job satisfaction/commitment at all levels.
>   Greater familiarity/more rapid fault recognition on equipment.
>   More rapid fault diagnosis.
>   Greater operator responsibility for QA – improved QA standards.
>   Greater motivation for performance improvement.
>   More rapid identification of performance inhibitors.
>   Maximize and sustain benefits of productivity improvement.
>   Maximize and sustain benefits of capital investment.
>   Increased machine running time/increased line output.
>   Shorter planning/material processing times.

Faster production throughput times/faster changeovers and elimination of waiting time.
  Elimination of delays from in-process QA testing/having a large pool of more technically competent people.
  Increase in available machine capacity/more efficient utilization.
  Reductions in raw materials/work in progress/finished goods inventories.
  Reduced capital expenditure.
  Increased workload/win business.

Costs examples:

  Training.
  Communication.
  Pay.

4 Visits

How can the visit notes/reports be collated for feedback?
How should the visit reports be fed back to the rest of department and to the site?

5 Summary

List all actions arising from the meeting.

6 Review of the meeting

How has the meeting gone?

7 Next meeting

Date and time of the next meeting.

Session 23. Communications and final report

1 Communications

Feedback on the interim report brief and follow-up sessions: what have we learnt? What can we do with the information? What were the reactions? (Go through dept by dept – packaging, filling/manufacturing, labs, engineering, inspection, other.)
Question and answer feedback – what are we going to do with this

Implementation 293

material? How should we feed it back? What about senior management input?
Do we need any further sessions other than those organized in the labs, in engineering and with the supervisors?

2 Timetable and final report

Review timetable and remaining tasks against proposed final report production timetable.
Plan timetable to the end of the study.
Some outstanding items:

> Development and challenging of organization structures.
> Development and challenging of roles and team members.
> Refinement of roles, teams and structures.
> Option selection.
> Option evaluation/costs and benefits.
> Visit report – learning points and summary.
> Implementation strategy/plan and timetable.
> Final report writing – summary and full communication of final report.

3 Summary

List all actions arising from the meeting.

4 Review of the meeting

How has the meeting gone?

5 Next meeting

Date and time of the next meeting.

Session 24. Communications, option development and evaluation, and final report

1 Communications

Have follow-up sessions for those people who were on holiday been organized/run yet?
Have answers been written up to the questions arising from the feedback sessions?

Have follow-up sessions with engineering craftsmen, labs, supervisors been run? The output?
Interim report misprints?

2 Organization options

Evaluation criteria development from terms of reference, e.g.

> Medicine Inspectorate.
> Health and Safety Executive.
> Food and Drug Administration.
> Inventory changes.
> Volume changes.
> Product changes.
> Pack type changes.
> Quality standards.
> Site charter.
> Communications.
> Benefits – company.
> Benefits – people.
> Training.
> Career progression.
> Implementation.

Also use design criteria, lessons learnt from visits, etc.
Apply the evaluation criteria.

3 Team task profile

What is the total task profile of the teams of the chosen option? e.g. for Option 3 it is:

> Packaging/planning (× 2).
> Filling/laboratory.
> Product coordination.
> Production support.

In this example, start with the 'packaging' and 'filling' teams.
What is the task profile in terms of task complexity, frequency and duration? What rules should be used to decide what to include within each of the teams? To what extent should they be autonomous? For everything or somewhere between day-to-day and, say, annual activities?
How many whole and part roles are there in the teams?

4 Individual role development

Build on the output of (3) above, and also add the existing role development work and the task comparison data in matrix form.
How many individual, full-time roles? For example, is it possible to justify a full-time fitter in the team?
Is the lab. role full-time in the filling/lab. team?
What is the team coordinator's role?
How do the new roles differ from existing ones?
What are the training implications?
How many levels of role?
New role titles?

5 Evaluation/cost benefits analysis

What are the costs and benefits of the new organization/teams/roles?
Benefits examples:

Reduced task duplication.
Reduced changeover times.
Reduced breakdown waiting time.
Improved material conversion/reduced wastage.
Shorter communication channels.
Greater responsibility/job satisfaction/commitment at all levels.
Greater familiarity/more rapid fault recognition on equipment.
Reduced wasted/dead time.
More rapid fault diagnosis.
Greater operator responsibility for QC – improved QC standards.
Greater motivation for performance improvement.
More rapid identification of performance inhibitors.
Maximised and sustained benefits of productivity improvements.
Maximised and sustained benefits of capital investment.
Reduced validation and commissioning times.
Reduced validation and commissioning costs – use of in-house resources.
Increased machine running time/increased line output.
Shorter planning/material processing times.
Faster production throughput times/faster changeovers and elimination of waiting times.
Elimination of delays from in-process QC testing/having more technically competent people.
Increase in available machine capacity/more efficient utilization.
Reductions in raw materials/work-in-progress/finished goods inventories.

296   *Changing Job Structures*

  Reduced capital expenditure.
  Increased workload/win new business.

Costs examples:

  Training.
  Communications.
  Pay.
  Knock-on of disruption due to changes.
(To be completed by Session 26.)

6 Implementation plan and timetable

Design criteria.
Lessons learnt from visits.
Communications.
Training.
Stages of introduction.
Timescale.
(To be completed by Session 27.)

7 Final report content

Content	*Action by whom in the group?*
Cover design	....
Contents	....
Summary	....
Introduction/picture/signatures	....
Terms of reference development	....
SWOT/5P analysis	....
Scope of the study	....
Study method	....
Information used	....
Visits	....
Interview data	....
Improvements projects	....
Option selection/evaluation	....
Selected option	....
Basis of design	....
Structure/organization	....
Team responsibilities	....
Roles in the teams	....
Implementation plan and timetable	....
Costs and benefits analysis	....
Conclusion/where next?	....

8 Visits to third-party sites

Summary of the lessons learnt from visits – generate list of points from each of the visits. Who will handle this?

9 Summary

List all actions arising from the meeting.
Draft tasks to be tackled at Session 26.

10 Review of the meeting

How has the meeting gone?

11 Next meeting

Date and time of next meeting.

Session 25. Final report

1 Role development

Engineering
Manufacturing/filling.
Labs.
Remaining roles:
   Team as a whole.
   Team coordinator.
   Support teams.

2 Final report

Costs and benefits.
Visits to third-party sites.
Study method and improvement projects.
Terms of reference, design criteria and existing structure.

3 Feedback

Roles.
Visits.
Study method.

Session 26. Final report

1 Role and team development

Engineering
  In production teams.
  In technical support team.
Manufacturing/filling/lab. team.
Team coordinator.
'Missing' quality tasks.
Packaging team.
Product coordination team.
(To be finished at this session.)

2 Costs and benefits

See agenda for Session 24 (to be finished at this session).

3 Final report

Visits.
Study method.

4 Summary

List all actions arising from the meeting.
List all remaining tasks to be tackled and put a date for completion of each.

Review of the meeting

How has the meeting gone?

6 Next meeting

Date and time of the next meeting.

Session 27. Final report

Progress on the following items:

1 Individual and team roles and responsibilities.
2 Visits – lessons learnt.

3 Costs and benefits.
4 Implementation: actions, plan and timetable.
5 Other contents of the final report.
6 Progress made against printer's timetable.
7 Remaining actions.
8 Date and time of next sessions to finish above.

These 27 sessions outline in detail the application of the method described in this book. The content of the 27 sessions also indicates the time taken to progress some items. Each of the sessions listed represents a day's work and requires supporting activities to be undertaken between the sessions.

In terms of facilities the following items are usually required:

1 Meeting room in a 'public area', e.g. near a canteen, entrance to the site.
2 Computer equipment, e.g. IBM Personal System/2, HP7475A Graphics Plotter or HP7550A Graphics Plotter, and HP Laser Jet IIP Printer. The total cost of these items at May 1990 prices was £8000.
3 Administrative support, e.g. typing and printing services.
4 Stationery.

Once the 27 sessions have been completed and communicated and an agreed option has been selected, three main support actions are required:

1 Training.
2 Pay and rewards system.
3 Monitoring and evaluation of the changes.

Training

It is not the intention in this section to provide details of specific training programmes, but to highlight the components of the training strategy necessary to the successful implementation of changes in organization and job structures.

Four main training initiatives are needed:

Strategic.
Human resource.
Human process.
Technical and structural.

Strategic

By far the the most important intervention here is to begin (if necessary) a reorientation of the company culture and dominant managerial style. This can be tackled through a mapping of the existing management style or culture using a proprietary organization profiling tool. In addition to this it is useful to begin to pose a few basic questions, e.g.

> How good do we *have* to be?
> What does it take to survive/succeed?
> How good do we really *want* to be?
> What are our internal performance objectives?
> Based on our expectations and our competitive position, how good do we fully believe we want/need to be?

It is questions such as these that will help to generate information relevant to the development of a mission and/or a series of value statements. The mission and value statements embody the beliefs and principles that the members of an organization plan to work by. They provide the basic principles that will be built upon in the formulation and application of policy and in the management and operation of the plant, business etc. This provides the beginning of a bridge which can be used to reach commitment to change.

Often this intervention is most appropriately achieved with the help of an external facilitator skilled in 'creating a vision' through a high level of participation. Because of the importance of fostering commitment and energy for the creation of a new, better organization it is often useful to train a selected number of people as 'change agents'. This has been successfully achieved in Exxon, the NHS, Digital Equipment, and Procter and Gamble, among others. In particular, these courses provide the platform upon which to develop ability to challenge existing assumptions and thinking, and create commitment to a jointly defined vision.

Human resource

A number of key abilities need to be developed, requiring:

1 The identification of core competencies (threshold, distinguishing and functional) for a particular job or jobs.
2 The translation of a set of core competencies into an appropriate assessment system.

3 The means for managing the process of performance improvement by an individual.
4 The design, development and application of an appropriate pay and rewards system.

Without all of these four interventions it is unlikely that both the culture/behaviour and technical job content changes will be achieved.

Human process

This refers to the skills and abilities which enhance the performance of people working with one another or in groups. In particular it is important that change agents and key job-holders leading changes can achieve/perform the following:

Communicating openly (and listening).
Collaborating.
Taking responsibility
Maintaining a shared vision.
Solving problems effectively.
Respecting/supporting.
Processing/facilitating interactions.
Inquiring.
Experimenting.
Generating participation.
Leading by vision.
Functioning strategically.
Promoting information flow.
Developing others (appraising and giving feedback).

It is the effective deployment of these skills that can achieve and sustain those behavioural changes which will provide the environment most conducive to changes in job and organization structure.

Technical and structural

By far the greatest effort of most organizations is devoted to the provision of technical training to develop specific job-related skills and knowledge. In addition to this there is a need to provide training in techniques and methods for the design and development of jobs, teams and organization, e.g. variance analysis, socio-technical systems analysis. The technical job-related training can draw directly upon the task data which can be used to develop the content of training programmes.

Training is one of the key interventions in changing any organization by adapting and improving individual standards of performance. It affects all new starters, trainees and all existing employees.

Specific points with regard to technical training

1. Acquiring the relevant training material and resources for operator craft, supervisory and management training takes much longer than usually expected – 9 to 12 months is not uncommon.
2. Tie any training inputs to clearly demonstrated requirements of the job in hand.
3. While trainability and learning rates will be an issue on most sites, the problems have not proved to be insurmountable; they require early recognition.
4. Training for implementation should be a mix of top-down, 'natural team', and cross-sectional training.
5. Training in 'technical job skills' should be highly focused on on-the-job training in the first instance, providing a high level of practice (a balance of 80:20 for on-the-job: off-the-job).
6. Training should be to standards at least as defined by the National Council for Vocational Qualifications or one of the other national standards-setting bodies, e.g. The City and Guilds of London Institute, Business and Technician Education Council, etc.
7. While most people can successfully complete training courses, protection will be required for the few who may have some difficulty for whatever reason.
8. Quite often technical colleges and further education colleges find it difficult to provide the appropriate training, and it may be necessary either to establish a new training resource on-site (e.g. Shell Chemicals at Carrington) or off-site (e.g. Albright and Wilson, Whitehaven), or to make use of other companies' resources (e.g. Crane Fluid of Ipswich using Perkins Diesel's facilities at Peterborough).
9. Training which is primarily aimed at raising competence in 'common skills', i.e. those falling into the TPM zone of commonality, should be delivered according to the principle 'a little often'.
10. Costs for training can vary greatly and need estimating from the outset. For example, one paper mill was spending £30,000 per candidate for the conversion of electricians into fitters, and vice versa. Those extending the role of craftsman (not quite to the full conversion of craftsmen into other trades) cost considerably less, e.g. in the range £1500 to £8,000 per individual.
11. Training should be an 'inclusive process' providing opportunities for all concerned.
12. Training must be continually monitored to ensure that progress is being

made, that the training is being effective and efficient and that standards are being maintained.

Pay and rewards

The first stage of any pay and rewards project must be the selection of a job evaluation method which is consistent with the promotion of the high level of individual development that is required if the jobs are designed by the method described in this book.

There are two main methods of job evaluation/measurement:

(a) Analytical. This is the quantitative method whereby jobs are measured against a number of elements to gain points which place them in rank order. The two main methods are *points rating* and *factor comparison*. In both of these approaches the job is broken down into its component parts and assessed against previously established factors.
(b) Non-analytical. This is the non-quantitative method of job evaluation which employs no formal measuring mechanism. Jobs are slotted into position often without the use of a panel procedure. The two main systems are *job ranking* and *job classification* and in both these systems jobs are measured as a whole rather than being broken down into their elements.

These four methods are described below.

Ranking method

In the ranking method, jobs are compared with each other, usually on the basis of judged overall worth. Most typically, these judgements are obtained by a simple ranking of jobs – hence the name 'ranking method'. However, jobs can be judged relative to others by the use of other procedures, such as the paired comparison procedure; this method could more appropriately be called the 'job comparison method'. The reliability of the evaluation usually is enhanced by having several individuals – preferably people who are already familiar with the jobs in question – serve as evaluators. When there are many jobs to be evaluated, however, it usually is impossible to find individuals who are familiar with all of them. Although there are ways of combining evaluations, with each rater evaluating only some of the jobs, this method is usually best suited to small organizations with limited numbers of jobs.

Classification method

The classification method consists of the establishment of several categories of jobs along a hypothetical scale. Each such classification usually is defined and sometimes is illustrated. The Civil Service System is essentially a classification system. In using this method, each job is assigned to a specific classification on the basis of its judged overall worth and its relation to the descriptions of the several classifications.

The classification method is a rather simple one to develop and use. However, unless special care is taken it permits a tendency to perpetuate possible inequalities in existing rates of pay if it is used for evaluation of existing jobs that already have designated rates.

Point method

The point method is without question the most commonly used procedure. It is characterized by the following features:

1 The use of several job evaluation factors.
2 The asssignment of 'points' to varying 'degrees' or levels of each factor.
3 The evaluation of individual jobs in terms of their 'degree' or level on each factor, and the assignment to each job of the number of points designated for the degree or level on the factor.
4 The addition of the point values for the individual factors to derive the total point value for each job.

This total point value then serves as the basis for conversion to the corresponding wage or salary rate.

Factor comparison method

In this method, 15 or 20 tentative 'key jobs' are first selected. These are jobs that have present rates not subject to controversy and that are considered by the job evaluation committee to be neither underpaid nor overpaid. These jobs are then compared with others in terms of factors common to all jobs. The 'key jobs' are first ranked on each of the factors (mental requirements, physical requirements, responsibility and working conditions), with all of the jobs appearing on each of the factor lists. The rankings usually are made independently by several people, and usually three times by each rater, with approximately one week intervening between each ranking session. Next, these jobs are subjected to a rating process in which the going rate (salary or hourly rate) is divided, for each of the tentative key jobs, into the amount being 'paid' for each of the factors. From these two independent procedures, two rank orders of the tentative key jobs on each factor are determined. The first ranking results from the direct ranking of the jobs on the factors. The second comes from the rank order of the monetary values that result from the rating process. Any of the tentative key jobs that do not come out with essentially the same rank orders in the two independent ranking procedures are eliminated from the list of key jobs. The jobs remaining constitute the framework of the factor comparison system for the company making the installation. All other jobs are compared with these key jobs, and each is located in its appropriate place on each of the factors included in the system. The amounts to be paid for the job for the various factors are then added, which gives the evaluated rate for the job. (McCormick, 1979, 314–316).

There has been tendency to pursue the non-analytical approach, with individual training and development influencing both within-grade and between-grade progression, being integral to the design.

It is therefore necessary to consider some form of job profiling approach which allows the existing jobs to be fairly slotted into any new structure, but which does not give undue weight to the present structure. The structure must also reflect the shift in the philosophy on pay, and be able to accommodate any foreseen working arrangements (shift patterns, hours of work etc.).

What factors should be used

Some possible factors include:

Qualifications required (vocational and non-vocational).
Working conditions.
Time-management pressures.
Experience required.
Complexity of tasks.
Independence of job.
Responsibility/accountability of job.
The nature and level of staff control.
The amount, level and nature of contacts.
Balance of routine and non-routine tasks.
Flexibility required within the job.

Accuracy demanded.
Dexterity required.
Access to confidential material.
Strength and stamina necessary.
Level of activity in the job.
Training required.

These factors will need to be reduced to between five and eight in total.

Five of the above list can be rejected for the simple reason that they are common to almost all jobs to a reasonable degree. *Accuracy* is a demand of all jobs; *training required* depends mainly on the individual, not on the job itself; *confidential material* is dealt with at all levels and abuse is subject to a disciplinary procedure; *dexterity* is rapidly becoming a required skill for all jobs, e.g. the use of computers; and the *level of activity* is very much a quality of all jobs, especially with the reduction in numbers.

Similarly, factors such as working conditions and strength and stamina can be eliminated because they often relate to the sex of the job-holder.

The remaining factors can be further reduced to the following five elements:

Factors	*Elements*
Qualifications	Qualifications and job knowledge
Experience	
Time management	
Independence	Responsibility
Accountability	
Complexity	
Routine and non-routine	Complexity
Contacts	
Communication	Coordination
Staff/team control	Staff

The factors most likely to need to be added to such a list are:

Standard and non-standard solutions: to *Complexity*.
Advice and influence: to *Coordination and planning*.
Initiative and judgement: to *Responsibility*.
Contractors/temporary staff: to *Staff control*.
Environmental conditions: to *Complexity*.

Once the list of elements has been agreed (explored through repeated testing to ensure that they cover the core components of every job), they can be subdivided into four or five levels.

Implementation

Thus, when the five or so elements have been derived, and the four or five levels within each element described, it is possible to translate each level within an element into a specific competency or range of competencies. It is these competencies which can be compared with an external measure of ability as operated by the National Council for Vocational Qualifications (see Figure 8.1).

Level	Qualifications and job knowledge	Responsibility	Complexity	Coordination	Staff
1					
2					
3					
4					
5					

Figure 8.1 *Factor–level matrix*

The task data can be slotted in either in the form offered, or the framework can be modified into a skills development matrix. In this type of matrix again three or four levels are used but the tasks are this time categorized by function or area of competence, e.g. production, science/quality, commercial, engineering etc. This type of pay structure is shown in Figure 8.2.

It is the application of these types of matrix or skill-based payment systems that has become popular. The classic example of this system is the Gaines Petfood plant (owned by General Foods) in Topeka (see Lawler, 1981:65–69) which has been in operation for more than fifteen years (see also Gupta *et al.*, 1986).

There is a range of pay and reward options and, no matter which option is chosen, the task data can be used to define the existing job families, the new jobs and structure, the possible remuneration structures etc. Again, the approach to the design and development of the pay and rewards structure should follow a logical system along the lines of the one used to design the jobs and organization. Figures 8.3 and 8.4 describe the typical methodology and project structure for a pay and rewards investigation. The key

	Leadership	Craft	Process	Science	Business	
A	Stand in for team leader. Using formal supv./mgt training.	Total breakdown. Diagnostics and pharmaceutics, various craft skills.	Flexible manf. op. with knowledge of product problems.	Fault diagnosis method problems/ services budget (a greater knowledge of chem. theory). ONC.	Planning/stock control. Customer services budget. ONC Business Studies	Recognized potential from Levels C–E or aptitude for specialism/ support.
B	Company supervisory courses and training.	PPM maintenance and troubleshooting. STA C & G.	Manufacturing skills.	Maintaining, setting analytical instruments (a greater knowledge of instruments). 'O' levels.	Scheduling. 'O' levels or C & G modules.	
C	Coaching and training of basic skills, i.e. trained trainers.	Machine set-up. Adjustment. Batch changes. Basic day-to-day maintenance.	Strip down and clean machinery.	Operating analytical methods (operating automated methods).	Collation. Materials' handling.	Selection into this group from Level D vs. business needs.
D		Cleaning machinery. V. basic change Parts.	Operating machinery. Packaging operator. GMP training. HASAW training.	Counting, weighing. Physical tests. Simple calculations, i.e. basic IPC and reconciliations.		Appraisal/ assessment. On-the-job training. 'Recognized potential. Plotting possible. Career maps vs. business needs.
E			INDUCTION			
	1	2	3	4	5	

Figure 8.2 *Skill–level matrix*

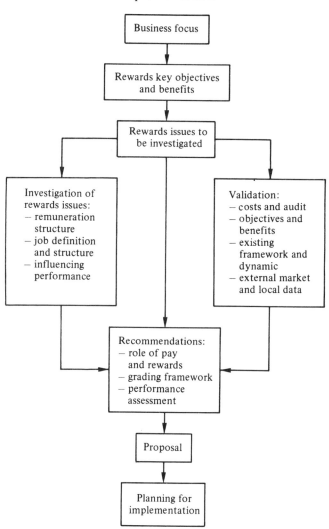

Figure 8.3 *Pay and rewards project methodology*

input into such an investigation is a clear indication of the content of the jobs and how they might be developed and maintained.

Monitoring and evaluating the changes

The final key aspect of the implementation is the development of an effective and efficient means of monitoring and evaluating the changes as they occur. They are two main reasons for creating a review system (monitoring and evaluating system):

1 The need in the short term to ensure that the changes are successfully implemented, and that successful implementation can be learnt from and transferred throughout the organization.

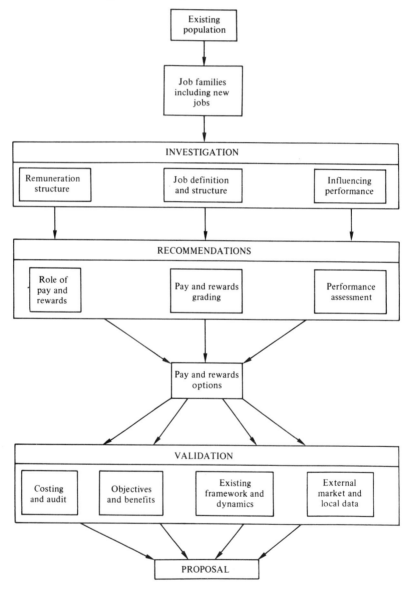

Figure 8.4 *Pay and rewards project structure*

Implementation

2 The need to create what Digital Equipment call the 'development cycle' of continuous change and improvement which is always trying to stretch the initial ideas developed in designing the jobs and organization structure and so yield on-going improvements.

For the successful review of progress it is necessary to install within the new organization a review process. Often this is not immediately possible and so an ad hoc or temporary body needs to be created which brings interested parties together. An example is useful here to illustrate this type of review system.

Example 1. Joint review mechanism at a UK oil refinery

With the rapid changes in the price for crude oil all of the oil companies introduced cost reduction programmes during the late 1970s and early 1980s. These cost programmes invariably included the closure of refineries, e.g. in the UK refineries closed at Ellesmere Port (Burmah Castrol), Milford Haven (Esso), Teesport (Shell), Isle of Grain (British Petroleum); distribution costs were cut by reducing the number of terminals, e.g. both Shell and Esso introduced quite major changes, while Conoco went to contract distribution; and finally, at most of the large refineries flexibility/productivity deals were introduced, e.g. Esso (1982 and 1983), Shell (at Stanlow in 1985), Mobil (1984) etc. This example draws upon the experience of Shell between 1985 and 1989.

Two major productivity deals were proposed at the Shell Stanlow refinery in March 1985 to introduce a series of changes in working practices within engineering (the 'craft deal') and operations (the 'process deal'). These two deals also called for large (30 per cent) reductions in both the engineering and production workforces on a voluntary basis. Similar cost reduction exercises and productivity deals had been introduced before at Stanlow. On previous occasions a temporary reduction in costs had been achieved, but no lasting changes in the way people worked. It was therefore in the minds of both parties, 'the management' and 'the unions', to ensure that the 1985 agreement lasted longer than, for instance, the honeymoon period of only 18 months or so which had been achieved at Fawley (Esso Petroleum) and Coryton (Mobil Oil). The solution arrived at was to introduce a Joint Review Board.

The Joint Review Board (JRB) was made up of four craft shop stewards, four managers from engineering and personnel (including the Site Engineering Manager/Chief Engineer) and two facilitators/organization development consultants (one internal, from Shell's UK head office, and one external independent adviser). This membership was held between

October 1985 and May 1987, when managers from operations were introduced and the most senior manager was drawn from operations.

While aspects of the role of the JRB were recorded in the signed agreement of 1985, its purpose and aims had not been agreed. Both of these were developed and agreed in late 1985 as follows:

Purpose: To contribute to the effectiveness and efficiency of the refinery/site by ensuring that the productivity aims of the deal are fully achieved.

Aims: To set objectives.
To communicate.
To provide resources.
To define progress measures.
To promote positive attitudes.
To assess progress.
To identify and resolve problems.
To transfer good practice.
To provide a long-term view.

In order to achieve its purpose and aims, the JRB agreed on a series of fixed review items which, taken together, would assess the health of the deal. The information required for these fixed review items came from three main sources:

1 Existing management information systems within engineering, operations and personnel.
2 A specific review board for craft training (the Craft Training Review Board).
3 Ad hoc surveys of craftsmen, operations management and supervisors etc.

The items which were reviewed with this information were:

Attitudes.
Efficient operations.
Service to operations.
Working practices.
Training.
Representation.
Consultation.
Contractors.
Overtime.
Costs.

Implementation 313

A little more needs to be said about each of these ten items to make them more understandable.

1 Attitudes: are attitudes positive towards the deal?
   This was measured by examining statistics on health and safety, absence etc. and by direct survey questioning.
2 Efficient operations: concerns the internal operations with maintenance.
   How efficient is the planning system?
   Measured by using internal information from planning, stores, workshop etc. backed up by survey data.
3 Service to operations: what does the the customer think of the service provided by engineering? Does it meet operation's requirements?
   Measured with reference to plant availability and reliability, and the level of utilization. Again, backed up by a survey of operations.
4 Working practices: are craftsmen sharing skills? Are craftsmen working on non-core trade jobs?
   Largely measured through survey data and with reference to specific jobs.
5 Training: is the training effective? Is the balance of off-the-job to the on-the-job right? Are people being released for training?
   Information collected by the CTRB from the training centre and from the training focal points and each of the plants in the form of individual training log sheets.
6 Representation: are the new representative structures working well?
   Reference here is to the change in the craft trade union representative structure to an area or constituency, rather than being trade based. Data provided by craft shop stewards.
7 Consultation: are the existing and new consultation structures working well?
   This is a general question seeking a measure of the quantity, quality and effectiveness of joint bodies, e.g. covering safety, training, etc.
   Again, information largely provided by shop stewards, but also from surveys of the communication systems.
8 Contractors: What are the levels? What are they being used for? Are their numbers reducing?
   It was accepted by both sides that the number of contractors and agency labour on site would need to be increased to cover training and to do some overhaul work. It was also expected from the outset that contract numbers would rise, then progressively fall as the on-site engineering craftsmen became increasingly skilled and productive.
   Most of the information was provided here from the existing maintenance and engineering systems.
9 Overtime: What levels of overtime are being worked? Is there real

equity of overtime opportunities? Is overtime being held to low, single figures?

Historically overtime was high on the refinery, especially in shutdowns, e.g. 30 per cent and trade related. It was further inflated by the use of overtime rather than shift premiums for non-day working. After the introduction of the deal it was planned to keep overtime below 5 per cent.

10 Costs: Is expenditure in line with budget? Are costs being contained/reduced?

The prime purpose of the deal was to reduce costs by significantly reducing resources and by improving the use of the existing ones.

These ten items were reviewed on a 6–8 week basis with major reviews of training and working practices every quarter. Arising from the findings of this review process, other issues emerged and were tackled:

1985 (3 JRB meetings held)

Role/purpose/aims of the JRB.

1986 (11 JRB meetings held)

Influence on longer-term, site-wide issues.
Materials availability.
Measurement survey of working practices (third survey).
Impact of proposed site organizational changes on training.
New maintenance organization for one part of the site.
Temporary foremen.
Temporary shifts.
Motivation/morale of craftsmen.
Use of training.
Update on site-wide developments relevant to the JRB.
Role and membership of the JRB.
Balance between expertise and flexibility – how far do we go either way?
Shutdown performance.
On-the-job training and practice.
Overtime.
Role of the supervisor.
Visits to other sites.
Priorities, planning and preparation of maintenance work when providing a service to operations.

1987 (10 JRB meetings held)

Minor maintenance/operations doing maintenance.

Operations review of the engineering deal.
Confined space standby procedures.
New maintenance measures/ratios.
Responsibility for training in the production units (combined engineering and operations organizations).
Setting-up of production unit review teams (PURTs), i.e. JRBs at local level.
Production unit role clarification.
Overtime guidelines.
Planning – access and quality problems.
Timekeeping.
Permits to work.
Validity of data being used.
Communication for training across the site.
Consistency of interpretation of training assessment.
Measurement survey of working practices (fourth survey).
Selling of the benefits of the JRB process – what has been learnt?
Availability of information on site.
Future of the central workshop.
Linkage of the JRB to the new production unit structure.
Role and contribution of the JRB.
Future of training in terms of needs, future skills profile, funding, facilities, validation, for teams and individuals, and end-point of the craft training in the production and service units.
Contractors.
Educating production unit managers about the craft deal.
Temporary foremen.

1988 (7 JRB meetings held)

Minor maintenance done by operators.
Minor operations done by craftsmen.
Future and current role of the JRB.
Management and equity of overtime.
Training in terms of focus, resourcing, responsibility for standards and management, and focal points in the production units.
Use of contractors.
Information requirements of the JRB.
The quality and relevance of the information used by JRB.
Measurement of success.
Communication of the JRB work.
Apprenticeships.
Job security.
Promotion prospects, e.g. quality assurance engineering positions.

Pay progression.
Measurement of performance.
External learning from other sites.
Operations review of the craft deal and the progressing of its findings.
Temporary shifts for shutdowns.
Role of the supervisor.
Confined space standby.
Listening and responding to complaints.
Change of trade union membership.
Content of the minutes of the meeting.
Labour mobility across the site.
Timekeeping.
Planning.
Permit-to-work procedures.
Knowledge of the craft deal among the production unit managers.

Over the period 1985–1988 the issues handled by the JRB can be divided into five main groups:

1 Issues directly related to the deal itself.
2 Issues related to the internal working of the JRB.
3 Issues related to engineering matters.
4 Issues related to boundary problems/interfaces with other departments.
5 Issues concerning the whole site.

In addition to those issues which fall completely into one of these five areas, there are those that overlap two of the five 'issue areas' (see Figure 8.5).

Achievements of the JRB

What did this JRB achieve? How does it show that the setting-up of a review body is worthwhile? First, let us look at the successes of this JRB.

1 It got the deal implemented.
2 It established adult craft training on site.
3 It provided an effective means for an open interpretation of the deal.
4 It offered the opportunity to develop the transfer and sharing of maintenance work with operators.
5 It created a pressure on the supervisors in engineering to think about their role.
6 It raised awareness of the deep-seated issues in engineering which were barriers to improvement.

Implementation 317

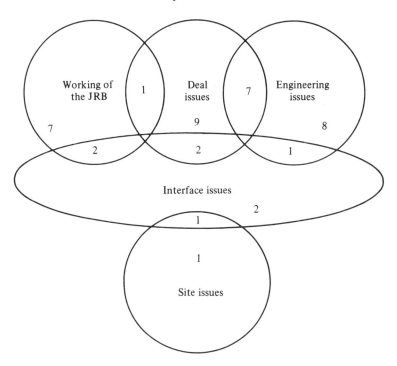

Figure 8.5 *Issues tackled by the JRB 1985–1988*

7 It provided a stimulation to others, especially in engineering, to take actions to introduce improvements.
8 It provided the means and opportunity for operations to review the progress and contribution of the craft deal to their activities. It therefore created bridges between engineering and operations and exposed misunderstandings and weaknesses on both sides.
9 It introduced the first regular review mechanism which built up information from the bottom of the organization about change at the individual level.
10 It introduced and produced regular communication channels up and down the engineering organization.
11 It provided the means by which the deal could be implemented over the next four years, and could be further developed on two occasions.
12 It prevented side issues from obscuring the key issues, and also minor issues from being blown up into major ones.
13 It provided a vehicle for the development, on a joint basis, of solutions to problems encountered.
14 It provided a role model for others in the organization to copy as the JRB showed that it had teeth and was worthwhile.

15 It provided the basis on which future changes in working practices could be discussed and developed across all of the departments on site.

The JRB therefore achieved its two overriding aims, the immediate implementation of the craft deal, and provision of a vehicle for development of the craft deal beyond engineering. In fact it provided during 1989 the basis for the creation of the Stanlow Working Arrangements Group (SWAG), which brought all parties together on site.

The following characteristics of the JRB over the period 1985–1989 are relevant in other contexts.

1 Legitimized by being integral to a joint agreement.
2 Tackled real problems, e.g. pay, training, organization changes etc.
3 Mirrored site organization.
4 Chaired by a senior manager who was a member of the site management team.
5 Directly linked to other bodies actively pursuing change and the implementation of the deal.
6 Respected by senior shop stewards and craftsmen.
7 Senior shop stewards on JRB have 'clout'.
8 Had a series of early successes.

The experience of this JRB also shows that such a body:

9 Must communicate widely and sometimes independently of existing channels.
10 Must be properly resourced in time to do its business.
11 Must change to match changes on site and establish relationships with new groups as they emerge.
12 Must seek to be pro-active, and not wait for problems to emerge.
13 Must be participative.

While the Shell JRB experience might appear restrictive and relatively slow, it does represent a realistic and pragmatic attempt to move the culture from being very short-term, confrontational and autocratic to one in which joint problem-solving is the norm. It also provided an example of the idea of continuous improvement being introduced and developed over a 3–4 year period.

Summary

Changing job and organization structures can be divided into two main components: the design of the new jobs and organization structure, and the implementation of the changes via three main interventions of training, pay and rewards, and regulation. Together these two components provide a meaningful way of successfully introducing and developing working practices. The third major component of the implementation exercise is communication, which forms the basis of the next chapter.

9
Communications

Introduction

The purposes of communications are many. At one extreme communications seek to raise awareness and contact with an idea or concept, while at the other end they seek to change the receiver of the information. Because the purposes of communications are many it is all the more important that they be considered in some detail. Communications form a key part of any change strategy. This chapter seeks to bring together some of the points raised in previous chapters, and to describe a few additional ones. This chapter is divided into three parts. The first considers a few questions to ask ourselves about communications, and the second poses the questions we should expect from the recipients of a 'change in working practice' message. The third draws together a number of more general points about communications in change situations.

Key questions about communications

1 Who is our 'market'? How is it made up? What do they know already?
2 What message are we trying to communicate? Where do we want the receivers of the communication to be once the message has been delivered? What reaction do we want from the receivers of the message?
3 What methods are available to us for delivery of our communications?
4 What form should the message take?
5 How frequently do we put out a message?
6 How do we know whether we are succeeding? What measures of success shall we use to assess whether the message we are communicating is being received, is being understood, and better still, acted upon?

Each of these questions should be posed and answered. The review system can be achieved in a number of ways. One is to organize structured feedback through syndicates and formalized information-sharing exercises. Another is to run surveys which elicit responses to the quality, quantity and content of communications. These audit exercises can be very effective means of collating data and judging 'where next'.

At the more informal level, small changes in the way meetings are arranged and agendas formed and in the style of the meeting can also communicate a series of points. It is possible so to structure meetings that people do contribute their ideas, and build on those of others. The way in which the minutes of a meeting are then used and the decisions agreed acted upon can also communicate the importance of the group meeting and the issues addressed. Not only the written, visual and spoken messages should be considered, but also the physical gestures and symbols – which can have a far greater impact.

In the specific case of changing job and organization structures it is vital to focus the communication on the individual and to consider his/her response to 'change'. Why should someone fear change and be unreceptive to communications about it? Let us consider a range of possible negative responses at the individual level – fifteen points can be readily identified (Plant, 1987: 18):

1 Fear of the unknown.
2 Lack of relevant information.
3 Misinformation.
4 Threat to existing core skills and competencies.
5 Threat to existing status.
6 Threat to existing power base(s).
7 No perceived benefits.
8 Lack of trust in the promoters of the change.
9 Fear of failure.
10 Fear of looking stupid.
11 Threat to the existing and trusted successful customs and practices.
12 Disbelief that the company is serious.
13 Threat to secure future employment.
14 Threat to earnings opportunities.
15 Fear of being excluded/being left behind.

This list of possible negative reactions to change helps in the design of any employee communications package. Each of these fears must be addressed in a positive fashion. Within the first employee communications the following individual doubts *must* therefore be addressed:

1 Security. What, if any, will be the impact on employment security?
2 Status. What will be the impact on existing job hierarchies and promotion opportunities? Will long-established pecking orders be challenged, e.g. the relationship between top process operator jobs and craft jobs?

3 Structure. By what series of steps will the changes be introduced? How will it be structured? Where do I fit into the new structure?
4 Support. Many people will have their jobs removed by the changes; what support will be offered to them?
5 Stability. Will all of the changes be introduced at once, or will we go through a series of manageable steps?
6 Safety. Both the content of the proposed changes and their introduction might challenge safety standards; how will they be maintained?
7 Consistency. How do these changes fit with the past? Are these changes part of a management whim, or are they real and long term?
8 Control. How can I get involved in the changes? I know most about my job which you want to change, and so can I have a say?
9 Career. Will training be provided to allow the changes to be introduced? Where next, if I succeed in the training?
10 Communications. Can I ask questions? Can I have time to think, and seek more information? Will there be any more communication sessions like this one?
11 Reward. What will be the impact on pay and rewards? When will the pay be discussed and agreed?
12 Rationale. Why change now? Why change in this way?

If the initial communications address these twelve issues and recognize the particular fears of individuals then the communications stand a high chance of succeeding.

Questions about change raised by those affected

One of the most fruitful sources of information about job and organization changes is the questions raised by people during the launch, development and introduction of the changes. What follows are two sets of such questions which are offered as an input into communications planning: communications should answer these questions.

Example 1. Reactions to proposals for new jobs and organization in a pharmaceuticals factory

The proposed new structure brought together all of the skills and knowledge necessary to produce a single product in single jobs where possible, or in teams. It created overlaps between craft jobs, between craft, process and quality jobs etc. What follows are the questions raised by over 300 people after two presentations and syndicate sessions in groups of 20 or so.

Communications

General

Will we need a factory pool of packaging labour to develop operators?
What is wrong with the way it is now? How did other staff react?

Team make-up

How many enhanced operators per team?
If analysts are going into a support group, where will extra staff come from to do their jobs?
What is the ratio of enhanced operators to general operators?
Are there enough staff to subdivide lab?
What happens when team members don't get on?
What will be the breakdown of the team?

Engineering

Technical support – where are the two fitters coming from?
Where does the new engineering grade come into this structure?
Can job rotation be built into the structure (ref. to fitters)?
How can fitters be in a technical support team when there are only two in the department?
Clarify electrician's role?
An electrician is also capable of fitting skills?

Payment

How soon after training will payment follow?
Will additional payment take money off our annual rise?
Once you have attained a higher skill level do you get paid for it all the time?
Will you only be rewarded when actually carrying out a particular skill?
How flexible are the pay grades going to be?
Will all enhanced operators be on the same pay?
What will a new pay structure look like?

The rest of the site

Will this approach be used elsewhere on site?
Will other departments undergo a similar reorganization?
How will it affect cleaners?
What happens if there is a spillage on line – will production stop to clean it or will cleaners be called?

Carrying out the training

How can we still meet budget outputs with staff being released for training?
When will training begin?
Who trains whom?
How will holidays and sickness be covered?
How will training be prioritized?
How long will it take to train a person?
How broad a skill is required before you are rewarded?
Will the emphasis on training be biased towards higher grades?
How will training be organized and can you re-visit if failed at first attempt?
Have we got the people we need?
Will training include further education (external)?
What type of education will it include?

Visits

What was learnt from visits?
Were options developed after visiting other companies?

Selection of option

Is the option already picked?
Who makes the final decision?
Do the study group members uphold everything in the interim report?
Why carry out a cost/benefits analysis on only one option?
Do we need other people to help the study group?
Who will select the option? Will there be a vote?
Which option is run closest to at present?

New roles

Who will be responsible for team discipline?
Who will decide on the overlap of skills?
How will the overlap of skills affect bargaining groups, i.e. how broad an overlap is envisaged?
Define team coordinator/enhanced operator.
Explain planning/scheduling own work.
How much role overlap?
Will people believe that an operator with packaging technology training has the authority to question component faults and beg answers?

We have people already capable but getting no recognition.
Will the team coordinator automatically be a supervisor?
What is the difference between general and enhanced operators?

Company perspective/union negotiation

Will other sites follow our implementation?
At what stage will the company involve unions?
When will the reward for new skills be discussed?
Will negotiations be held at site or group level?
How will the system be monitored to ensure that it is on the right path?

Content of skill blocks

Where do existing skill levels fit into the new structure?
Do cleaners feature in this structure (matrix)?

Facilities and equipment

Who decides who goes on new high speed lines?
Who selects the operators that will be quicker than others to go on high speed lines, and will it cause friction?
Will there be more pay for running high speed lines?
Have we had the OK for the new room?
Will we still get new machines even if we don't get approval for the new room?
How many lines will the new room have?
Will it affect staff numbers?

Implementation

When will new structure be implemented?
Have roles already been earmarked for certain people?
Can the options still be implemented in the old facility?
Where next from interim report?
Flexitime or shifts?
Will the structure be implemented only when the new room is ready?

Selection criteria

Who decides in which direction operators move and how are they selected?
Does age come into it? Will there be an age limit?
Can opportunities be equal for male and female in all options?
What if everybody wants to become enhanced?

Will everybody be allowed to train to their fullest potential?
How will they decide who does what job?
Will there be tests?
What happens to those who don't fit in?
Why the swing from qualifications?
Will the pay structure be fair (it takes the whole team to get the work out)?
Will the number of people for training be restricted for any new skills?
Is everybody expected to go up or will some be expected to do lesser skills, e.g. supervisors?
How do they expect to train everybody?
Who chooses enhanced operators and how?
How do cleaners progress up the pay scale?
Does experience count when it comes to analytical support?
What opportunities will lab. people have to go into production and at what level?
Is a lab. technician going to end up an enhanced operator?
How will the coordinator be selected?
Will personnel determine who goes where?
What if you want to stay put?

Example 2. Reactions to new engineering roles in a food factory

In this case a series of eleven meetings was held to discuss a proposal to introduce a minor form of overlapping of craft roles. The presentations were made by the Chief Engineer and the Maintenance Manager. Both the questions and the answers are recorded in this example.

Meeting No. 1 – Workshop mechanical and stores

Question. With the possibility of more people being involved with their own plant handling will there be a lowering of safety standards?

Answer. There will be no lowering of standards, the work will only be carried out by competent persons.

Question. Why can't we be paid the full amount now if we are so flexible?

Answer. There is no agreement at this site other than for payment of the common craft rate.
 Our other site has accepted other schemes and moved up the pay ladder to its present position.

It is not possible to pay the full offer amount at the outset because of the 'knock on' effect with other groups on the site.

Question. Where will reliefs come from in the future?

Answer. The aim for the future is to have all skilled staff in maintenance, giving the opportunity for semi-skilled staff to be retrained for work in other engineering department groups.

Question. Will the flexibility payment be consolidated and will it form part of pensionable pay?

Answer. The payment will be kept separate, allowing for a two-pronged wage negotiation in the future. It will also be pensionable and form part of the O/T calculator.

Meeting No. 2 – Site services operators: Site shift fitter and mate, Production shift fitter and mate

Question. With so many on technician grade, why maintain the craft grade?

Answer. 1 It is used as a benchmark to which to relate other payments.
2 A craftsman in his probationary first year is less effective.
3 Very few people are affected by this.

Question. Who decides if a person is capable of a task?

Answer. His manager/supervisor is the best qualified to decide; obviously the person must highlight his own reservation if he has any.

Question. Will shift fitters' mates continue to be relieved from semi-skilled?

Answer. The company will use natural wastage to reduce shift mates and with more emphasis on skill it is likely that we shall eventually move to a 100 per cent skilled crew.
In the meantime the choice of skilled or semi-skilled reliefs will be determined by what is the most effective solution for a particular situation.

Question. If the company feels shift mates are so useful, why don't they get 90 per cent? What about the chargehand rate for the shift fitter if the shift fitter and production fitter are combined?

Answer. The 90 per cent rate is considered for those operators who provide a continuous service and do a job on their own, e.g. without the immediate availability of a craftsman. Chargehand rate will carry on as a leading hand will be required.

Question. Site services operators currently show a great deal of flexibility so surely new rate should be 90 per cent of the new craft rate? Some of the financial savings do not match in any way the rewards offered.

Answer. These savings would be considered anyway.

Question. Semi-skilled can contribute as much as a tradesman, so why shift the balance?

Answer. A skilled tradesman is capable of far more in different areas so, with the differential of 10 semi-skilled to 9 skilled for the same money, the latter is more effective.

Question. Will the power-house operator be included in the proposed boiler-house crew for holiday/sick relief?

Answer. Yes.

Question. If the number in a self-relieving crew falls below the minimum, will the other shifts with spare reliefs cover?

Answer. This has yet to be considered in detail; reliefs could come from either other shifts or daywork, whichever is more effective.

Question. What happens to crewing if we go back onto oil?

Answer. In the event of the gas supply being interrupted we would revert to the three-man crew for the period of interruption.

Question. Too much is being considered at one time with flexibility being confused with manning.

Answer. It is only fair to put all the cards on the table; the money is fixed, all that can be considered are the requirements.

Question. The reward for the boiler crew does not compensate for potential loss of earnings.

Answer. Changes in agreements are being considered anyway as the situation in the boiler house has changed.

Meeting No. 3 – Electrical department

Question. Is the paging system on order?

Answer. Yes, the system is for use by management as well as shop floor personnel.

Question. How much money do continental workers get by comparison?

Answer. Approximately 100 per cent more, with manning levels at 50 per cent of the UK average.
   However, with only 10 per cent reduction in engineering staff levels over four years and a much higher inflation rate than on the continent, this differential has considerably narrowed.

Question. How can a reduction in shift strengths be financially beneficial to the shift relief man currently earning £520 minimum for this service?

Answer. Overall, the deal will pay out more than the losses. Reliefs will still be required to a lesser extent.

Question. Will there be redundancies if the scheme is thrown out?

Answer. There will be no enforced redundancies but the proposals will still be 'nibbled' away at over a period of time through economic necessity.

Question. Are we not quick enough getting to the job?

Answer. We have no complaints about the service as it stands. What can be improved is effectiveness, i.e. – a reduction in the time it takes to get information relayed.
   Acceptance of the use of a paging system will improve the situation. More effectiveness means less people for the same work.

Question. Will there be fewer contractors on site?

Answer. We always look at our own staff to cover the work in the first instance as far as is practicable, particularly where 'in house' skills are involved, but we cannot cope with the variable project load and maintain time schedules solely with our labour. The contract work load will be variable.

Question. Will there be any problems in getting approval for payment of phases II and III of the proposals?

Answer. No, it is seen as a rubber-stamping exercise if people co operate.

Meeting No. 4 – Oil production and site services

Meeting No. 6 – Site services operators: Site shift fitter and mate, production shift fitter and mate

Meeting No. 11 – Site services operators: Site shift fitter and mate, production shift fitter and mate

Question. Painters and fabrication sections have been given the opportunity for voluntary redundancy. Would there be any enforced redundancies?

Answer. There will not be any enforced redundancies as a direct result of these proposals. Two areas have been highlighted, i.e. painting and fabrication, where skills outside the site are readily available at competitive rates.

Question. With more painting and fabrication going to contract, will this also apply to mechanical work?

Answer. No. At present the overall fitting strength is less than required. If losses occurred in the painting and fabrication sections the opportunity would be taken to shift the balance of trades and correct fitting shortfalls in certain areas.

Question. Why 18 months before the full amount of money will be paid?

Answer. Paying the full amount initially could cause problems with other groups. So it will be introduced in steps.
Management have agreed with head office that we will have parity with our other site in 18 months from acceptance date.

Question. Will acceptance of the deal mean that every change to a job has to be negotiated?

Answer. No, if they are capable they would be expected to carry out assigned tasks.

Question. With flexibility would any work done by engineering department be transferred to production department?

Answer. Flexibility has only been considered within the engineering department. The transfer of work from engineering to production would be the subject of separate discussions.

Question. Would overtime be compulsory?

Answer. No.

Question. Will it be compulsory to work through meal breaks?

Answer. No, but people would be expected to work in an emergency.

Question. If the boiler house were operating with only two men, at certain periods (collecting meals, transferring samples to the lab. etc.) only one man would be in the plant.

Answer. This is something that will be discussed, but manning of plant cannot be planned at levels to cover these isolated periods. With the introduction of the paging system communication will be much improved, so contact with supervision and management will be available should problems occur.

Question. At the moment planned maintenance in most departments is minimal. How would flexibility affect this?

Answer. It is really the furtherance of self-relieving shift crews that will enable a more stable daywork crew to be established. This in turn will allow more planned work to be undertaken which ultimately will improve plant reliability. Improved maintenance strategies are being prepared for the site with a view to use of computer techniques.

Question. The distribution of monies available between craft and semi-skilled seems unfair.

Answer. Discussions with head office on money available and distribution had been very difficult. Management's aim that all should benefit from the flexibility proposals was achieved but it is not possible to make the payments the same for everyone.

Meeting No. 5 – Maintenance daywork: production daywork, stores, some boiler house personnel

Question. Why did we not get higher rates for redundancies, similar to Mobil for flexibility?

Answer. We are not financing our flexibility by redundancy.

Question. Since the grading scheme was turned down there have been considerable savings, could some of that money be put on the table?

Answer. We can't go backwards, our engineers rejected the scheme and that is all water under the bridge. The scheme at our other site has advanced in return for improved flexibility and fixed job losses of semi-skilled over predetermined periods.

Question. Could there not have been a fairer distribution between the groups?

Answer. 'Fair' is different for every individual; the structure proposed is designed to move closer to fit market rates.

Question. Will there be more grading splits in the future?

Answer. We are seeking to broaden the flexibility/skills of all trades, therefore we do not envisage creating further grades.

Question. Is it pensionable?

Answer. It is pensionable, and contributes to the overtime calculator. It has been kept separate from the basic to try to create a ladder for future negotiations to enhance real pay on the site.

Question. If a person is asked to work through a meal break, who defines an emergency and how is he paid?

Answer. Management/supervision decide on an emergency. While the current embargo has been on there has only been one known case. Current rules will still apply regarding payment.

Question. Does flexibility reduce costs?

Answer. This is difficult to extract, as many different factors affect the final cost.

Question. What about administration and management reductions?

Answer. The percentage reduction in management and supervision over the past four years has been greater than on the shop floor. A large proportion of engineering management and supervision is concerned with on-going projects with current spending at £5M per year.

Question. With manning in the boiler house down to two men, at some stage one occasionally will work on his own. Is this safe?

Answer. We do not intend to operate unsafely; however, we cannot arrange continuous manning to cover the very occasional situation. If a person is unsure he should call his supervisor and with the paging system this will be even easier.

Question. As certain skills are immediately required, will total numbers increase?

Answer. The head count will not increase but the balance between trades will shift.

Question. What will happen to existing skilled staff as multi-skilled general-purpose apprentices come through?

Answer. Ample training opportunity will be given to existing tradesmen to broaden their skills and apprentices will still be classified in a trade but with bolt-on skills to help them with their job.

Question. If the stores delivery system is implemented will extra men be provided?

Answer. This hasn't been discussed and nothing is decided.

Meeting No. 7 – Mechanical (shift)

Meeting No. 10 – Mechanical (shift)

Question. What is the future manning level of mechanical shifts?

Answer. In the future the manning will be six fitters self-relieving to five fitters/shift. However, this will be a gradual process and will involve the cooperation of all shift members. There will be periods when shift crews will comprise five fitters and one auto-attendant. As permanent shift semi-skilled vacancies occur in other sections, the younger auto-attendants will be given the opportunity to fill those positions. This will be a matter of personal choice and it is not intended to force this situation.

Question. Will flexibility reduce overtime?

Answer. It has been and will continue to be the aim of the department/company to reduce overtime level. However, approximately half of the overtime currently worked is for production requirements.

Meeting No. 8 – Fabrication and civil sections

Question. Is the ultimate aim to shut down the fabrication section?

Answer. No, a small competent and flexible crew will still be required.

Question. How far ahead can you see?

Answer. The company works to a five-year plan.

Question. What about the continuous use of contract labour on 'borderline' work, i.e. alterations and improvements?

Answer. There is no way we could permanently employ sufficient people to do both maintenance and investment work. If profitability stops, projects stop. It is necessary to maintain tight permanent labour strength to keep fixed costs down.

Enforced redundancy is not the company's aim. We are not in the 'hire and fire' business and there will always be a need to use contractors.

Question. What is the proposed ultimate strength of painters?

Answer. Two.

Question. What is the proposed ultimate strength of the pipe trades?

Answer. Three.

Question. Are the proposals with respect to mates carrying out fire cover duties covered by the company liability insurance?

Answer. More information required.

Question. Why can't painters receive all the offer?

Answer. The company will not allow the full rate to be paid. Comparisons have been made with other schemes and with the various trade groups outside the company.

Question. Why, for the total sum on the table, have we got to wait 18 months?

Answer. Flexibility must be demonstrated. We have got to start somewhere.

Our other site accepted grading proposals and staff reductions some time ago. (Explanation of difficulties of negotiations with head office.)

Question. Will payment increase with inflation?

Answer. Yes.

Question. What about the future with possible changes in management?

Answer. Once the situation is agreed, it will remain unless changed by negotiation.

Question. Will there be the possibility of an 'additional skills payment' separately?

Answer. No.

Question. If the scheme is not accepted, what will happen?

Answer. We have still got to be more effective. Shift strengths will still be reduced but the whole business will be more painful and slower.
There are not many opportunities to install a scheme such as is proposed and which was put forward by our management. Nobody is forcing the scheme in.
There are no proposals for alternative ideas.

Question. Will the call-out system be scrapped?

Answer. No – there are some difficulties but these will be discussed separately.

Question. Will other trades be involved in welding operations?

Answer. This point has not been included in any discussion. 'Allied trade' skills are points for separate counselling.

Meeting No. 9 – Instrument department and mechanical (shift)

Question. Who will decide who is capable?

Answer. This will be down to the section manager/supervisor – growth in capabilities is recognized as a slow process and must be carried out sensibly.

Question. What form would any training take?

Answer. This would be arranged out of discussion; courses can be organized – needs could be met by exposure with other personnel – requirements must be identified by personal counselling.

Question. What would happen to existing chargehands with a merger?

Answer. We will still require people who can lead. There is a need to honour current chargehand status.

Question. What about relief chargehands?

Answer. This needs to be fully discussed.

Question. Will fitters be expected to take over the duties of auto-attendants?

Answer. Changes in practices will mean this work could be carried out by operators – other tasks could be carried out as daywork activities.

Question. What about the 'safety' of auto-attendant jobs as stated when greasing activities were changed?

Answer. The emphasis was now changing from semi-skilled to skilled. The three young men could be absorbed across the three shifts.

Question. If the sixth man is an auto-attendant, will he be paid the same as the fitters?

Answer. No.

Question. Is it possible for the three-man crew of instrument mechanics to be reduced to two?

Answer. It could be. If we were wrong in our assessment of the situation we will find out in a self-relieving situation.

Question. What if the total shift balance changes due to sickness etc.?

Answer. The shift will need to be adjusted by judgement, using an extra man working days if necessary. Better planning, flexibility and the use of a paging system will help to improve effectiveness.

Perpetual faults need to be designed out to ease the total work load. (Comparison made with other companies re shift strengths.)

Question. Can we ask for more money next year?

Answer. Yes there are extra rungs on the pay ladder for extra skills.

Question. Why do we have to wait for 18 months for the money?

Answer. Comparison with the other company site, we turned down previous proposals. Money not available overnight; must be seen to earn it; 'knock on' effect: best deal negotiated.

Question. Did our other site's mates get anything?

Answer. No.

Question. How will the scheme affect overtime?

Answer. The overtime calculator will be increased. We can't manage without overtime, some 50 per cent is dictated by production needs. However, there is always the need to minimize overtime. Non-productive overtime will be saved.

Question. What about the problems of releasing plant?

Answer. A better scheme means more credibility with production management. It's a 'chicken and egg' situation – a more stable daywork workforce is required.

Question. What about spares availability?

Answer. This should not present a problem. Flagging up of problems is required from tradesmen etc.

In this second example some very specific questions forced out a series of commitments which the company later could not honour. It showed that the company concerned had not really prepared its communications effectively. The example and the list of questions do provide useful material. Again, communications should be able to handle these questions.

Lessons learnt about communications from companies introducing new jobs and organization structures

Here is a series of points learnt from the experiences of 140 companies during the 1980s.

Communicate 'like you have never communicated before' Don't allow the grapevine to take over.
Remember the power of agendas and the way meetings are run. Both can indicate changes in managerial style.
Meetings are important. Consider their purpose and structure them appropriately in process terms to achieve the relevant outcomes.
Remember that what you think an employee knows and understands might not (and in all probability does not) coincide with what the organization thinks the employee knows and understands. Information needs must be assessed.
Information priorities are in operation with most individuals. They start with information relevant to personal needs, then there is the information relevant to the job and immediate work situation, and finally, there are the wider information needs relating to the broader company issues, e.g. training, investment etc.
Any information being communicated should be understood, apposite and relevant.
Match the means of delivery information with the purpose of the communication e.g. a verbal presentation can persuade, explain, instruct and update.
Share as much information as possible. Do not operate a 'need to know' policy.
Do not hedge. Say 'No,' if you mean 'No'.
Use language that describes reality, is relevant and is in everyday use.
Do not dress up ideas to give them a false rationale.
Record and write down *all* communications.
Do not rely on single channels or single deliveries of a key message. Repeat key messages frequently.
Downward and feedback communications sessions should be organized.
Effective communications is a key managerial competence – audit it via the appraisal system.
Management should be visible and act out communications, i.e. 'They do what they say'.
Make use of all communication techniques, e.g. audio-visual, video shows, surveys etc.

Multi-channel communications are vital and senior management support must be 'visible and physical'.

'On-going communications inputs are necessary in terms of the logging of progress etc. which can be channelled down existing lines of communication.

Understanding at all levels through constant and consistent communications will help to provide a common base on which to build.

The process of developing a company mission/vision statement and its translation into realizable actions is a key step for the building of a common understanding of the direction of the changes, at least at senior management level. This is also important for the shop stewards committees to go through. Provide a clear focus on the aim of the exercise and make sure that this is widely shared.

Changes must be needed and seen as such by those involved – a rationale must exist.

Some of these points may seem a little like stating the obvious, but they are rarely recognized and acted upon. Developing communication skills among *all* managers is vital and must form part of the training for managers and supervisors prior to implementation.

Summary

Without the ability to 'sell ideas' in a clear and understandable way, any change initiative will flounder. Auditing and developing communication skills at the individual and organizational level is a key intervention. In this chapter we have considered a number of questions to be considered and examples of the demands for information by employees embarking on a process of change.

10
Where next?

The preceding chapters have addressed the design, content and application of a task-orientated job and organization design and development method which has been empirically developed over the ten years leading up to the 1990s. At this point, it seems appropriate to speculate on the future, with particular attention to the application of the approach described in this book.

In three recent texts, this 'Where next?' question is posed. They provide a useful input into our thinking about how jobs and organization methods and their outputs might develop in the future. William Pasmore (1988) identifies two key areas for development: values, and some possible changes in the socio-technical systems paradigm. Under values, he identifies:

1 Ownership and commitment through participation.
2 Developing people.
3 Making technology more compassionate.
4 Sharing rewards.
5 Becoming more comfortable with change.
6 'Reaching out' versus 'closing in'.
7 Cooperation versus competition.
8 The ultimate value.

Pasmore also identifies some possible changes in the sociotechnical systems paradigm:

1 New applications for sociotechnical systems thinking.
2 Changes in how sociotechnical system thinking is applied.

In a sharply focused book on job analysis, Michael Pearn and Rajvinder Kandola (1988) identify six areas in which job, task and role analytical methods might develop in the future:

1 Computer-based systems.
2 Computer-assisted systems.
3 More emphasis on processes.
4 Complete systems.

Where next? 341

5 Synthetic validity.
6 Employment legislation.

Finally, Thomas Cummings (1989) identifies eight specific developments for organization development in the future:

1 Broader conceptual boundaries.
2 Integrative contingency perspectives.
3 A science of changing.
4 Large-scale transformation change.
5 Managing environments and creating strategic alliances.
6 Action learning.
7 General management and business concerns.
8 Greater accountability and rigorous assessment.

Several common themes emerge from these three lists of future developments in the general field of job and organization design and development. The main areas are:

1 Comprehensiveness of the approach.
2 Greater application of methods and techniques to assist organizations to improve their jobs and structures.
3 Scale of issues tackled.
4 Greater effort to ascribe costs and benefits from organization development intervention.
5 Changes in the 'process' skills of individuals and organizations.

In addition to these five general areas of agreement, the following developments are foreseen.

Relationship with job content and long-term skill/competence development

At present, jobs are developed in an incremental way 'on top of' an existing core of skills. It is not clear what are the long-term implications of failure to understand fully whether damage is caused to individuals whose core skill base is never developed. How adaptable will they be in the long term? What are their employment prospects?

Organization development as a key management competence

As more and more organizations realize that the skills to develop and design jobs and organizations, and the improvement of the internal processes that bind them together, are vital to long-term success, they will seek to develop organization development skills among an increasing number of managers.

Ready assessment matrices for organization design

An increasing number of organizations are applying the method described in this book and this is resulting in a large pool of task data which can be collated and modelled. In time this will allow ready-reckoner charts to be developed to speed up the initial design of appropriate jobs by task sampling.

Learning organizations

With the repeated application of job design and organization structure development methods, organizations will begin to internalize them so that they become part and parcel of everyday working. This, over time, will be a key input into the creation of 'the learning organization' which is continuously seeking to improve and raise its performance.

Spill-over effect of self-improvement

The provision of work environments in which an increasing number of individuals play an active part and take an increasing responsibility for improvement will have a direct effect upon career expectations and trade union representation. Companies will have to apply the notion of career development to more and more of their employees, while trade unions will be forced to examine their strategic and tactical role as their members take charge of more and more issues formerly handled by shop stewards.

Raising individual and organization adaptability

While they are at present only a relatively small number of organizations actively applying job and organization design methods, those that are doing so are developing increasingly robust organizations which can adapt to technical, commercial and social pressures.

All organizations need to identify more appropriate job and organization structures. Not all organizations recognize this need yet, but more and more are doing so. In particular, increasing numbers of individuals are realizing that they can change their organizations by redesigning their jobs and their immediate work areas. I hope that this book has provided material, methods and ideas which will fuel this process for the benefit of all of us.

Bibliography

Aguilar F.J. (1988). *General Managers in Action*. Oxford: Oxford University Press.
Bailey J. (1983). *Job Design and Work Organization*. Englewood Cliffs, NJ: Prentice Hall.
Buchanan D.A., McCalman J. (1989). *High Performance Work Systems – The Digital Experience*. London: Routledge.
Campbell A., Sorge A., Warner M. (1989). *Microelectronic Product Applications in Great Britain and West Germany: Strategies, Competencies and Training*. Aldershot: Avebury/Gower.
Cherns A. (1987). Principles of sociotechnical design revisited. *Human Relations*, **40**, 153–162.
Commonwealth of Australia (no date). *Participative Work Design. Module 5*. Canberra: Department of Employment and Industrial Relations, Working Environment Branch.
Cross M. (1985). *Towards the Flexible Craftsman*. London: Technical Change Centre/Policy Studies Institute.
Cross M. (1986). Multi-skilling. Costs and benefits. *Work Study*, **34** (4), 23–27.
Cross M. (1988). Changes in working practices in UK manufacturing 1981–1988. *Industrial Relations – Review and Report*, (414) May, 2–10.
Cross M., Mitchell P. (1986). *Packaging Efficiency – The Training Contribution*. London: Technical Change Centre/Policy Studies Institute.
Cummings T. (1976). Sociotechnical systems: an intervention strategy. In *Current Issues and Strategies in Organization Development* (Burke W., ed.) New York: Human Science Press.
Cummings T. (1989). *Organization Development and Change*. 4th edn. St Paul: West.
Doray B. (1988). *From Taylorism to Fordism. A Rational Madness*. London: Free Associated Books.
Foster M. (1987). *Developing an Analytical Model for Sociotechnical Analysis*. Documents Nos HRC7 and HRC15. London: Tavistock Institute.
Gael S. (1983). *Job Analysis*. San Francisco: Jossey-Bass.
Galbraith J. (1973). *Designing Complex Organizations*. Reading, Mass: Addison-Wesley.
Goodstein L.P., Andersen H.B., Olsen S.E., eds. (1988). *Tasks, Errors*

and Mental Models; A Festschrift to Celebrate the 60th Birthday of Professor Jens Rasmussen. London: Taylor and Francis.
Goranzon B., Josefson I., eds. (1988). *Knowledge, Skill and Artificial Intelligence*. Heidelberg: Springer-Verlag.
Gupta N., Jenkins G.D., Currington W. (1986). Paying for knowledge: myths and realities. *National Productivity Review*, Spring, 107–123.
Jackman J.R., Oldham G.R. (1975). Development of the diagnostic survey. *Journal of Applied Psychology*, **60**, 159–170.
Heller F. (1989). On humanizing technology. *Applied Psychology: An International Review*, **38**, (1), 15–28.
Herbst P.G. (1972). *Sociotechnical Design*. London: Tavistock.
Hill P. (1971). *Towards a New Philosophy of Management. The Company Development Programme of Shell UK*. London: Gower Press.
Hunt J.W. (1986). *Managing People at Work*. 2nd edn. London: McGraw-Hill.
Johannsen G. (1988). Categories of human operator behaviour in fault management situations. In *Tasks, Errors and Mental Models* (Goodstein et al., op. cit.).
Keyser V. de et al., eds. (1988). *The Meaning of Work and Technological Options*. New York: Wiley.
Lawler E.E. (1981). *Pay and Organization Development*. Reading, Mass: Addison-Wesley.
Lawler E.E. (1982). Increasing worker involvement 'to enhance organizational effectiveness. In *Change in Organizations* (Goodman P., ed.). San Francisco: Jossey-Bass.
Leighton P., Syrett M. (1989). *New Work Patterns. Putting Policy into Practice*. London: Pitman.
Lupton T., Tanner I. (1987). *Achieving Change*. Aldershot: Gower.
McCormick E.J. (1979). *Job Analysis: Methods and Applications*. New York: Anacom.
McLaughlin I., Clark J. (1988). *Technological Change at Work*. Milton Keynes: Open University Press.
Mintzberg H. (1983). *Structures in Fives. Designing Effective Organizations*. Englewood Cliffs, NJ: Prentice-Hall.
Mitroff I. (1983). *Stakeholders of the Organizational Mind*. San Francisco: Jossey-Bass.
Mumford E. (1981). Participative systems design: structure and method. *Systems, Objectives, Solutions*, (1), 5–19.
National Council for Vocational Qualifications (1989). *Staff Development Handbook*. London: NCVQ.
Office of Technology Assessment (1984). *Computerized Manufacturing Automation*. Library of Congress No. 84–601053. Washington, DC: Government Printing Office.

Organization for Economic Cooperation and Development (1989). *New Technologies in the 1990s – a Socio-economic Strategy*. Paris: OECD.
Pasmore W.A. (1988). *Designing Effective Organizations: The Sociotechnical Systems Perspective*. New York: Wiley.
Pearn M., Kandola R. (1988). *Job Analysis*. Wimbledon: Institute of Personnel Management.
Peters T., Waterman R. (1983). *In Search of Excellence*. New York: Harper and Row.
The Planning Exchange, Glasgow (annual publication). *Paying for Training: A Comprehensive Guide to Sources of Finance for Adult Training*. London: HMSO.
Plant R. (1987). *Managing Change and Making It Stick*. London: Fontana/Collins.
Savage P. (1987). *Who Cares Wins*. London: Mercury Books.
Schermerhorn J.R., Hunt J.G., Osborn R.N. (1985). *Managing Organizational Behaviour*. 2nd edn. New York: Wiley.
Schermerhorn J.R. (1986). *Management for Productivity*. 2nd edn. New York: Wiley.
Taylor J.C. (1971). High technology leads to more democracy: some effects of technology in organizational change. *Human Relations*, **24**, 105–123.
Toon D. (1979). Job design through participation (unpublished paper). Melton Mowbray, Leics:, Pedigree Petfoods.
Waterman R.H., Peters T.J., Phillips J.R. (1980). Structure is not organization. *McKinsey Quarterly*, Summer, 2–20.
Whitmore D.A. (1987). *Work Measurement*. 2nd edn. London: Heinemann.
Zuboff S. (1988). *In the Age of the Smart Machine*. Oxford: Heinemann.

Index

Ability, requirement scales, 16
Absence, counselling, 176; monitoring, 176, 221
Accident, investigation, 178; reports, 135
Accountability/responsibility imbalance, 41
Accounts, 175; monthly, 95
Activity, sampling, 16, 18
Adaptability, individual, 342; organization, 342
Adapting, 9
Aerosol, can manufacture, 96–106, 123–4
Agreement, development, 71
Aguilar, F.J., 4
Albright and Wilson, xi, 302
Alcan Plate, xi
Amalgamated Engineering Union (AEU), 85, 216
Ambassadors, for company, 39
Applefords, xi
Apprentices, multi-skilled, 333
Apprenticeships, 68
Appraisal, management system, 23
Appraisals, conduct, 176
Appraising, skills, 301
Ashford, Kent, xi
Asset, register/fixed asset list, 95, 123
Assumption surfacing, 72
Audit coordinator, 175
Australia, 3, 25
Automation, 2
Awareness raising, 11
Aylesford, Kent, xii

Banking, 6
Bar coding, 61
Barclays Bank, xi
Bargaining, structures, 41–2
Barnard Castle, xii
Barnsley, xii
Batch coding, 221
Batchelors Foods, xi
Behavioural change, 12

Belgium, 54
Birmingham, xi
Birtley, xii
BP Chemicals, xi
Breakdown, waiting time reduction, 215, 219, 222, 224–5
British Nuclear Fuels, xi
British Petroleum, 38, 311
British Pipeline Agency, xi
British Standards Institution, 114
British Steel, 38
British Tissues, xi
Bromborough, xii
Budget, preparation, 178
Burmah Castrol, 311
Business centre, 44–8; control information, 47; culture, 48–9; definition, 50–1; external relations, 49; key characteristics, 44–5; manager role, 46; people, 48; principles, 51–2; organization roles, 46–7; resources, 48
Business, linking, 9; plan, 14, 95; unit development, x
Business and Technician Education Council (BTEC), 302

Cadbury, xii
Cambridge, xii
Capacity, utilization, 178; under utilization, 40
Capenhurst, xi
Capital, expenditure reduction, 220
Car manufacturing, 2
Career, paths, 85; progression, 12; system (participative), 195
Carrington, xii, 302
Change, acceptance of, 32; evolutionary, 45; initiation of, material, 109; initiation of, output, 110; initiation of (process), 32, 109; maintenance department, 326–37; monitoring and evaluation, 309–18; overcoming barriers to, 71; preparation for, 33; rationale for, 71;

realization of, 32; rules for and their development, 73–7
Change management, 7–8
Change process, 8–9; design criteria, 30; implications for involvement, 31; job design method, 14–15; participation, 31
Change strategy, empirical–rationale, 11, 13; force–coercion, 11, 13
Changeovers, 179; time reduction, 215, 219, 221–2
Changing job structures, balance sheet, 241–9; benefits, example, 215–29; costs, 229–41; costs, example, 232–41; final report, 293–9; management costs, 239–41; payback period, 242–3; step-by-step implementation, 251–99; training and development costs, 235–8
Charter, site, 32, 107–8; development, 77–8
Check list method, 16
Checks, elimination, 219
Chemical manufacturing, 6
Chemicals, fine, processing and packaging, 62
Cherns, A., 25, 189
Cheshire, 8
Chlorofluoro carbons (CFCs), 90
Ciba-Geigy, xii
City and Guilds of London Institute (CGLI), 3, 217, 302
Civil service, pay system, 304
Cleaner, 175, 207
Clerical, integration with operators, 39
Coaching, 176
Coca-Cola Schweppes Beverages, xii
Collaborating skills, 301
Collator, 175
Combination job analysis method, 16
Commissioning, cost reduction, 215
Committees, chairing, 176
Commonwealth of Australia, 25
Communicating skills, 301
Communication, channels (short), 219; costs, 231
Communications, 45, 253–8, 260, 263, 268, 270, 272–3, 275, 278–85, 287–97, 320–39; initial design criteria, 321–2; key lessons, 338–9; key questions, 320; quality, 12; questions about change, examples, 322–37

Competencies, distinguishing, 300; functional, 300; threshold, 300
Competition, x
Competitor information, 324
Conceptual education, 54
Condition monitoring, 178
Conditions of work, 12
Conflict resolution, 51
Conoco, 311
Consensus systems design approach, 21
Consultation, 313
Content analysis, 16, 18
Contract management, 177
Contractor, base work load, x
Contractors, 23, 45, 313, 334
Core activities, 187, 191, 193; business, 45; and non-core work, x
Corrective action teams, 156
Coryton, xii, 311
Cost, and benefits analysis, 23, 34, 82; control, 40; information, 44
Counselling, absence, 176
Courages, xii
Courtaulds, 38
Cowley Hill Works, xii
Craft, integration with operators, 39; operator partnership, 245; role, 46; Training Review Board, *see* Joint Review Board, 312–13; working practices communication, 326–37.
Crane fluid, 302
Critical incident technique, 16
Crosfield Chemicals, xii
Cross, M., 113
Cryoplants, xii
Culture, 42; reorientation, 300
Cummings, T., 29, 341
Cummins Engines, xii
Cussons, xii
Customer care, 67; complaints, 95, 178; service, 54, 59–60; service improvements, 227–8; service levels, 42
Cycle times, 59

Dalry, xii
Darlington, xii
Data, analysis, 34; collection, 34, 111–53
Dead time, reduction, 215
Decision statement, 214, 216

Demarcation, 41–2, 48, 64–5, 67, 69, 199, 201; trade, 216
Denmark, 54
Department of Employment and Industrial Relations, Australia, 25
Design principles, 283–5
Development, of subordinates, 176; cycle of continuous change, 311
Diagnostic skills, 237
Diary method, 16
Digital Equipment Corporation (DEC), 1, 3, 5, 300, 311
Disciplining, 176
Doray, B., 21
Dornay Foods, xii
Downtime analysis, 221
Drug prescribing, 84
Dual skill/skilling, 213–14, 216–18

Edinburgh, xii
Edmonton, xii
Education, economic, 195
Electrical, technicians, 68
Electrical, Electronic, Telecommunications and Plumbing Union (EETPU), 216
Electricians, 64, 68, 174
Elements, definition, 114
Elida Gibbs, xii
Ellesmere Port, 311
Employee involvement, 3
Employment stability, 195
Engineer, plant, 175
Engineering, departmental weaknesses, 64–7; industry, 6; multi-disciplinary, 68; organization design criteria, 69–70; steering group, 62–70; work planning, 176; work requests (EWRs), 95; work scheduling, 176; working practices–communicating changes, 326–37
Equipment, changeovers, 44; familiarity, 215; performance monitoring, 221; purchase, 178; running time, 215; utilization, 178
Esso Petroleum, xii, 311
Establishment numbers, 85
Europe, 54; western, 3
European Economic Community (EEC) Social Fund, 230, 232
Experimental, engineers, 67; projects, 11

Experimenting skills, 301
Expert conferences, 16
External demand assessment, 2
Exxon, 2
Exxon Chemicals, xii, 3, 7, 13

Fabricator group, 214
Facilitator, external, 300
Factor-level matrix, 307
Factory, manager role, 46; pool of labour, 323
Fault analysis, 16, 18
Fault, diagnosis, 219; finding, 131, 177; recognition, 219
Fault management matrix analysis, 16
Fawley, xii, 13, 14, 311
Feedback giving skills, 301
Fibreglass, xii
Filling, manager, 175
Fire fighting ability, 40
First line management, 38
Fitters, 64, 175, 206, 214
Flexibility, x, 39, 43, 61, 200, 334–5; communicating changes, 326–37
Flexible, approach, 39; craft system, 214, 216–18; craft systems, costs and benefits, 242–3; work practices, x; workforce, 37; working, 31
Focused factories, x
Food and Drug Administration (FDA), 87, 294
Food manufacturing, 6
Foster, M., 29
France, 54
From Taylorism to Fordism: A Rational Madness, 21
Functional job analysis, 16

Gael, S., 116
Gaines Petfoods, 307
Galbraith, J., 7, 10, 40
General Foods, 1, 3, 5, 307
General, operator, 215, 224–5; practitioner market, 84; worker concept, 218
Germany, West, 3, 54
Glasgow, 232
Glaxo Operations, xii
Good manufacturing practice (GMP), 135; audit, 181–2
Goods received notes (GRNs), 95
Goodstein, L. P., 21

Goranzon, B., 21
Gorseinon, xii
Grangemouth, xi
Greasing, 177
Greece, 54
Greefield approach, 19
Greenford, xii
Greengate works, xii
Grimsby, xii
Group working, x; see also Team; Work group
Gupta, N., 307

Hackman, J.R., 16, 189
Harlesden, xii
Harrison and Crosfields, Chemicals Division, 7
Harrow, xii
Hartlepool, xii
Hazard spotting, 178–9
Hazardous goods movement, 61
Health and Safety Executive (HSE), 87, 294
Heinz, xii
Heller, F., 25
Hemel Hempstead, xi
Herbst, P. G., 25
Hewlett-Packard (HP), equipment, 299
Hierarchy level reduction, 219
Hill, P., 25–9
Holiday monitoring, 221
Housekeeping, 64
Hunt, J.W., 7–8, 10
Hygiene services, 175

Ideal organisations, 3
Imperial Chemical Industries (ICI), 7–8; Pharmaceuticals, xii
Implementation, constraints, 203; iterive approach, 203; plan, 80; risks, 203; timetable, 80.
Improvement, focus, 9, 199; projects, 257–8, 260, 262–8, 272, 275, 278, 281, 283–4
In Search of Excellence, 3
In-process control, 41, 44; inspector, 175; technical assistant, 175
Income security, 81
Individual role development, 295
Industrial relations structures, 41–2, 49; supportive of performance objectives, 43

Industrial engineering, 44
Industry worker concept, x
Inflation, 83
Informate, 2
Information system, 4, 189; decentralized/team based, 195; flow promotion, 301; participative, 195
Inquiring skills, 301
Institute of Personnel Management, 15
Instrument, calibration, 177; for change, 4; mechanic, 175; overhauls, 177; technicians, 65; 68
Inter-site cohesion, 40
Interaction, facilitating, 301; processing, 301
International Business Machines (IBM), equipment, 299
Interviews, conduct, 176
Inventory, control, 59; forecast, 59, level, 60; management, 41, 54; method, 16; policy, 95; reduction, 54, 92, 220
Involvement of people, 37
Ipswich, 302
Isle of Grain, 311
Isolation, of equipment, 177
Italy, 54, 91

Job, anchors, 23; descriptions, 95, 135; evaluation criteria, 159–66; high performance, 1; ideal, 171–2, 189; manufacturing, 172–3; manufacturing skills profile, 188; performance improvement, 215; quality, 189; rotation, 323; security, x, 81, 321
Job analysis, 7; methods and approaches, 15–19
Job Analysis: A Practical Guide for Managers, 15
Job analysis interview method, 16–17
Job components inventory, 16
Job design, x, 1, 41; bottom-up, 163, 189, 192–3; criteria, 19–22, 162–4, 270; evaluation criteria, 194–214; outputs, 22–4; participative, 195; principles, 159–66; teaching manual, 25; top-down, 163, 188–9; self-managing teams, 195; structure, 29–35; survey, 273, 276, 279
Job diagnostic survey, 16
Job element analysis, 16

Job evaluation, 23, 62, 95, 303–9; factor comparison, 303–5; factors, 305–7; job classification, 303–4; job ranking, 303; points rating, 303–4
Job information matrix system, 16
Job learning analysis, 16
Job role, matrix, 164–5; 190; possible new combinations, 171–85
Job task rotation, 342
Johannsen, G., 16
Joint, commitment, development of, 216; problem solving, 318
Joint Review Board (JRB), achievements, 316–18; characteristics, 318; issues tackled, 314–17; learning points, 318; membership, 311; purpose and aims, 312; review items, 312–14; review process, 311–18
Josefson, I., 21
Just-in-time, 2, 57–8, 61

Kandola, B., 7, 15–16, 340
Kellogg, xii
Kepner Tregoe decision analysis, 214
Key account, involvement, 54; performance, 60
Key issues, identification, 253
Keyser, V. de., 21
Kimberly-Clark, xii
Kings Lynn, xii
Kirkby, xii
Kitt Green, xii
Kodak, xii, 3
Komatsu, xii
Knowledge, Skill and Artificial Intelligence, 21

Laboratory, manager, 175; steward, 175; tests, 182–3
Labour, availability, 2; displacement costs, 231; overload, 221; shortages, 2; site mobility, 316; transferability, 201; underload, 221
Lawler, E.E., 195–6, 307
Lead time reduction, 92, 215, 219, 227–8
Leadership, 4; training, 236
Learning, collective, 199; organization, 342; rates, 302
Leeds, xii
Leighton, P., 21

Lever Brothers, xii, 38
Line, dedication, 64–5; downtime reduction, 224–5; extensions, 90; logs, 95; serviceman, 175; utilization, 47
Listening skills, 301
Log Method, 16
London, x; Business School, 7
Lostock, 7–8, 10, 21
Lubrication, 177
Lupton, T., 21
Lyons Tetley, xii

Macclesfield, xii
Machine, availability, 215; complexity, 2; maintenance, 2; operation, 2; performance improvement, 219, 222–3; running time, 220; setting skills, 39
Macrae, J., 7, 10
Maidstone, xii
Maintainability Centred Approach, 19
Maintenance, 9, 177, 187; monitoring, 221; planned (PM), 135; planned preventative (PPM), 95, 177, 181; whole machine approach, 68; work sharing, 316; *see also* Total productive maintenance (TPM)
Management, man, 38; process, 40; reduction, 219, 226; stability, 44; structure style, 12, 38, 46, 62, 300
Management of change, 11; communication costs, 233; enabling programme, 239–41; labour reduction costs, 234; management costs, 233–4, 239–41; salary costs, 234–5; system costs, 235; training, 232–3, 235–8
Manager, section, 46
Managerial competence, 42; *see also* Competencies
Manchester, xii
Manpower, planning, 42, 176
Manufacturing, strategy formulation, 37; team membership, 236
Manufacturing Centre, 45–6, 70, 199; definition, 50–1; design principles, 45; formulation, x; key principles, 51–2
Marketing-research relationship, 41
Mars, 1, 5
Mars Confectionery, xii

Index

Material, control, 54–62, 59–60; conversion improvement, 219–20, 223, 226; loss reduction, 178; processing time reduction, 220; usage, 44; wastage reduction, 47, 221
McCormick, E. J., 16, 20, 305
McKinsey, 61; 7S Model, 10, 61–2
Meaning of Work and Technological Options, The, 21
Mechanization, 2
Medicine inspectorate, 87, 294
Meetings, running, 176
Melton Mowbray, xii
Metal Box, xii
Michelin, xii
Milford Haven, 311
Minimal critical specification, 189
Mission, company, 32, 49; core, 14; site, 32, 49; statements, 18, 300; *see also* Charter; Value; Vision
Mitroff, I., 55
Mobil Oil, xii, 311, 331
Monsanto, 3
Mossmorran, xii
Multi-skilling, x, 31, 214, 216–18, 244–5; individuals, 68, 198; operators, 224–5; teams, 69, 198
Mumford, E., 21, 26

National Council for Vocational Qualifications (NCVQ), 3, 130, 302, 307
National Health Service (NHS), 84, 90, 300
Near misses, 95; reports, 135
Neath, xii
Negotiations, location, 325; single site, 217
Netherlands, 54
New process introduction, 42, 44
New products, 94; introduction, 42
New site, design, 4; project management, 4
New technology, 1
New work patterns, 21
Newcastle, xii
News International, 3
Nineteen Ninety-Two (1992), 83, 90
Nissan, 3, 38
Normative-re-educate, 11
Norsk Hydro, 3
North West England, 77

Nottingham, xii

Observation method, 16
Occupation analysis inventory, 16
Occupational testing, conduct, 176
Office services, 175
Oil refining, 6
Oldham, G.R., 16, 189
Open Systems Analysis, 25
Operation, definition, 114
Operations, manager, 175; maintenance partnership, 244
Operator, 206; basic engineering maintenance, 44; filling, 175; general, 174; in-process control, 44; integration with clerical, 39; integration with craft, 39; integration with secretarial, 39; integration with technical, 39; job enhancement, 39; mechanics, 68; multi-skilled, 235; packaging, 175; role, 46; technical, 174; upskilling, 92
Optimized operations, 57
Option, benefits, 289, 291–2, 295–6; costs, 290, 292, 296; development, 284–92; evaluation criteria, 289; selection, 34, 324
Order management, 61
Organization, culture, 1; development, x, 341; effectiveness workshops, 77; evaluation criteria, 159–66; existing-desired comparison, 50; high performance, 1, 26; ideal, 3; layers, 8; learning, 41; levels, 44–5; option selection, 85; principles for effective, 39; profiling, 300; roles, 46; strengths, 39–40; weaknesses, 39–42
Organization design, x, 1–2, 186–93; concepts, 40; criteria, 30, 162–4; evaluation criteria, 194–214, 216–18; principles, 159–66; structure of the approach, 29–35
Organization structure, 1, 4; design outputs, 22–4; levels, 38; manufacturing, 172–3; matrix, 164–5, 190; participative, 195; possible new combinations, 171–85; team based, 195
Overhead costs, 44
Overtime, 313–14, 327, 332, 337; reduction, 216, 333
Oughtibridge, xi

Pack proliferation, 41
Packaging, manager, 175
Paisley, xii
Paper manufacturing, 2, 6
Parallel importing, 90
Participant observation, 16
Participation, generation, 301
Participative system, features, 194–5
Part-time staff, 48
Pasmore, W.A., 25–9, 340
Pay system, 12, 43, 301, 303–9; common grade structure, 39; for change, 327; design, 37–9; development, 79; pay progression, 316, 326; project study structure, 307, 310; structure, 40; study method, 307, 310; training link, 323
Pearn, M., 7, 15, 16, 340
Pedigree Petfoods, xii
People assumptions, 12–13
Perception surfacing, 72
Performance, awareness, 219, 227; improvement, 301; information, 44; management system, 23, 38; measurement, 316; monitoring, 178; related pay (PRP), 84
Perkins Diesel, 302
Permits-to-work procedures, 178, 316
Personnel, assistant, 175; Institute of Personnel Management, 15; officer, 175; participative policies, 195; records, 95
Peterborough, 302
Peters, T.J., 3
Pharmaceutical engineers, 68
Pharmaceuticals manufacturing, 6, 30, 187
Physical layout, egalitarian, 195; participative, 195
Pilkington Brothers, 38
Pilkington Flat Glass, xii
Pirelli, 3
Planner, 175, 207
Planning, 178; engineering work, 176; resource allocation system, 4; system improvement, 220–1; time reduction, 220
The Planning Exchange, Glasgow, 232
Plant, R., 321
Plant, availability, 19; productivity, 200; utilization, 19
PLM Redfearn, xii

Polyvalency, x
Port Sunlight, xii
Portugal, 54
Position analysis questionnaire, 16
Positive reinforcement techniques, 38
Power and control group, 214
Presentations, make, 176
Problem, definition, 19, 33, 252–3; identification, 63; incident method, 16, 18; scoping, 33; solving skills, 237; solvers, 41
Process, 'bad running' state, 116; documentation simplification, 220; 'good running' state, 116; mapping, 115–16, 256–8; technologies, 1; understanding of, 39
Procter and Gamble, 300
Product, costing, 221; development, 187; proliferation, 38; rationalization, 41, 49, 56; uptake, 1; wastage reduction, 215
Production, apprenticeship, 236; cells, 187; centre, 70, 199; engineering partnership, 68, *see also* Total productive maintenance (TPM); load smoothing, 221; maintenance partnership, 69, 198–9, *see also* TPM; process integration, 2; process mapping, 88, 96–106; storage points, 187; transformation points, 190; unit review teams (PURTs), 315
Productivity, improvement, 82–3, 219; paradox, x
Professional profile, 67–8
Project, authorization, 177; engineering, 187; handover, 177; management, 40
Prudhoe, xii
Purchase orders, 95
Purchasing, strategic, 183
Purfleet, xii

Quality, assurance responsibility of operators, 219; assurance testing delays, 220; audits, 178; circles, 40, 86, 105, 156; control, 175, 187; control administration, 175; control manager, 175; control packaging material, 175; index, 43; information, 44; integration, 38; review, 175

Rainbow collar worker, 2
Raising capability, 9

Rating scales, 120
Raw material testing, 175
Reactions to change, 321–2
Reading, xii
Reasonable person, 11
Recession, 4
Recognition rights, 49
Redates, 60
Reed Corrugated Cases, xii
Reliability Centred Approach, 19
Renault, 2
Repertory grid, 16
Representation, trade union, 313
Research and development, 94
Responsibility taking, 301
Review measures of change, 312–14
Reward, increases, 231; – systems, 4, 189; egalitarian, 195; participative, 195; skill based, 195, 307; supportive structure, 199; *see also* Pay systems
Rework stock reduction, 47
Roche Products, xii
Role, clarity, 43; culture, 45; definition, 324–5; development, 297–8; in-process quality assurance with operator, 219, 226–7; integration of engineering with operator, 219, 226; supervisor, 316
Ross Foods, xii
Rothmans International, xii
Rowntree, xii

Safety, 42–3, 52; audits, 95, 178; certificates, 177; circles, 156; index, 18; inspections, 177; projects, 178; standards, 326, 332–3; task, 192
Saint Helens, xii
Savage, P., 7, 9, 13
Scheduling, 184; conformance, 59; engineering work, 176; system improvement, 220–1
Schermerhorn, J.R., 7, 11
Scottish and Newcastle Beer Production, xii
Second order techniques, 18
Secretarial, integration with operators, 34
Selection, participative, 195
Self, containment principle, 44; description method, 16; improvement process, 342; inspection, 38
Sellafield, xi

Service levels, 92, 95
Seven (7) C Model, 7
Shell Chemicals, xii, 3, 302
Shell Lubricants, xii
Shell UK, xii, 26, 311
Shift working, 81
Shop floor, knowledge under-utilization, 41
Shutdowns, 177
Single status, 39
Site, business centre relationship, 49; centre relationship, 42
Skill, based payment system, 195, 307; blocks, 325; development – job content link, 341; development matrix, 307; dilution, 217–18; interpersonal, 195; level matrix, 308; mix, 2; payment, 335; primary and secondary, x; project, 199
Slough, xii
Socio-technical, analysis approach, 27–8, 107, 189–90, 301; assessment survey, 25–6; change model, 28; design approach, 25–6; paradigm, 340; potential weaknesses, 26–7; redesign method, 25
Somerdale, xii
Southampton, 13
Spain, 54
Specification of user requirements (SOURS) process, 254
Speke, xii
Spennymoor, xii
Staff utilization, 176, 179
Staffing, and people development, 4
Stakeholder analysis, 55
Standard, operating procedures (SOPs), 95, 135; – checking, 180; initiation, 177; monitoring, 177; training, 177; writing, 178; product costs, 184
Stanlow, xii, 26, 311; Working Arrangements Group (SWAG), 318
Start-ups, 177
Statistical process control (SPC), 38, 245
Steel manufacturing, 2
Stock, control, 184; materials controller, 175; outs, 59–60; taking, 178; turnover, 59; write-offs, 95
Stoke-on-Trent, xii
Stores, receipt and despatch, 175

Strategic functioning, 301
Study, approach, 254; group membership, 79; method application, 255
Sub-contracting, 4
Supervision, minimal direct, 70
Supervisor, 207; collation, 175; filling, 175; laboratory, 175; packaging, 175; role of, 316; structure reduction, 219, 226
Suppliers, approval, 181; audit, 181, 183; auditor, 175; liaison with, 177
Support, activities, 187; activities direct, 187; congruence, 189–90; system enhancement, 220
SWOT/5P analysis (strengths, weaknesses, opportunities, threats/ plant, people, programmes, process, procedures), 55–9, 88–93, 95–6, 109, 158–9, 204–6, 252–4, 279
Syrett, M., 21

Tacit skills, 2
Tanner, I., 21
Task, batch type, 132; complexity, 128–31, 168–9; continuous, 155; contractors, 156; core, 167, 187–8; cover, 155; culture, 45; definition, 20, 113–16; description, 114; direct manufacturing 166; direct support manufacturing, 166; distribution, 191; distribution, geographic, 192; distribution, temporal, 192; duplication reduction, 127; duration, 127; environment, 1; equipment non-specific, 168; equipment specific, 167; frequency, 126, 170; hierarchical analysis, 16, 18, 115–16; impact, 132; indirect support manufacturing, 166; integration, 191–2; known, 9; listing development, 134–48; location, 132; overlapping, 155; performer, 125; profiles, 174–85; safety, 192; site/ support, 167; sources, 135; statement writing, 116–23; support, 132; support resources, 192; training, 156; transferability, 188–9, 192–3, 245–8; type, 133; verb list, 120–2; volume, 131, 191–2
Task data, 301; analysis, 154–93; 276–83, 285–6, 293–9; cleaning, 154–60, 266–77, 280; collection, 150–2,

255–7, 259–71, 274, 277, 280; loading, 271, 274, 277; output, 167–70; plotting, 157–8, 171, 186; reduction, 158; rules for analysis, 166–71; validation, 156
Tasks, Errors and Mental Models, 21
Tavistock Institute for Human Relations, 25, 27
Taylor, J.C., 25–6
Team, building, 59, 77, 176; business focused, 51; coordination, 45; coordination role, 236; design, 45; development, 298; leader, 46, 215, 236; line structured, 207–9; management, 51; manufacturing, 51, 208, 211; membership, 172–3, 323; membership interaction, 323; mobility, 70, 199; multi-skilled, 198; operating, 186; operational, 45; process structured, 209–12; product based, 206–7; product coordination, 208, 212; reliability, 186; size, 46; support, 45; task profile, 294; technical, 208, 211; training, 79, 236, 251; working, x, 38, 56, 67
Technical, change, x; integration with operators, 39; operators, 215, 236, 224–5; operator apprenticeship, 235
Technicians, 174, 207; laboratory, 175
Technological, change, 3; diffusion, 3; fix, 27; imperative, 27
Technology, dependency, 2; deskilling effects, 23; failure, 2; fix, 25; imperative, 25; keeping up-to-date with, 177; use and enhancement, 1
Teesport, 311
Temporary, labour, 4; staff, 23, 45, 48
Terms of reference, 33; completion, 74–7; definition, 73–7; development, 33, 77–88; examples, 78–9, 86–8
Thatcham, xii
Third world, 83
3M, xii
Throughput time, 215; reduction, 220
Time, ability and safety (TAS) principle, 69–70, 199; savings worksheets, 245–8; study, 16
Toon, D., v, 189
Topeka, 307
Total, management system, 61; productive maintenance (TPM), x, 3, 185, 243–9, 302; quality control

Index

(TQC), 38; quality management (TQM), 2
Trade union, barriers, 66; involvement, 325; membership, 49, 316; representation, 66; *see also* Unions
Trainability, 302; assessments, 23
Trainee protection, 302
Training, 299–303; budget, 231; costs, 235–8, 302; development opportunities, 12; distributed, 302; human process, 301; human resource, 300–1; imparting, 176; inclusive process, 302; investment in, 3; job link, 302; material acquisition, 302; modules, 23, 95; monitoring, 302–3; needs analysis, 77; participative, 195; programme development, 176; records, 95; resourcing, 302, 324; review, 176; selection criteria, 325–6; standards, 3, 302; strategic, 300; technical and structural, 301–2
Training agency, 230, 232
Training and Enterprise Councils (TECs), 3, 230, 232
Transportation industry, 6
Transition management, 3
Transitional organization, 189–90
Transportation, analysis, 25–6; physical, 187
Trebor, xii

Understanding, developing, 71
Unilever, 38
Unions, company relationship with, 38; *see also* Trade unions
Unit cost, reduction, 43, 46
United Biscuits, xii
United Kingdom (UK), 3, 54
United States of America (USA), 3, 25
Uxbridge, xii

Validation, coordinator, 175; cost reduction, 215; protocol, 95; work, 178

Value, statement, 14, 18, 300; system, 42
Van den Berghs and Jurgens, xii
Variance, analysis, 26, 301; control, 189
Vision, generation, 36–73; leading by, 301; maintenance, 301; selling, 53; statements, 18, 194; statement (manufacturing), 52–3; statement (personal), 39, 42–52; value statement; *see also* Value statement; Mission; Charter
Volvo, 1

Waiting time reduction, 216
Ware, xii
Warehousing, network, 54; serviceman, 175
Warrington, xii
Wastage reduction, 219–20, 223, 226
Waterman, R.H., 3, 10, 61
Western economies, 2–3
Whitehaven, xi, 302
Whitmore, D.A., 112
Work, group (semi-autonomous), 160–2; high performance system, 5, 25; -in-progress, 184, 215, 220; measurement, 16, 112–15; performance survey system, 16, 18; restructuring, 25; sampling, 16, 18; scheduling, 178; study data, 135; study reports, 95; system, 2
Working, flexible system of hours, 43; practices, 314–35; shorter life, 2; shorter week, 2; shorter year, 2
Workshop, for 'shop floor', 78; trade unions, 78
Wrexham, xi

York, xii

Zone of commonality, 245; *see also* Total productive maintenance
Zuboff, S., 2